A RIBBON OF HIGHWAY

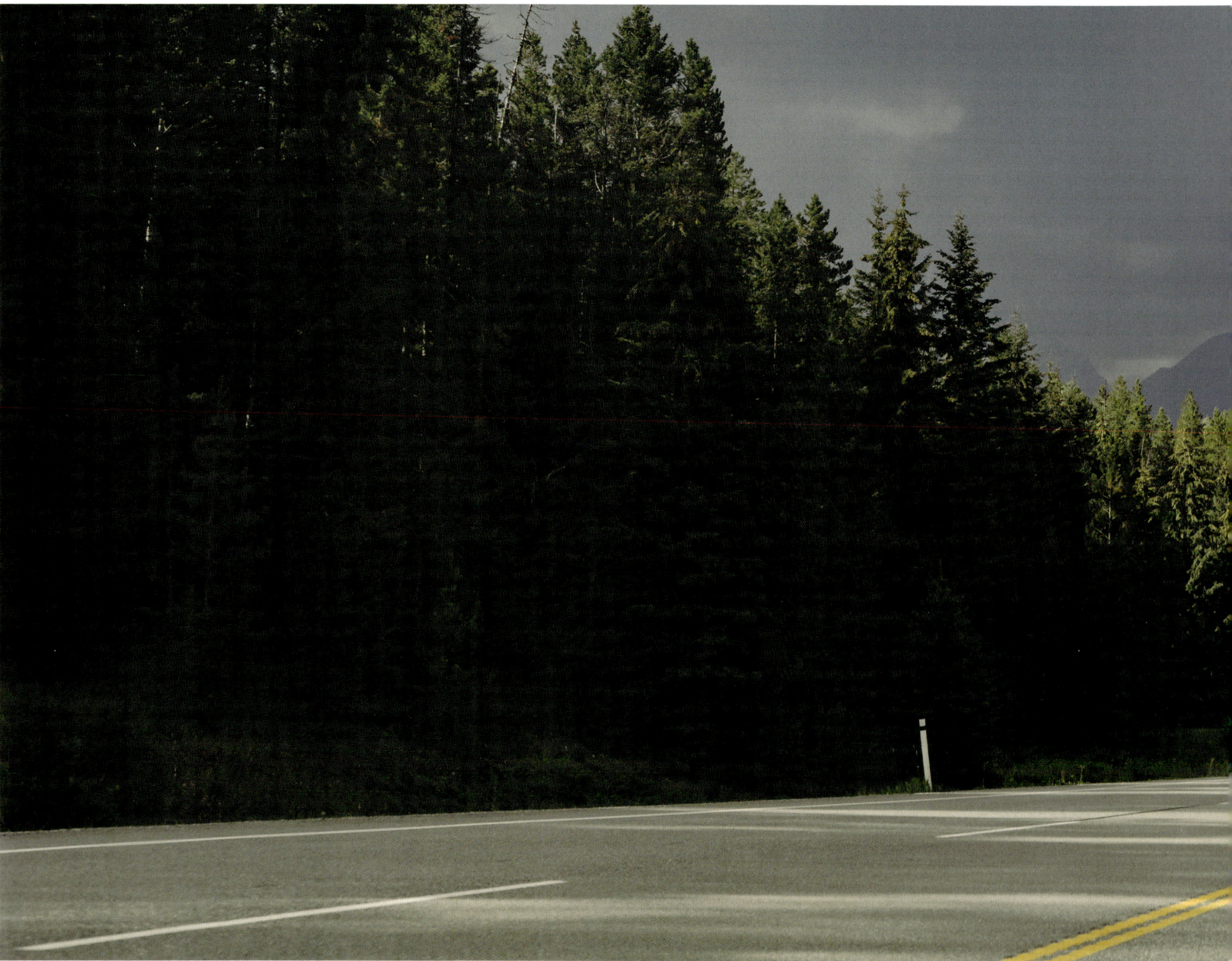

A RIBBON OF HIGHWAY

A PHOTOGRAPHIC EXPLORATION OF CANADIAN IDENTITY

TAYLOR ROADES

FOREWORD BY JACQUELINE SALOMÉ

RMB

For information on purchasing bulk quantities of this book, or
to obtain media excerpts or invite the author to speak at an event,
please visit rmbooks.com and select the "Contact" tab.

RMB | Rocky Mountain Books Ltd.
rmbooks.com
@rmbooks
facebook.com/rmbooks

Cataloguing data available from Library and Archives Canada
ISBN 9781771605793 (hardcover)
ISBN 9781771605809 (electronic)

All photographs are by Taylor Roades unless otherwise noted.

Design: Lara Minja
Printed and bound in China

We would like to also take this opportunity to acknowledge the
traditional territories upon which we live and work. In Calgary,
Alberta, we acknowledge the Niitsítapi (Blackfoot) and the people of
the Treaty 7 region in Southern Alberta, which includes the Siksika,
the Piikuni, the Kainai, the Tsuut'ina, and the Stoney Nakoda First
Nations, including Chiniki, Bearpaw, and Wesley First Nations. The
City of Calgary is also home to Métis Nation of Alberta, Region III.
In Victoria, British Columbia, we acknowledge the traditional
territories of the Lkwungen (Esquimalt and Songhees), Malahat,
Pacheedaht, Scia'new, T'Sou-ke, and W̱SÁNEĆ (Pauquachin,
Tsartlip, Tsawout, Tseycum) peoples.

We acknowledge the financial support of the Government of Canada
through the Canada Book Fund and the Canada Council for the
Arts, and of the province of British Columbia through the British
Columbia Arts Council and the Book Publishing Tax Credit.

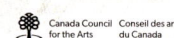 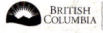 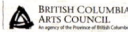

For Maddy, Paul and Deb, who showed me

that being a photographer is possible

and brought me to Roderick Lake

like a member of their family.

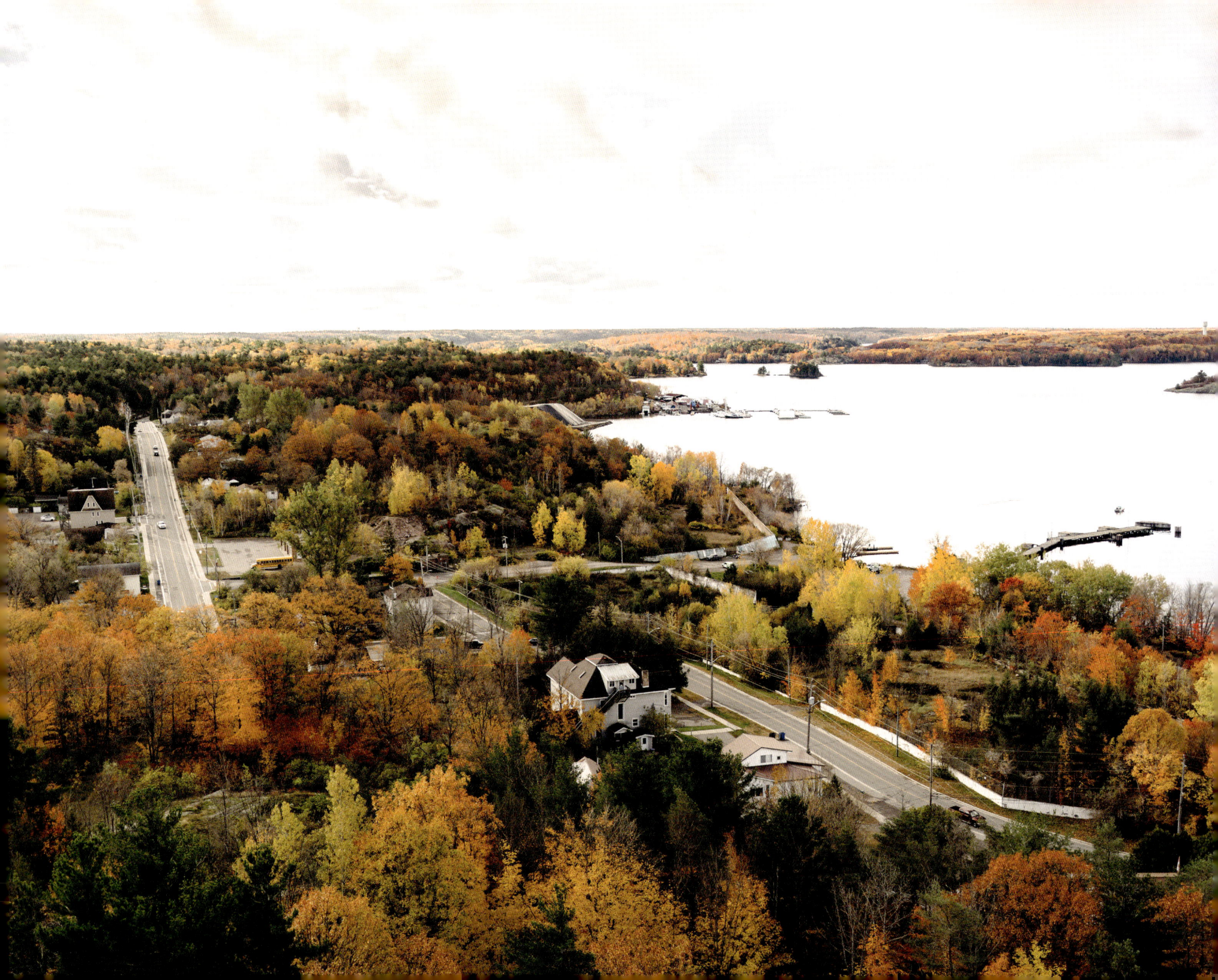

THE MOST CANADIAN THING ABOUT CANADA

IS THAT WHEN THEY RAN A CONTEST THAT WENT

"FINISH THIS SENTENCE. AS AMERICAN AS APPLE PIE.

AS CANADIAN AS BLANK," THE WINNING ANSWER

WAS "AS CANADIAN AS POSSIBLE UNDER

THE CIRCUMSTANCES."

— MARGARET ATWOOD

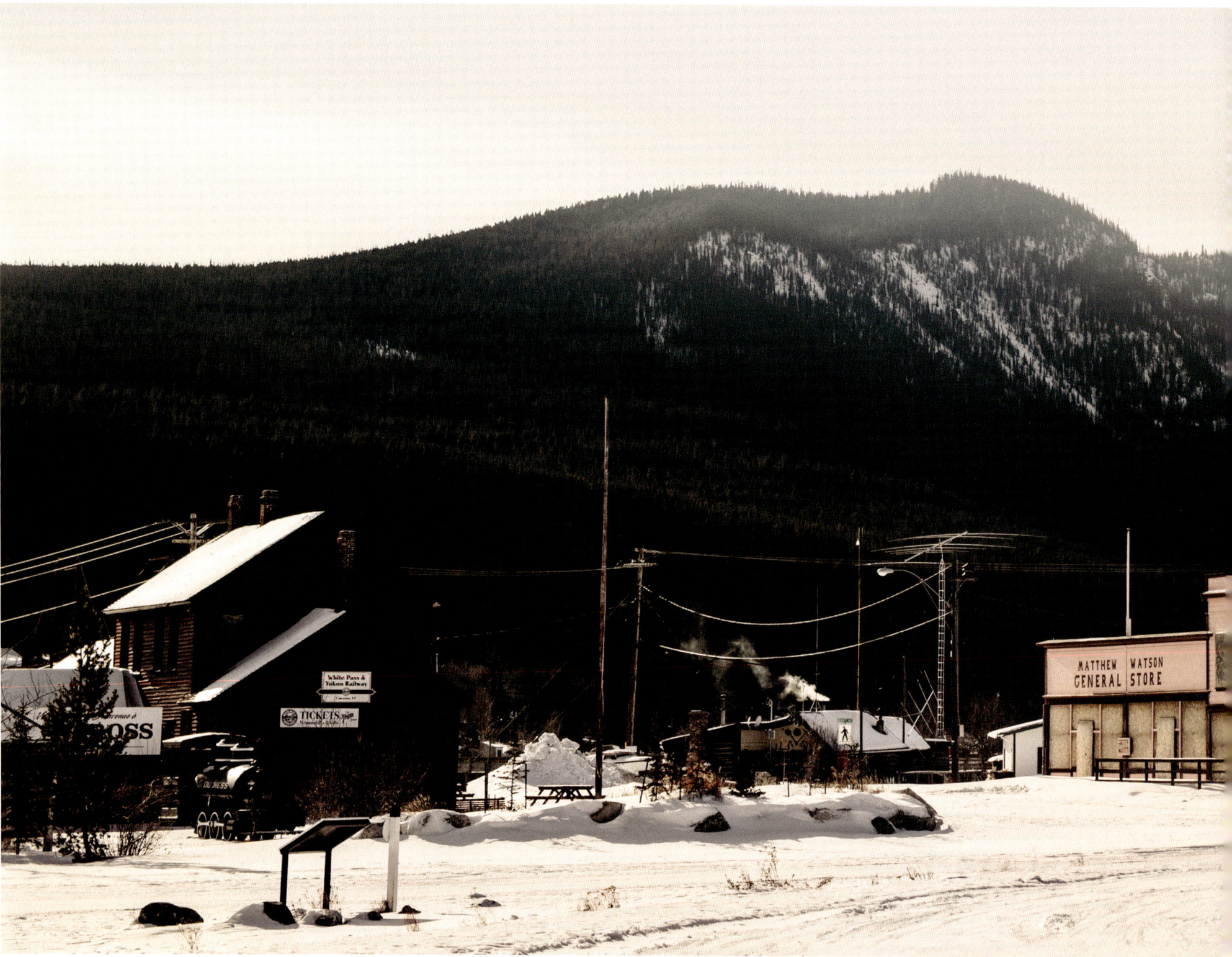

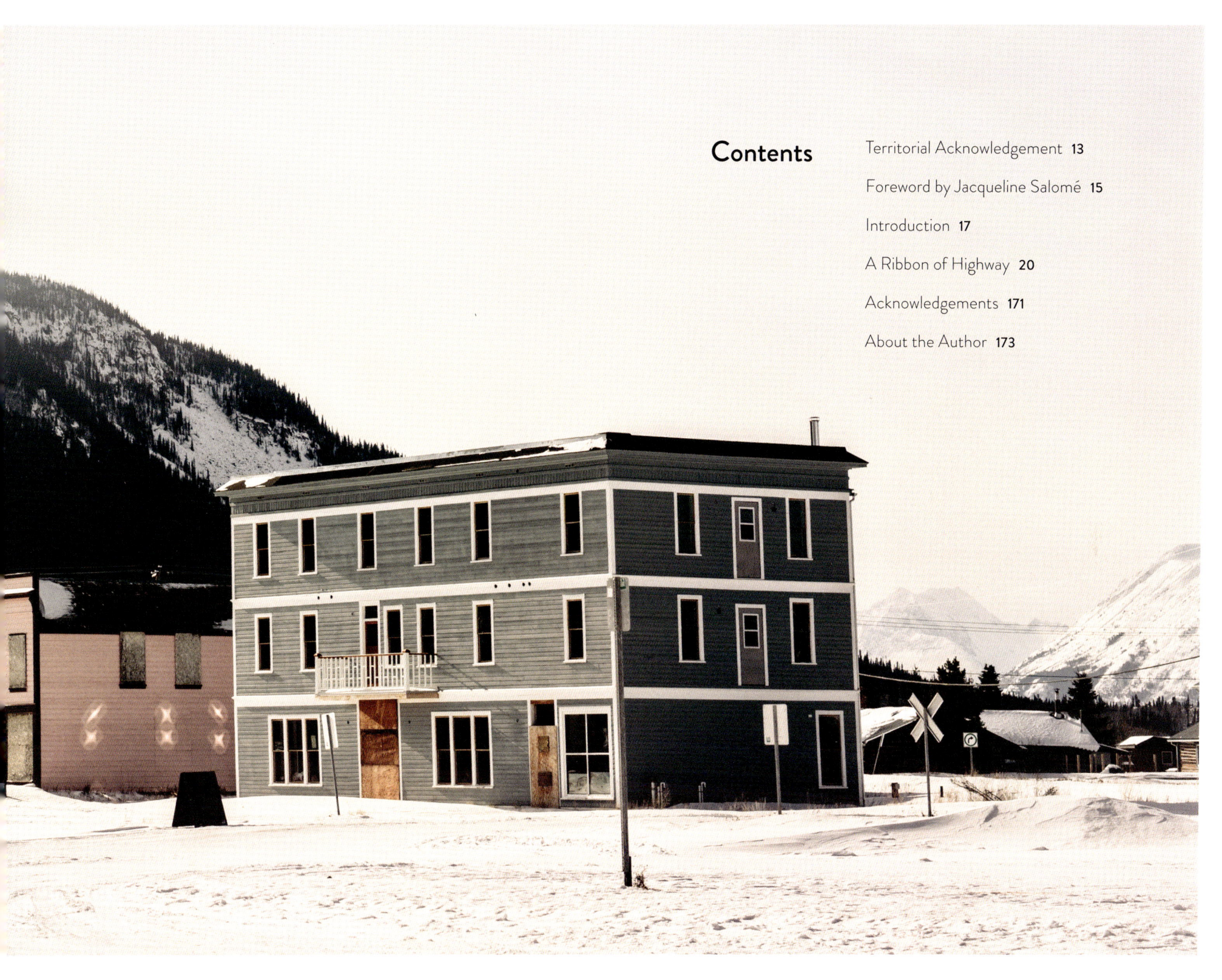

Contents

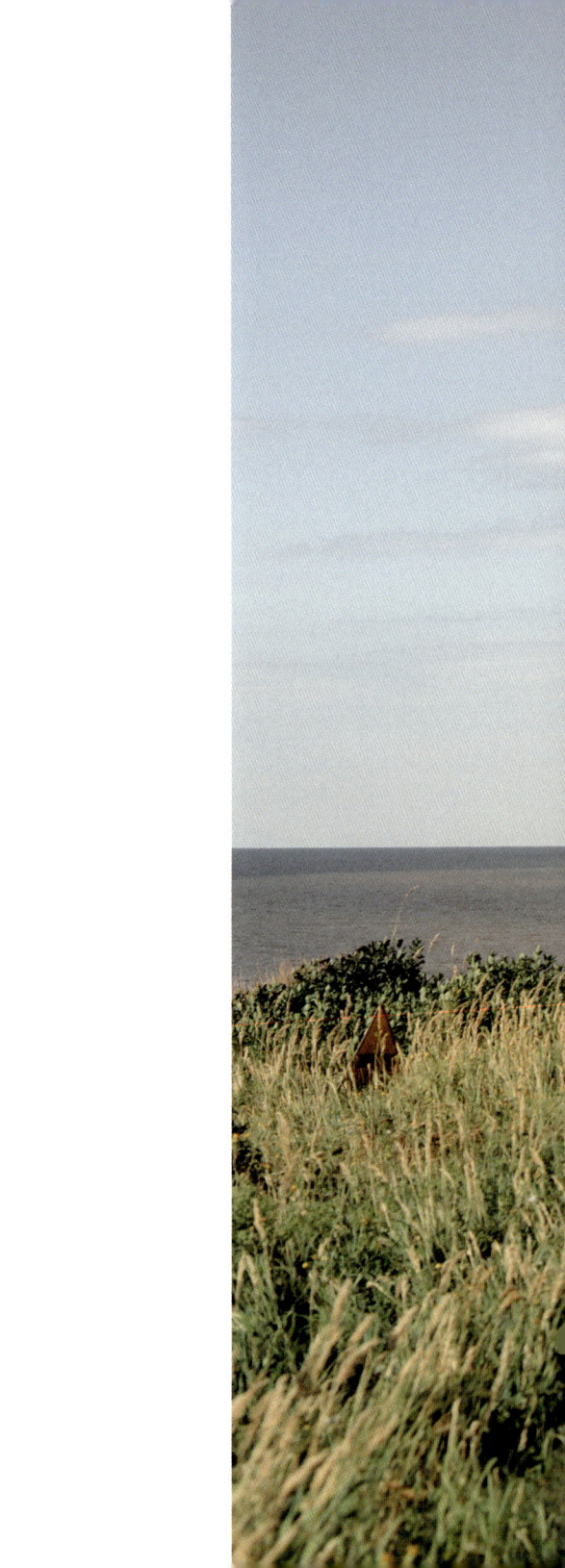

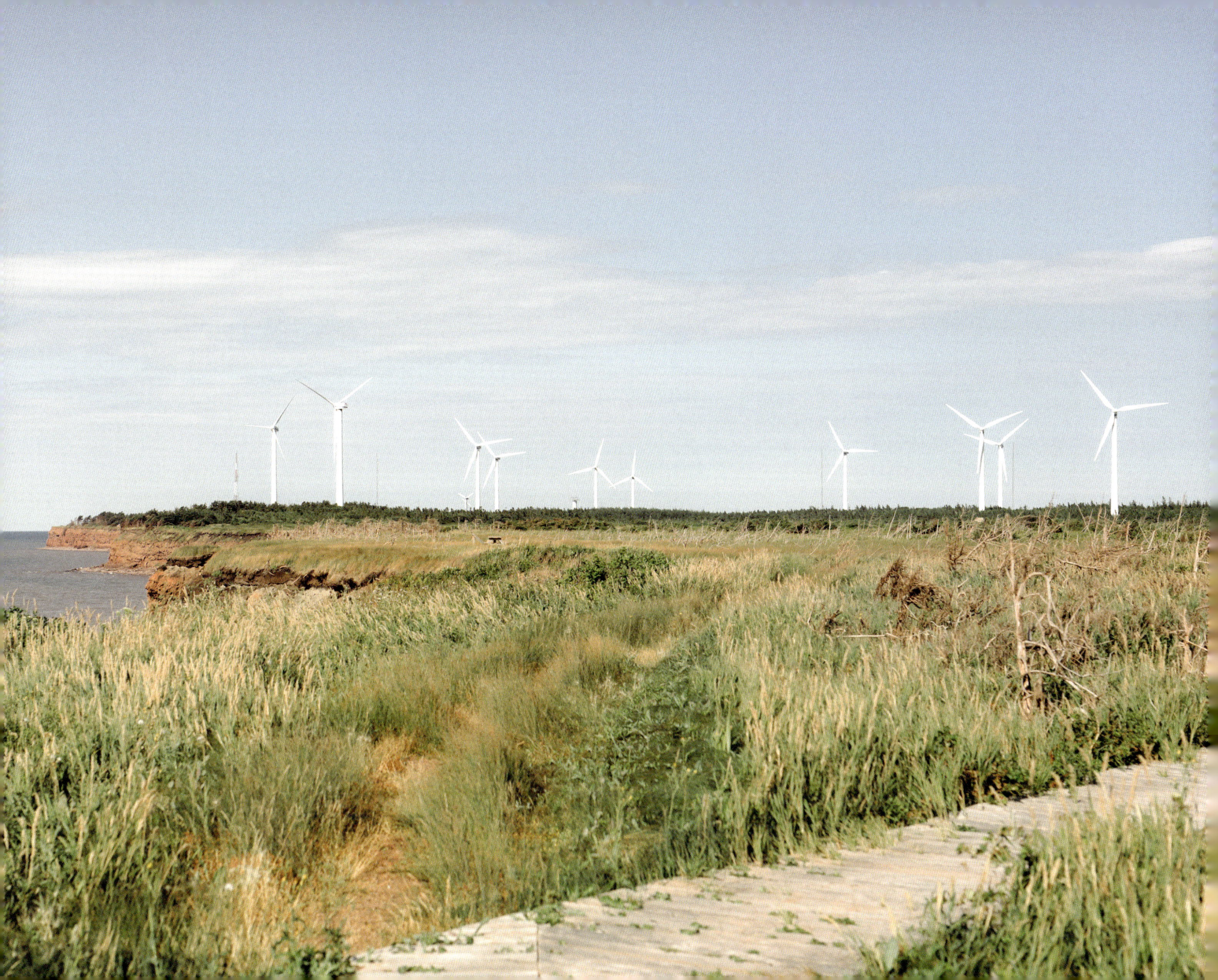

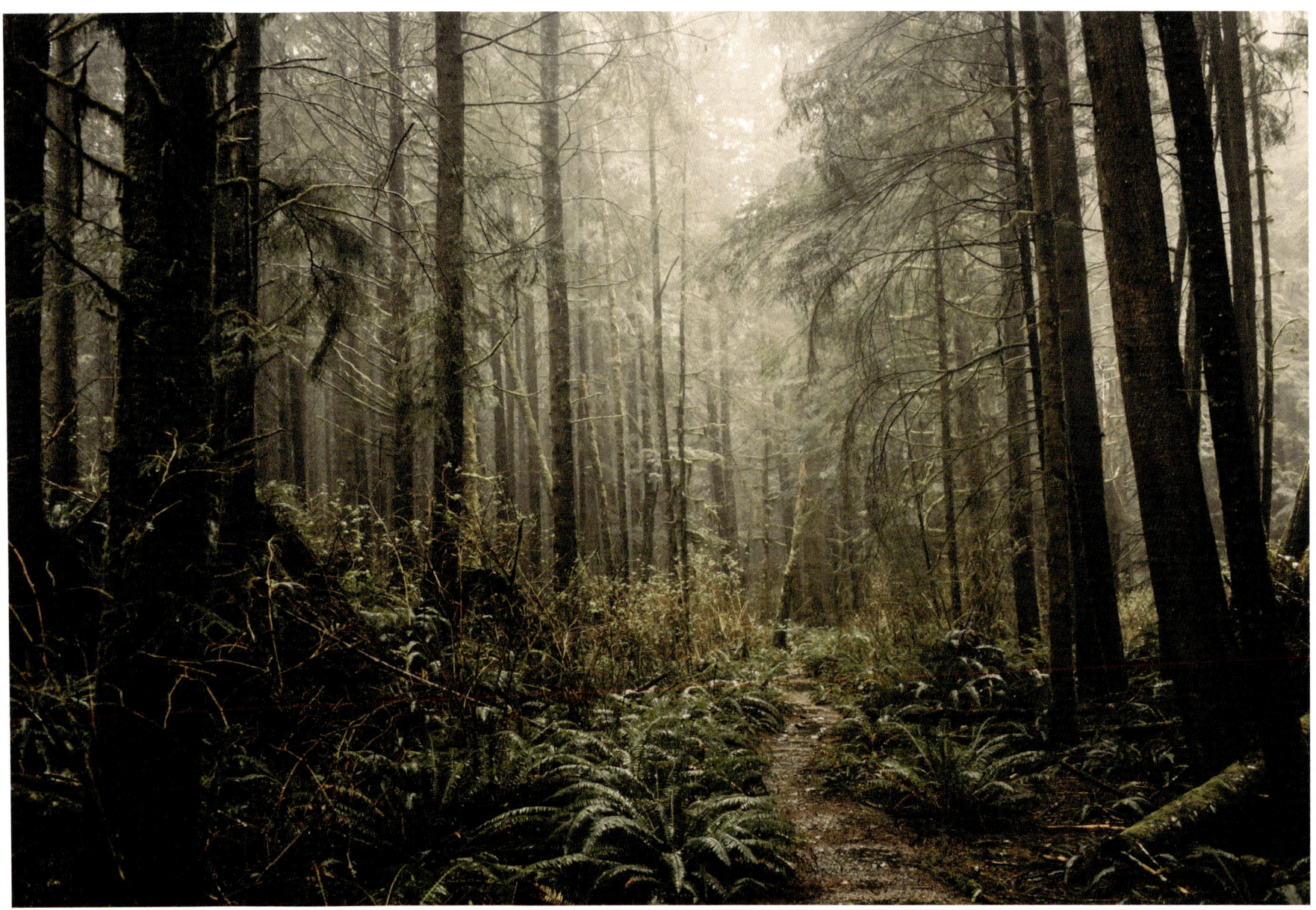

Territorial Acknowledgement

This book was compiled on the land of the unceded territory of the lək̓ʷəŋən People, known today as the Esquimalt and Songhees Nations. Specific Nations are mentioned in select captions, but photos included in this book span dozens of First Nations, Métis and Inuit territories across the country.

There is no proper or adequate way to atone for the actions of our ancestors, but to do our best to acknowledge what occurred, honour the legacy of those lost, and maintain a profound caring for the land and resources they once cared for.

—FOGO ISLAND INN WEBSITE

← JUAN DE FUCA MARINE TRAIL, VANCOUVER ISLAND, BRITISH COLUMBIA, MARCH 2015.

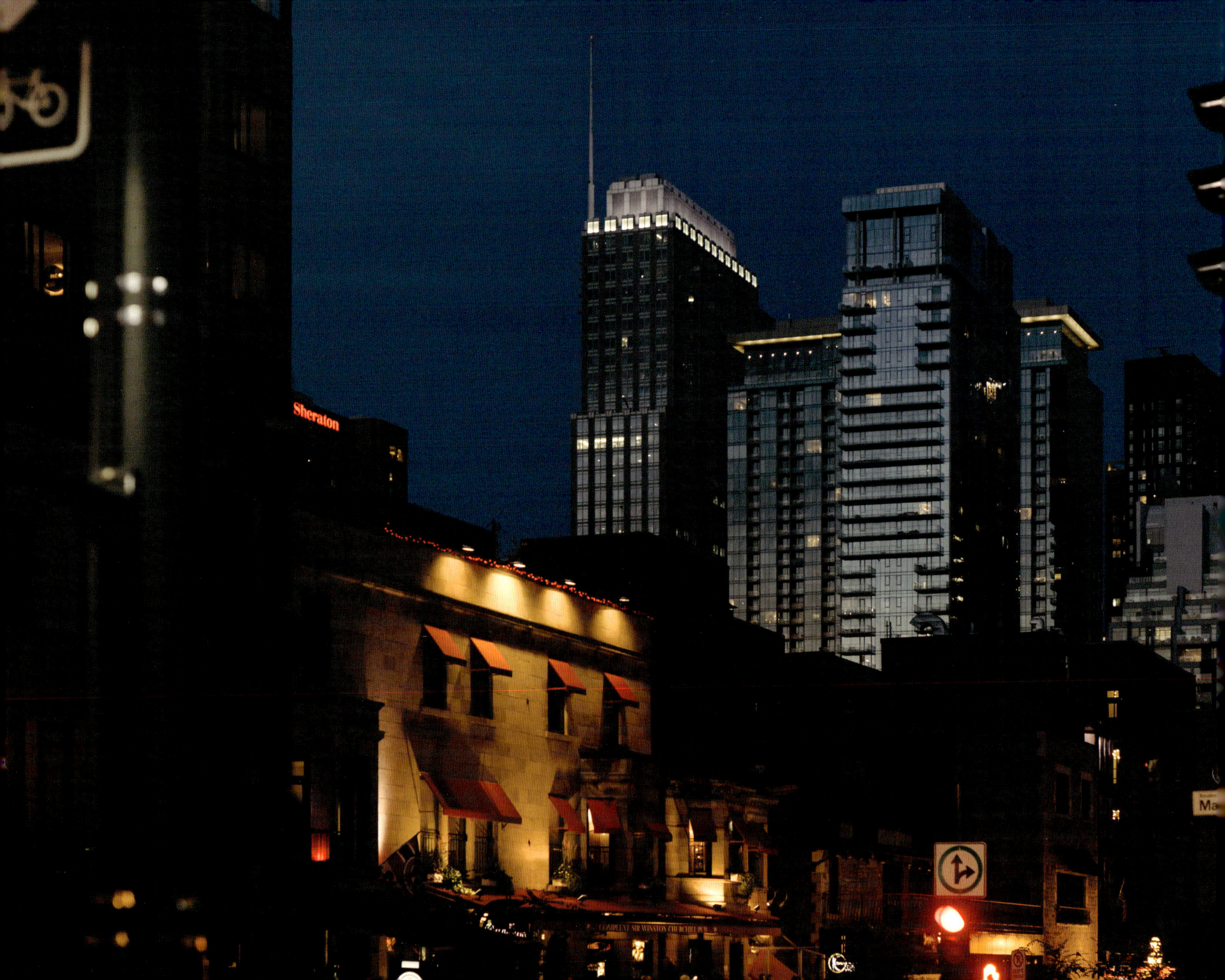

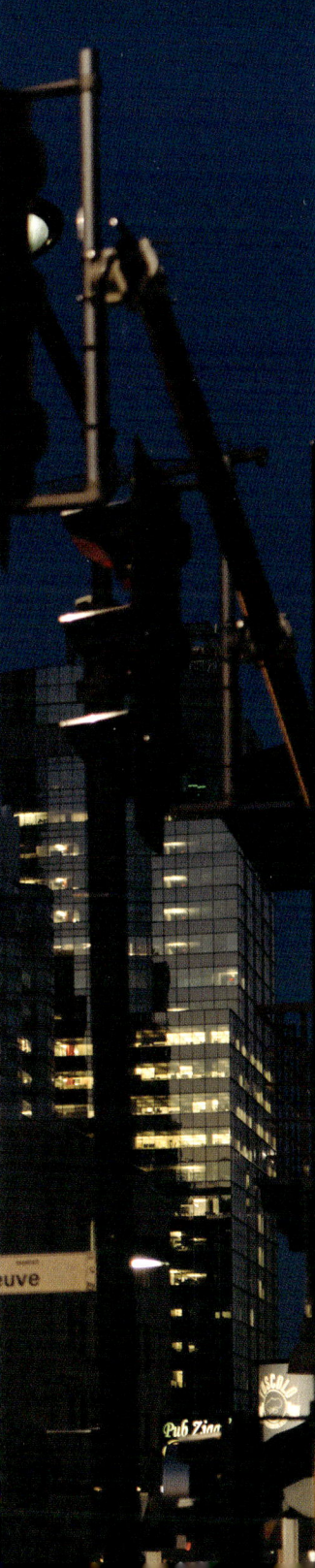

Foreword

Hop in the window seat folks, this is a road story.

It's a tale told in visions, captured in a blink as this big country flash-flashes by, the way it does when you're travelling down the Trans-Canada Highway.

This is a story about Canadian identity. But you won't find any firm answers here, just experiences, interpretations. Looking through photographer Taylor Roades's eyes, but seeing with your own.

In *A Ribbon of Highway*, you may find something you know. The frosty-face feeling of racing sleds down a backyard hill in winter, the slice-slice sound of skates on ice, the sweet smell of gasoline and cedar in a roaring bonfire. A plane taking off from some somewhere to a far domestic somewhere else, or geese flying just about anywhere. Fur pelts, dead maybe, or alive if you're lucky enough to glimpse it.

That feeling of shock-awe humbleness that envelops you at the foot of a colossal mountain or towering tree; you know, the one that reminds you just how small you are against the sheer magnitude of this land. A plaid-jacket neighbour chop-chopping wood and punctuating her sentences with "eh" like an un-ironic stereotype.

There are gas stations, bus stops, cheap old motels in every small town from here to there. Every cabin wall with dark knots in the wood, and maps with so much blue, blue that comes to life as rushing rivers, loon calls reverberating over lakes, and fishing boats afloat on great oceans, with waves thrashing on sandy beaches, frozen beaches, rocky beaches awash with driftwood, kelp, starfish and seashell treasures.

There's that vast, beautiful nothingness between destinations on the road in Canada – just you, the yellow line dash-dashing under your tires, and those unforgettable strangers you meet with their hats-off kind of kindness.

Maybe you've seen it, or maybe you're about to for the very first time. In either case, I bet you will *feel* it. And that's the point. Influenced by her keen interest in tasting the flavours of local life, Roades's images are like visceral portals taking you into every hometown, every living room across this country. You know what they say: home is not a place but a feeling.

There may not be any clear verdict on that nebulous thing we call Canadian identity. But what a delightful, liberating conundrum! Answers can be killjoys. It's that shape-shifting wonder that inspires us, drives us like the road itself.

As author Tom Robbins says in his hitchhiking road story, *Even Cowgirls Get the Blues*, "let us live in the beauty of our own reality."

And that's exactly what the eyes-wide-open photographer and veteran traveller Taylor Roades has done in this gift of a debut photo book. Inviting you to ponder life's curious questions with her as she rides the Greyhound bus from Ontario to British Columbia and back again, asking you to take the wheel on one of those long, cross-country road trips she's taken too many times, and buying you a ticket to gaze upon the jagged-sharp Rockies, or the vast subarctic tundra of the northern territories as you fly overhead.

Through photos like tattoos in time, Roades is welcoming you into her reality, offering you a vantage point from which you can piece together our complicated puzzle of Canadian-ness.

So what I'm saying is don't be fooled, folks. You're just as much a driver here as Roades herself.

But before you hit the gas, allow me to let you in on a little secret, one that will help you navigate the purposeful yet meandering journey contained in this book. It's a secret that can only come from knowing Roades since the two of us were kids growing up in small-town Ontario, one that's inspired me to become somewhat of a yes-person myself, a "let fate take the wheel" kind of explorer just like my dear friend.

Taylor Roades travels to get lost. You find more that way – more detours, mishaps and quirky characters, more sights, sounds, smells, and more feeling, knowing, loving and dreaming – all of which are key ingredients in the recipe for spontaneous adventure and a good story, just like the one you're about to embark on.

And I'll let you in on one more secret, informed by Roades's travel ethos: if you're not travelling to get lost, you might already be more lost than you think.

So, as you take a trip down *A Ribbon of Highway*, take a page out of Roades's book, quite literally. Take a look through her viewfinder and get lost in these photos, this visual wonderland of meticulous artistry. Allow yourself to feel at home here on this land known as Canada, wherever that may be.

—JACQUELINE SALOMÉ

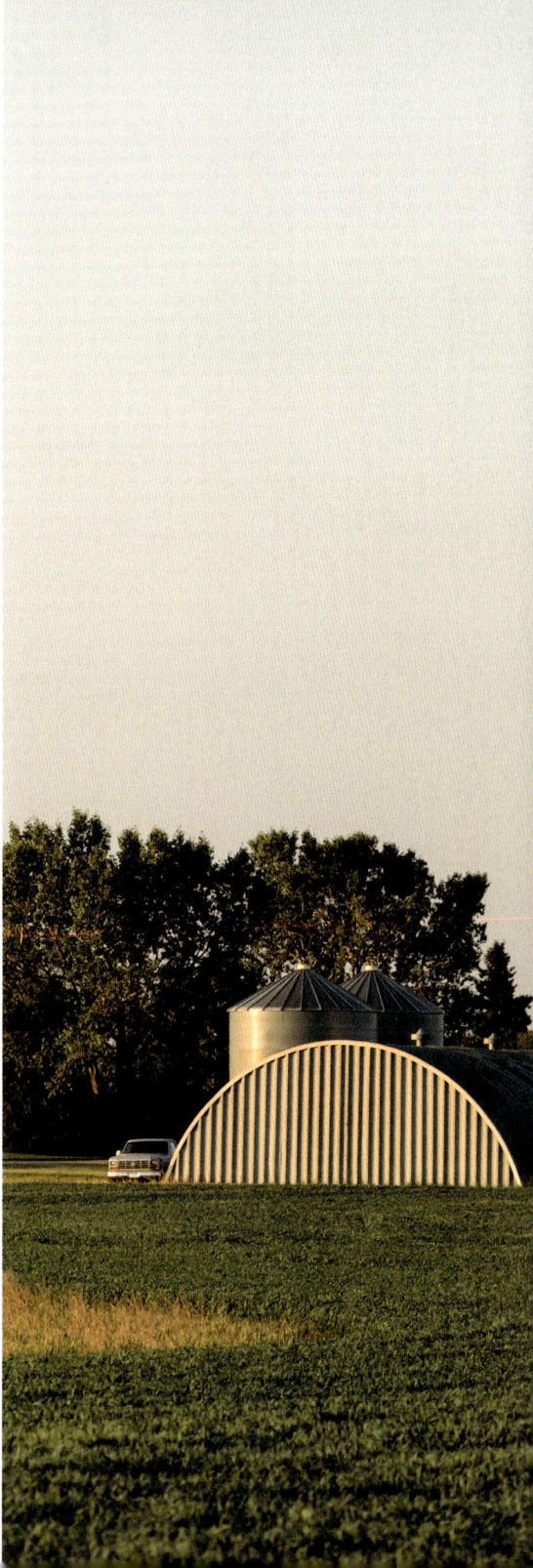

Introduction

I was born and raised in the suburbs of Toronto at the edge of where the city fondly meets rural life, and in my mind both worlds mixed seamlessly. I skated on ponds, rode horses and canoed on crystal-clear blue lakes, while being devoured by mosquitoes. On the other side of the coin, I explored the Royal Ontario Museum on school field trips, and my Baba and Didi took us to see *The Lion King* at the Princess of Wales Theatre in the city. I did the classic Ontario kid's road trip at 18 to Montreal, Quebec, where I stuck my feet into plastic grocery store bags before I put them into my boots and pulled myself up a rope to get to the top of an icy hill somewhere near McGill University. These I thought were quintessential parts of the Canadian experience, until I actually began to explore the rest of Canada in earnest.

My first real destination, which may make some laugh, was New Brunswick. I drove there from Toronto. I also got my first speeding ticket somewhere past Kingston on the way, and then spent two full weeks between Moncton and the Atlantic Ocean. We didn't have the gas budget to make it any further.

I returned to university in Waterloo, where I sat in a first-year lecture room and took a course called "Canada on a Global Perspective." The class was known famously on campus to have a section on beer and donuts, but it was really about the symbols, ideas and notions that make us Canadian, separate from our American counterparts – better even. The course took these ideas and turned them promptly on their head. We knew Canada had a global reputation as a racially diverse place, where immigrants were welcome, but learned the historic Chinese head tax was a government-endorsed example of systemic racism, and First Nations had endured worse at the hands of the residential school system. Each week in this class we came together and asked questions: Are corporations trying to sell us an identity? (This was the famous beer and donuts lecture, using Molson Canadian and Tim Hortons as the example.) And can we have a unified idea of what Canada is in the face of grand-scale inequality, a wildly diverse landscape and infinite subcultures coast to coast?

I was shocked by our violent history and intrigued by a country so big that I could barely begin to comprehend it. I had more questions than answers, and so what would any good student do, you ask? I promptly dropped out. I was interested in photography at the time and adamantly disinterested in most of my other courses. I began shooting full-time and left the university setting behind. But those questions continued to linger. They lingered until I moved out to British Columbia, taking the Greyhound bus to get there, where they intensified. They hung in the air when I visited distant family at a reunion on the prairies, and as I began to photograph assignments in the northern territories.

This book – my first – is a collection of all the photographs I took during this time. It is both a personal retrospective and an exploration of a Canadian identity. It is a collection of photographs taken between 2010 and 2022, a decade of my 20s when I moved and travelled extensively across the country, coming of age and questioning both my own value systems and what being Canadian might mean. The photographs depict my individual lived experience, visiting landscapes that vary drastically in geography, history, socio-economic status and overarching lifestyle.

If there is one thing I've learned for certain, it is that Canada is vast. I have photographs from every province and territory, except Nunavut. I took three trips across the country on a Greyhound bus over this time, and drove many kilometres more in my own vehicle. I know there is more I'm missing. I won't claim this collection to be all-encompassing of "Canadianness"; it is a reflection of the place and the person I was when I took the images.

These photos were not taken with a final goal in mind; the scenes were interesting to me in the moment. I did not think at 20 that I would one day make a book with all my images from across Canada. But since my days as a formal student, I've always been deeply intrigued by the cultural threads that hold Canada together, and perhaps subconsciously I was collecting.

Our patriotism is steeped in contradictions. We are friendly, even if we don't want to be friends. We are hardy people, but we collectively complain about the weather more than anyone I've ever met from another country. We have feelings of moral superiority to the United States, with a robust public health care system, and yet we have a history of deeply unequal and morally horrific policies when it comes to the treatment of Indigenous Peoples on this land.

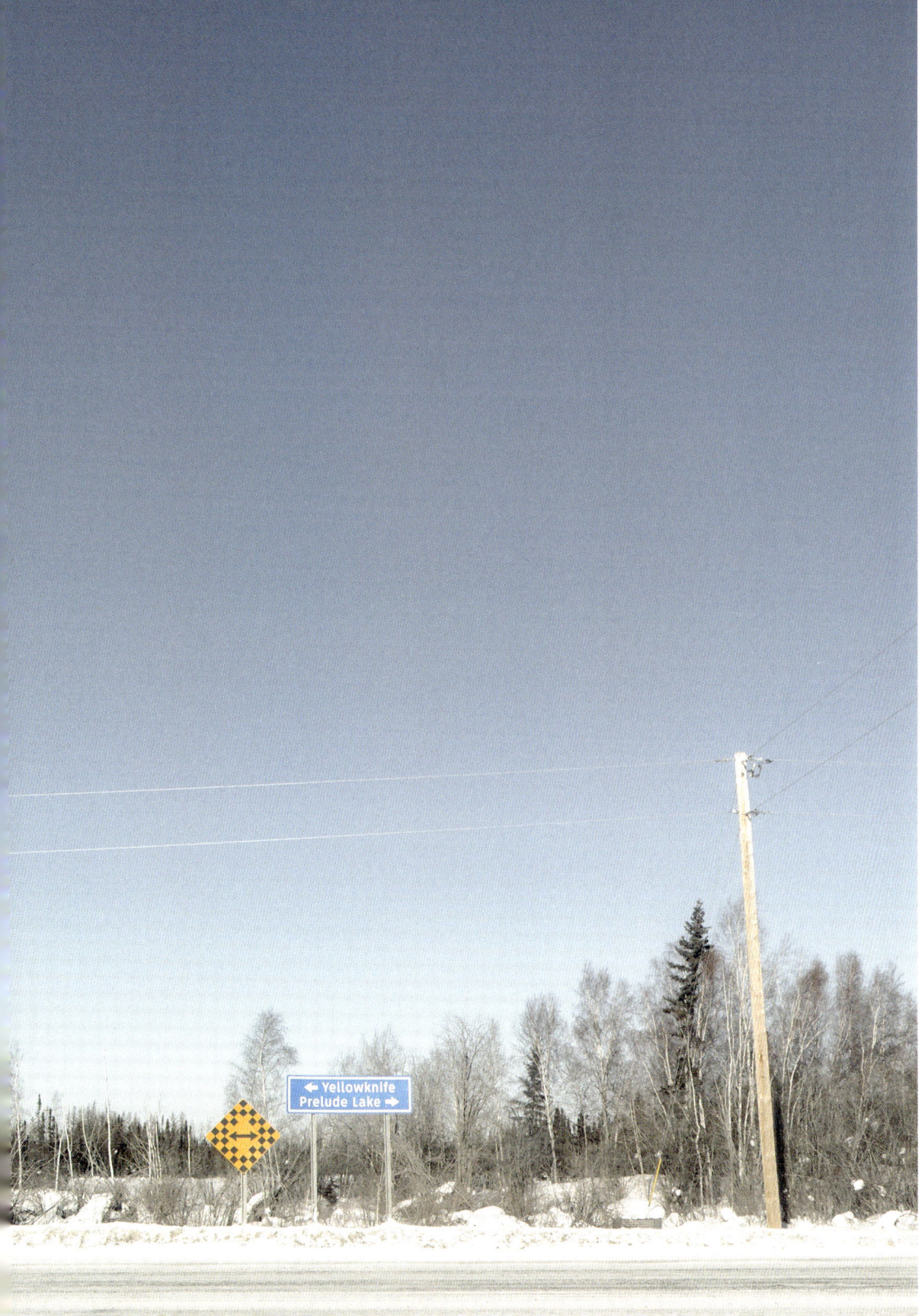

It is my hope, if you have spent time in this country, you will see your own experience, even if only partially. Canada, as we know it, emerged from a series of outposts, and in a sense still operates this way. As I found growing up in a small town on the edge of a city, there is a pull between the provincial and the cosmopolitan. No matter where you lay your head in this country, we are all existing and moving in the space between the places we go – the highway, the city centre pavement, or the backcountry gravel or ice roads that make up most of this country. With these photos, we can enjoy that thread of shared experience together.

19

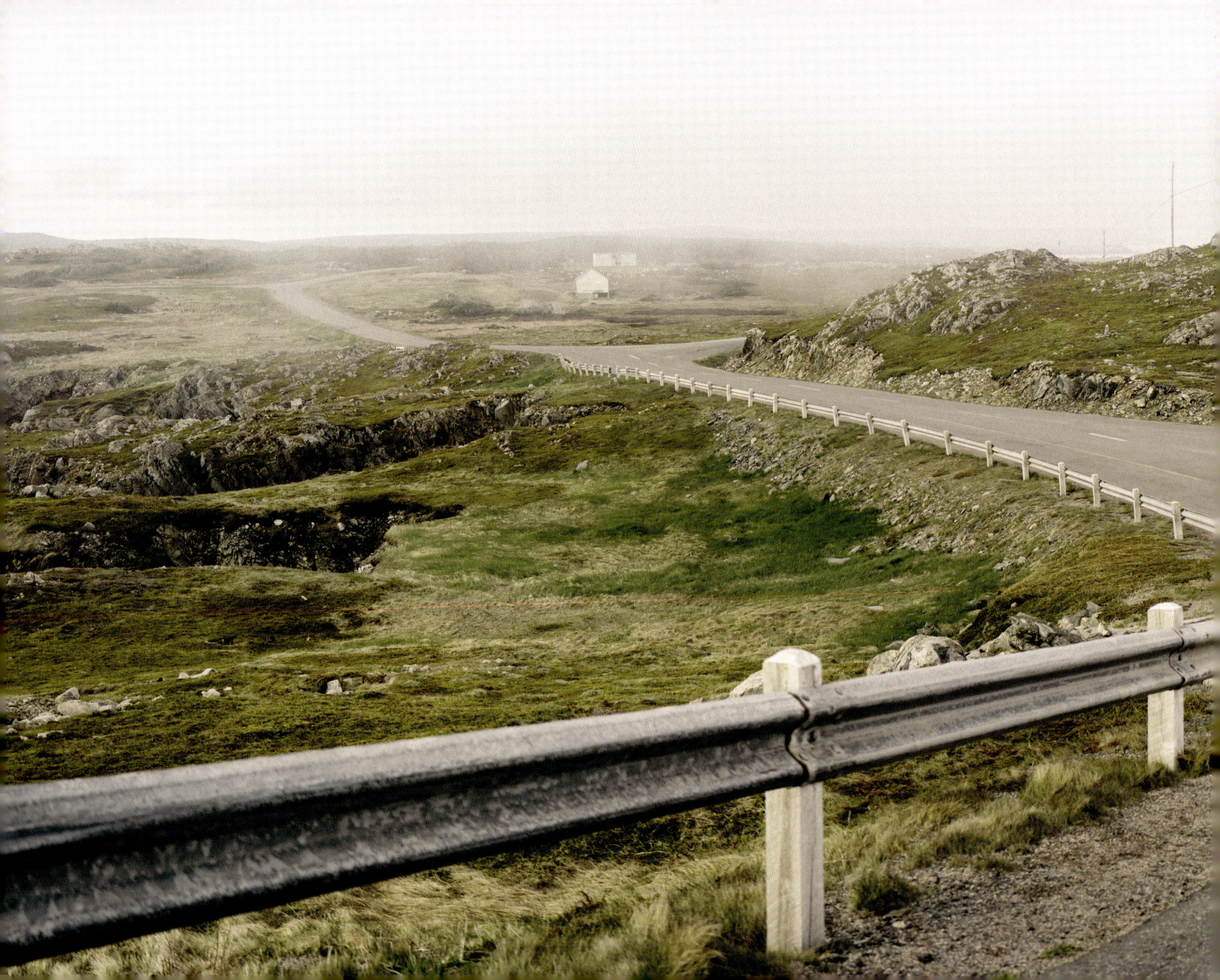

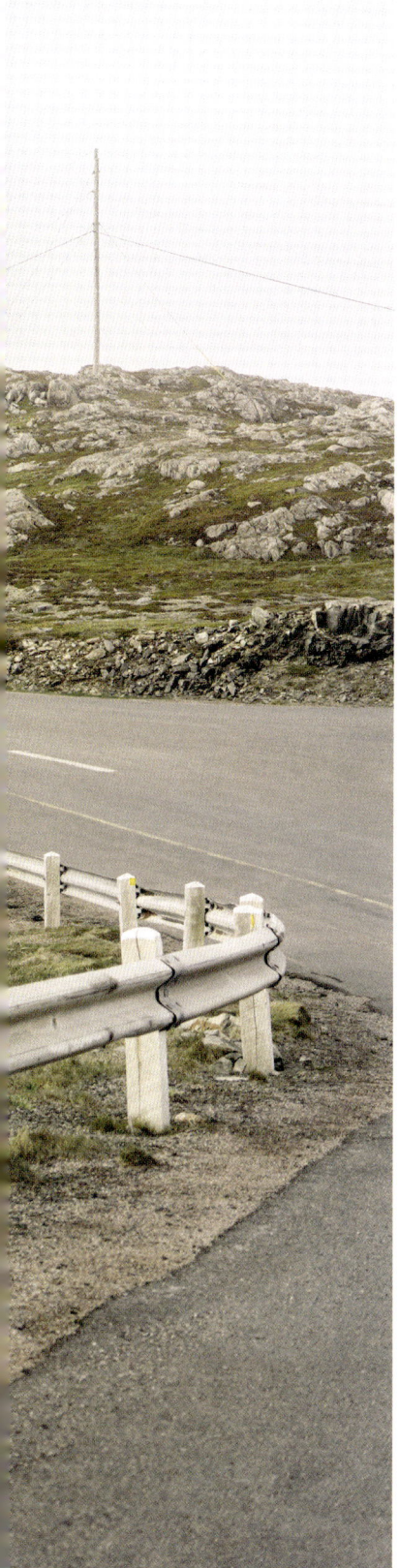

COMMUNITY PASTURES LOOK OUT OVER
THE ATLANTIC OCEAN. BONAVISTA,
NEWFOUNDLAND, MAY 2022.

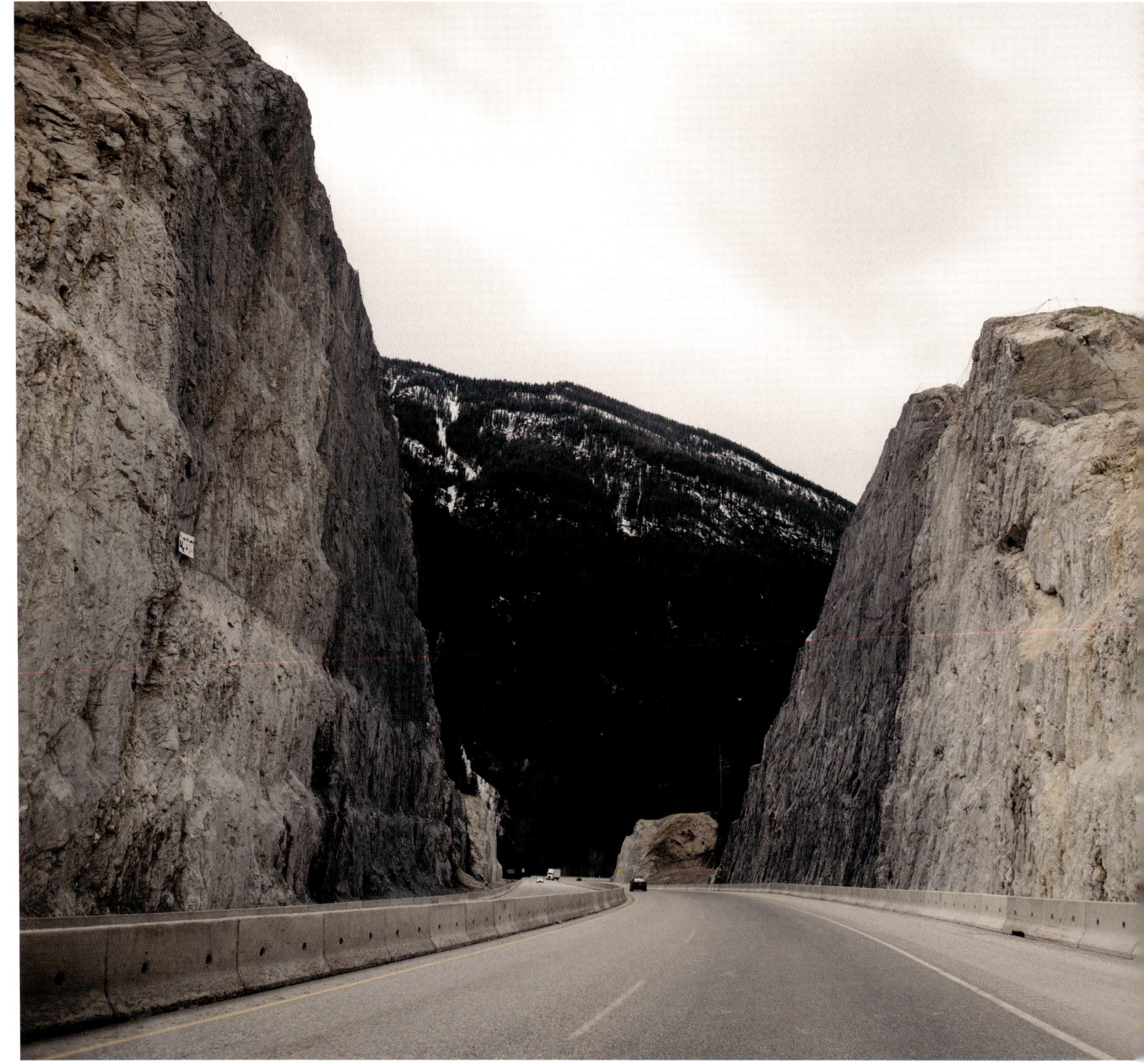

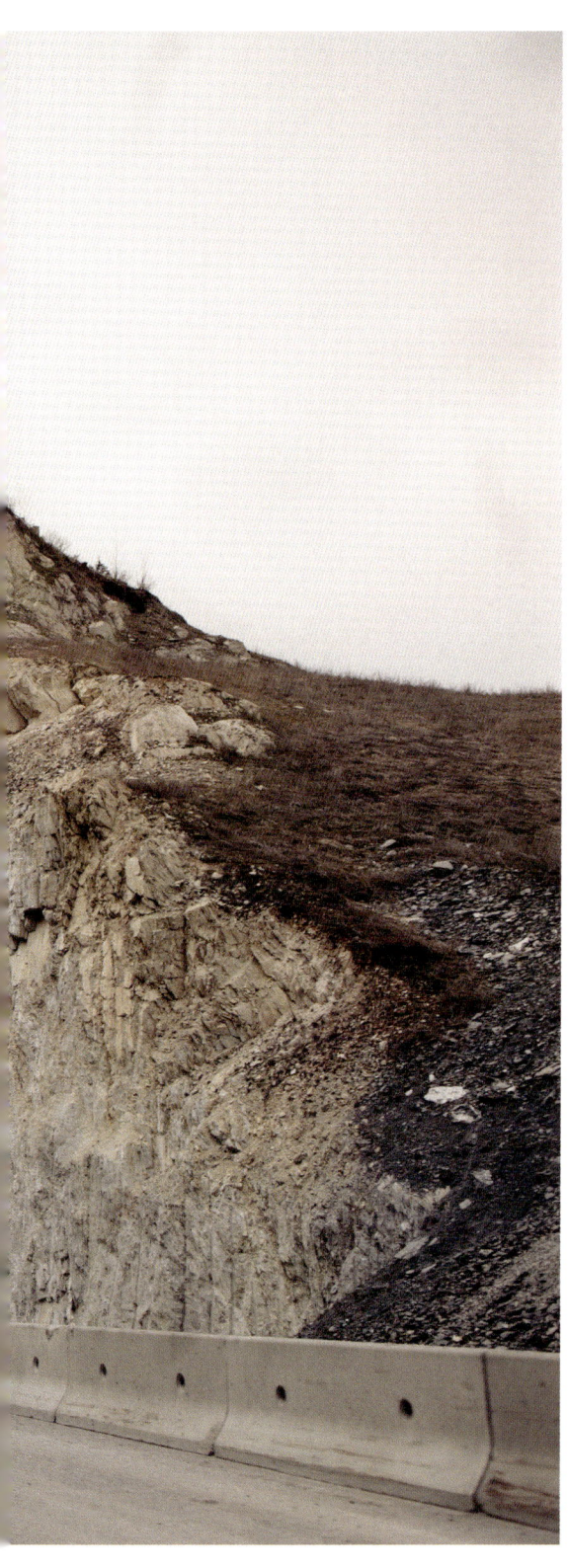

IT IS A MONUMENTAL ENDEAVOUR TO
CROSS A CONTINENT, AND THE SHEER
SENSE OF SCALE CAN REALLY ONLY
BE APPRECIATED WITH TIME SPENT
ON THE ROAD. ROGERS PASS,
BRITISH COLUMBIA, APRIL 2013.

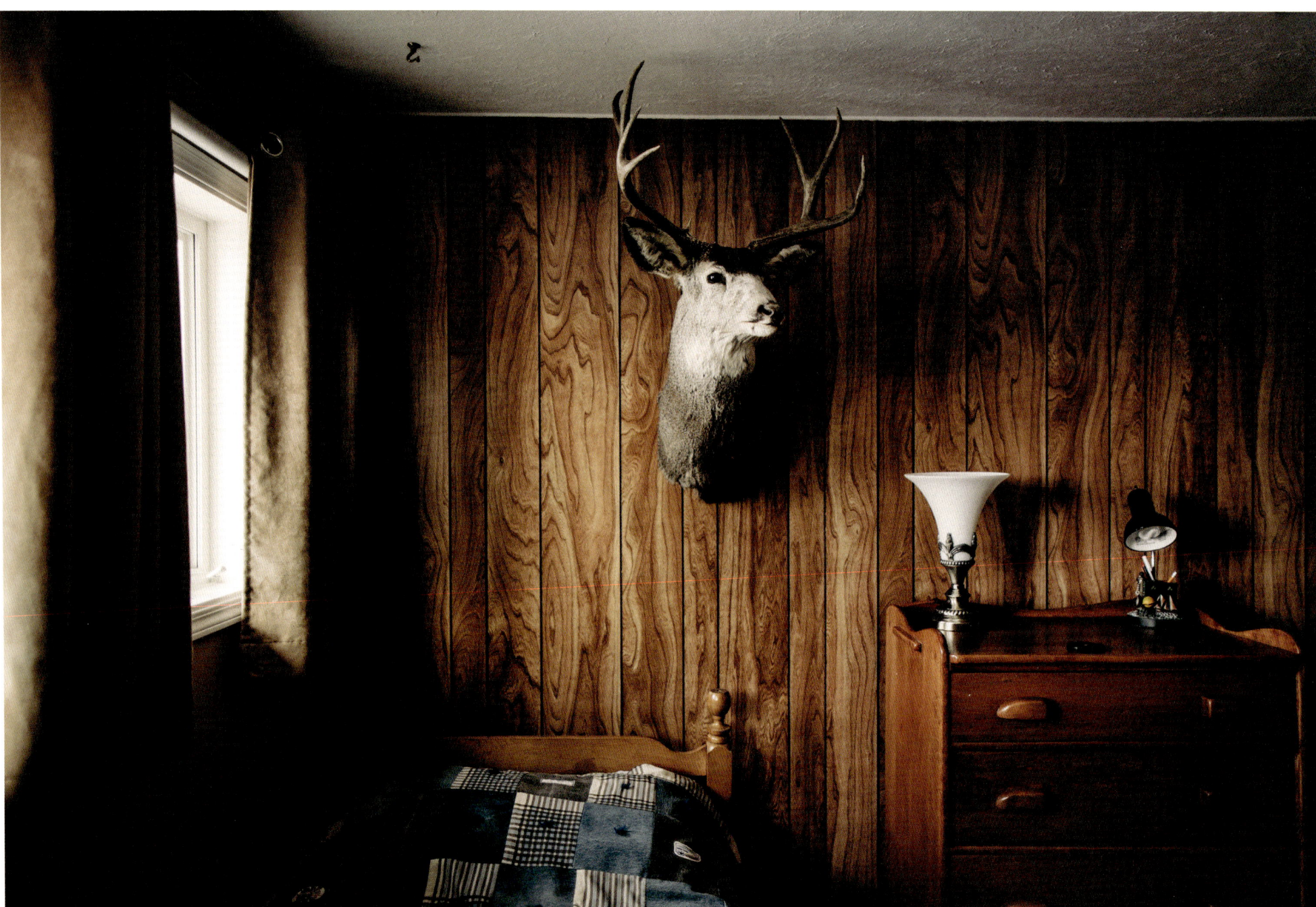

LIKE MANY OTHER FAMILIES, MINE LEFT EASTERN EUROPE AND INITIALLY SETTLED IN SASKATCHEWAN. WE DISPERSED FROM THERE, BUT A FEW RELATIVES STAYED. I'VE BEEN BACK TO VISIT MANY TIMES. THIS IS MY COUSIN'S SPARE ROOM IN CLAYBANK, SASKATCHEWAN, APRIL 2013.

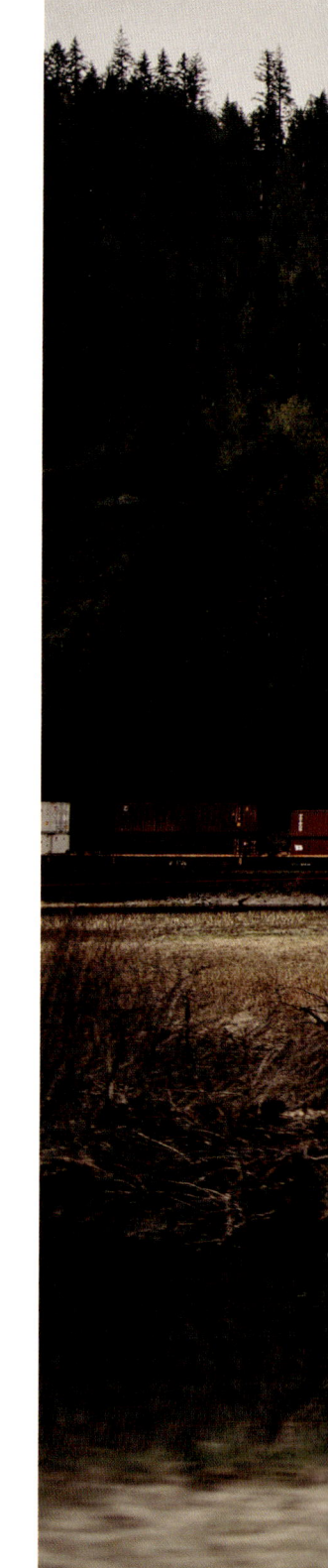

TRAVELLING ALONGSIDE THE TRAIN
ON THE TRANS-CANADA HIGHWAY
IN BRITISH COLUMBIA, APRIL 2013.

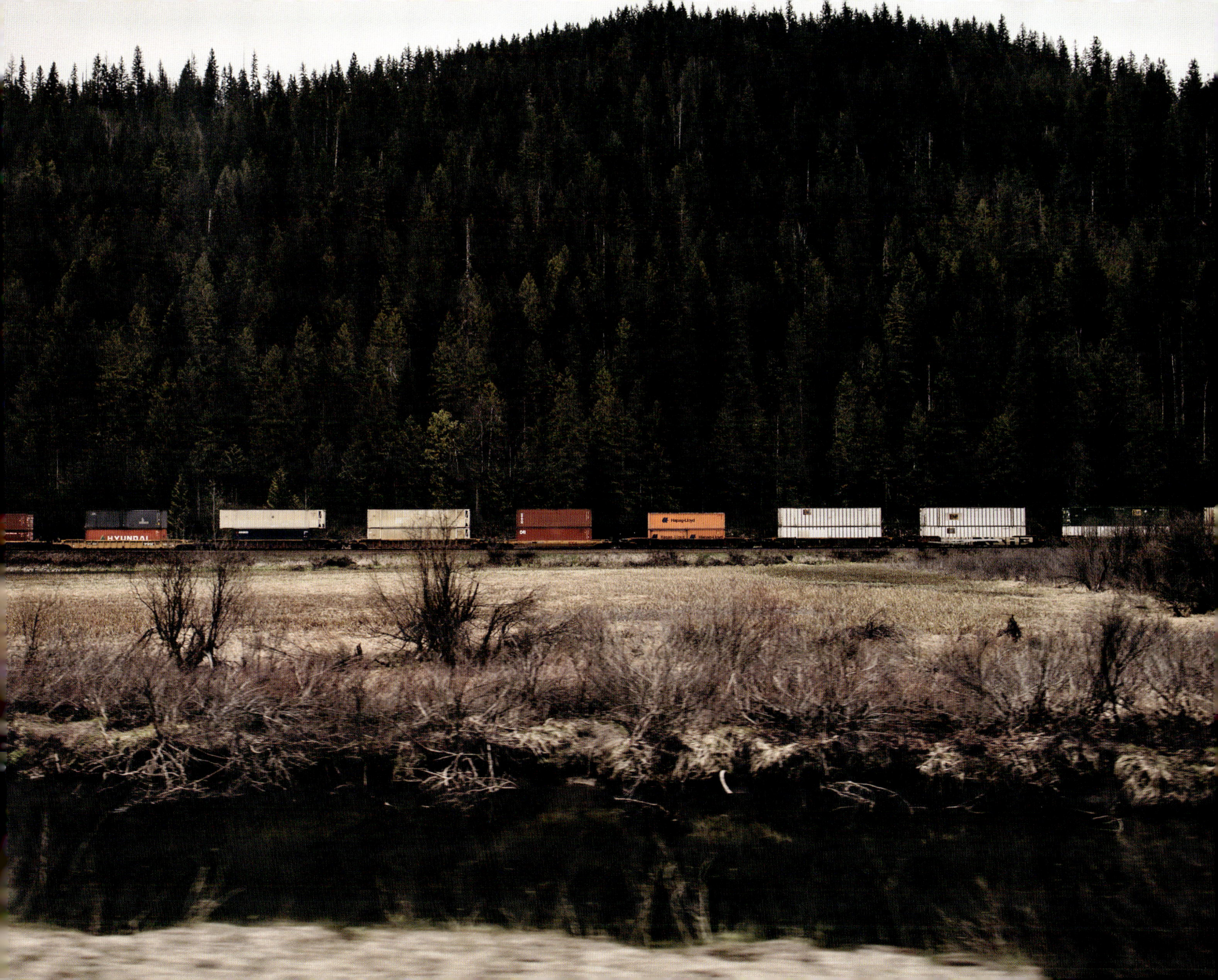

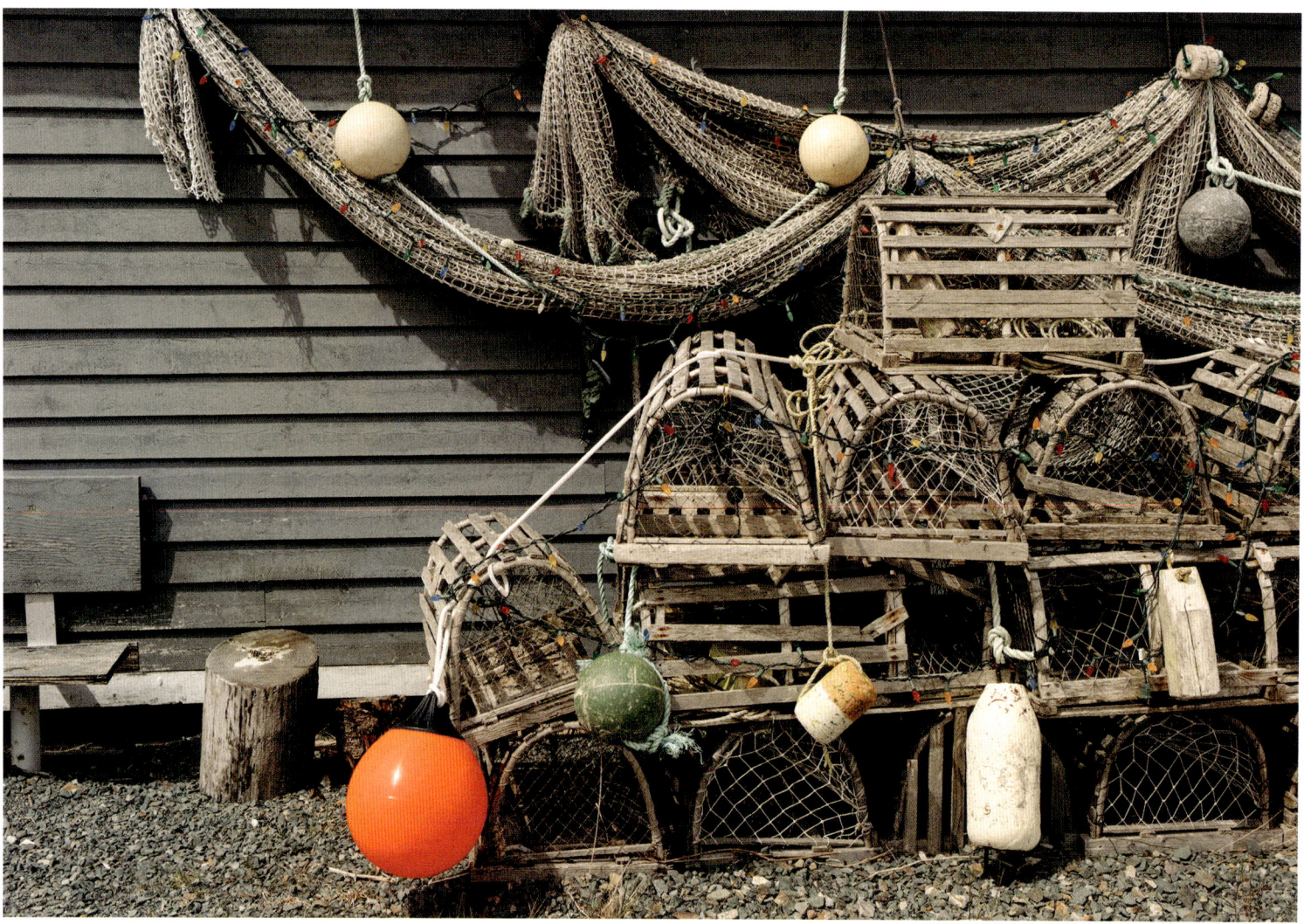

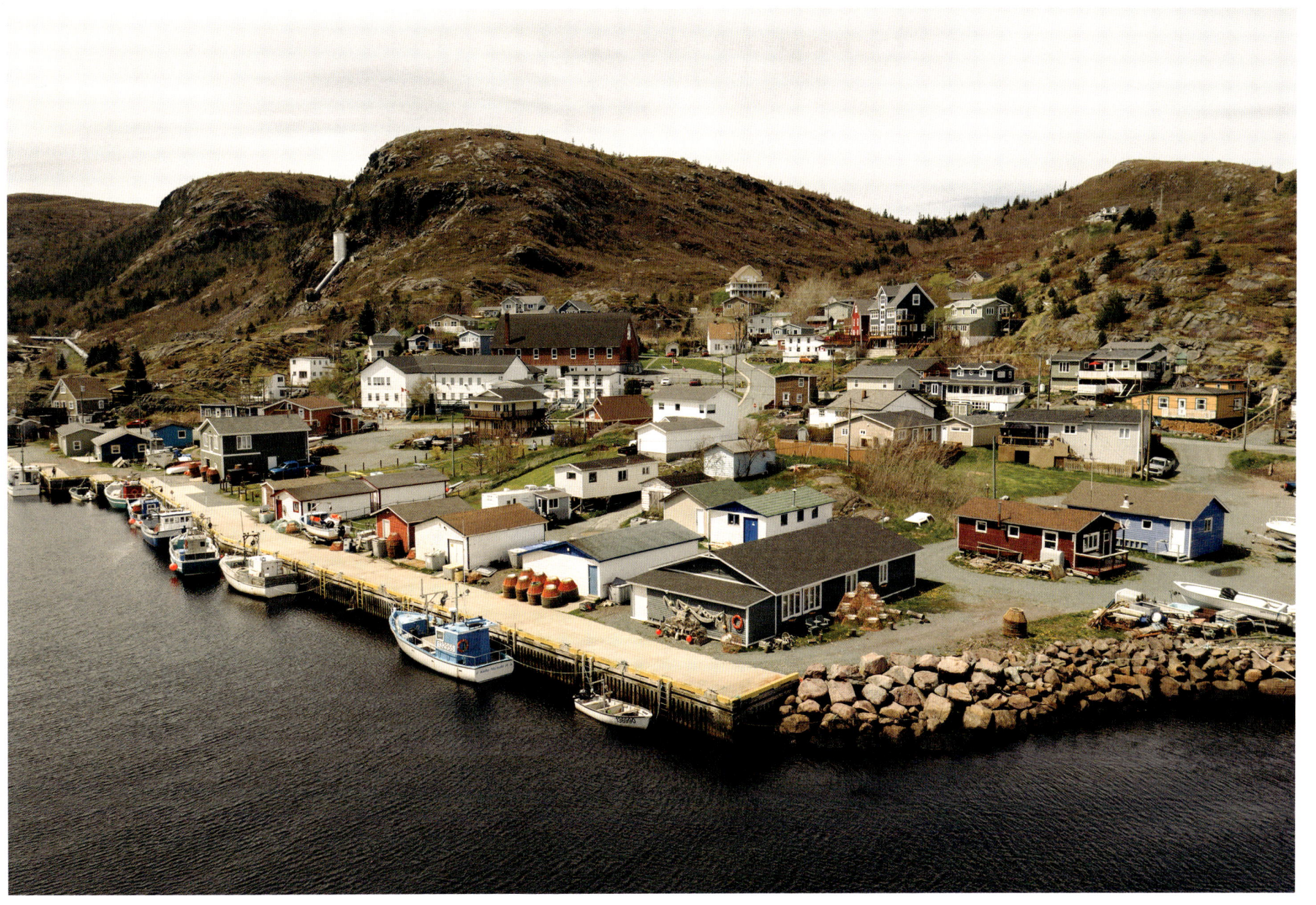

SPREAD PETTY HARBOUR, NEWFOUNDLAND, MAY 2022.

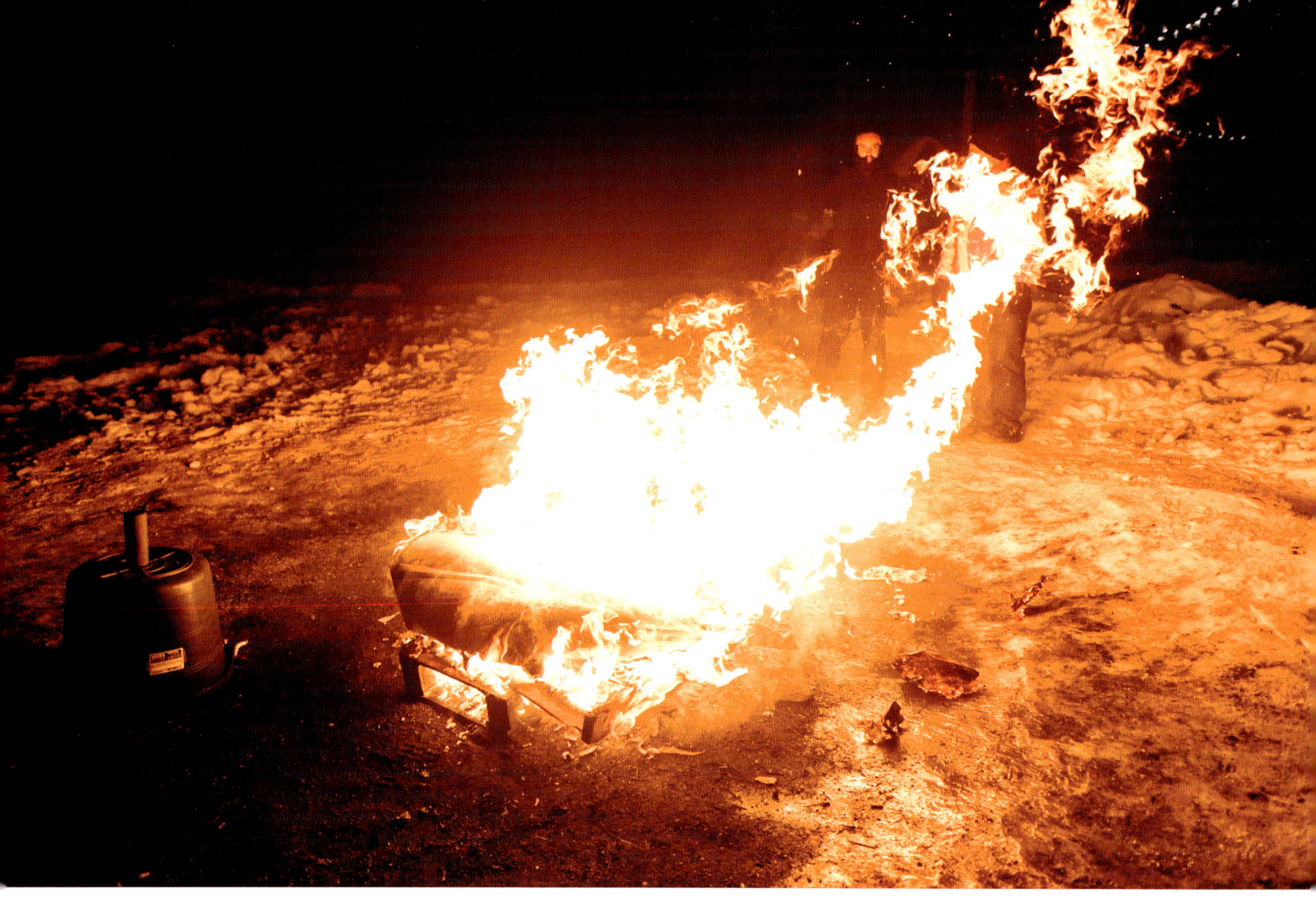

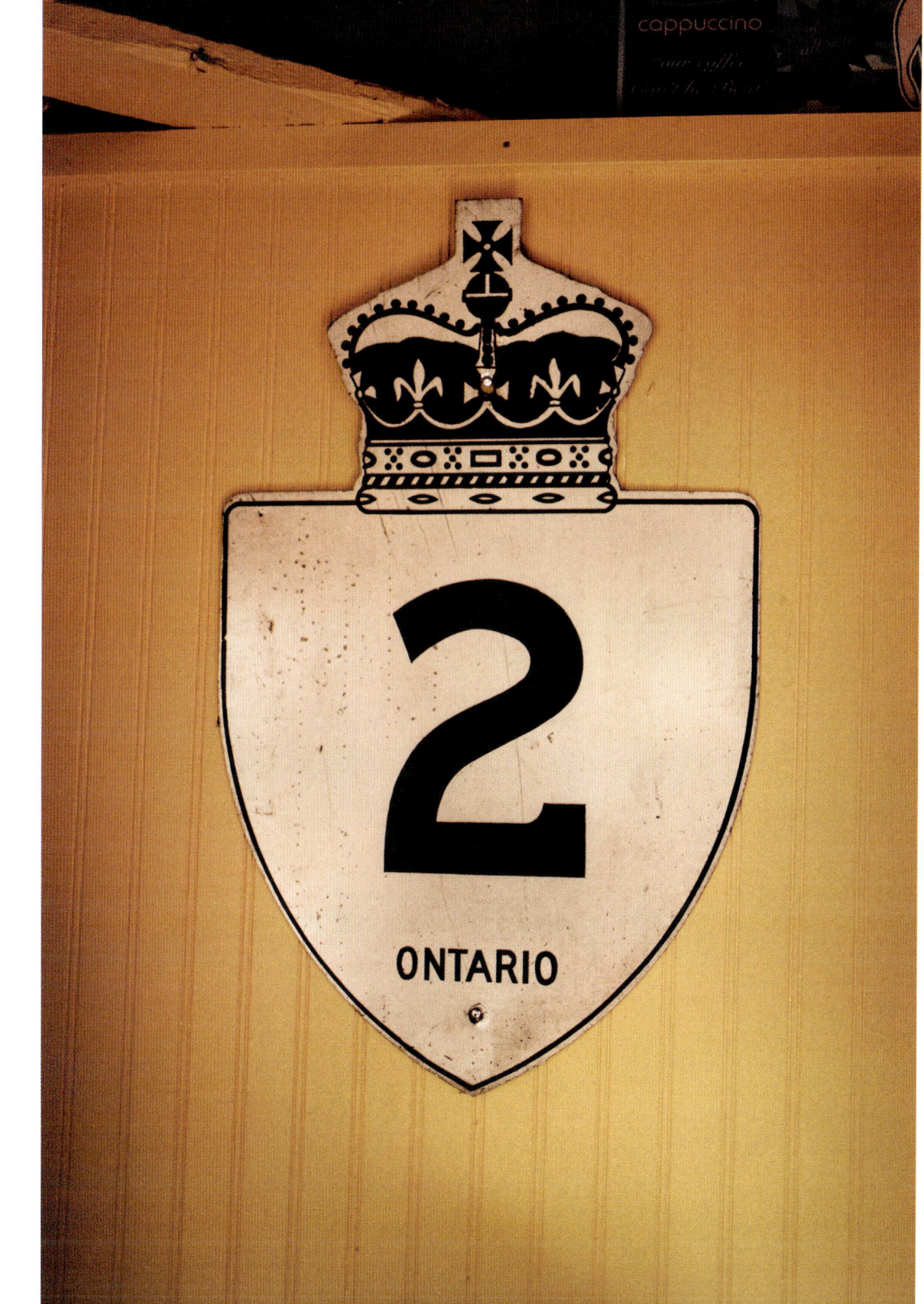

← NEW YEAR'S BONFIRE, SUNSHINE VALLEY,
BRITISH COLUMBIA, JANUARY 2016.

→ ROAD SIGN, MACTIER, ONTARIO, OCTOBER 2012.

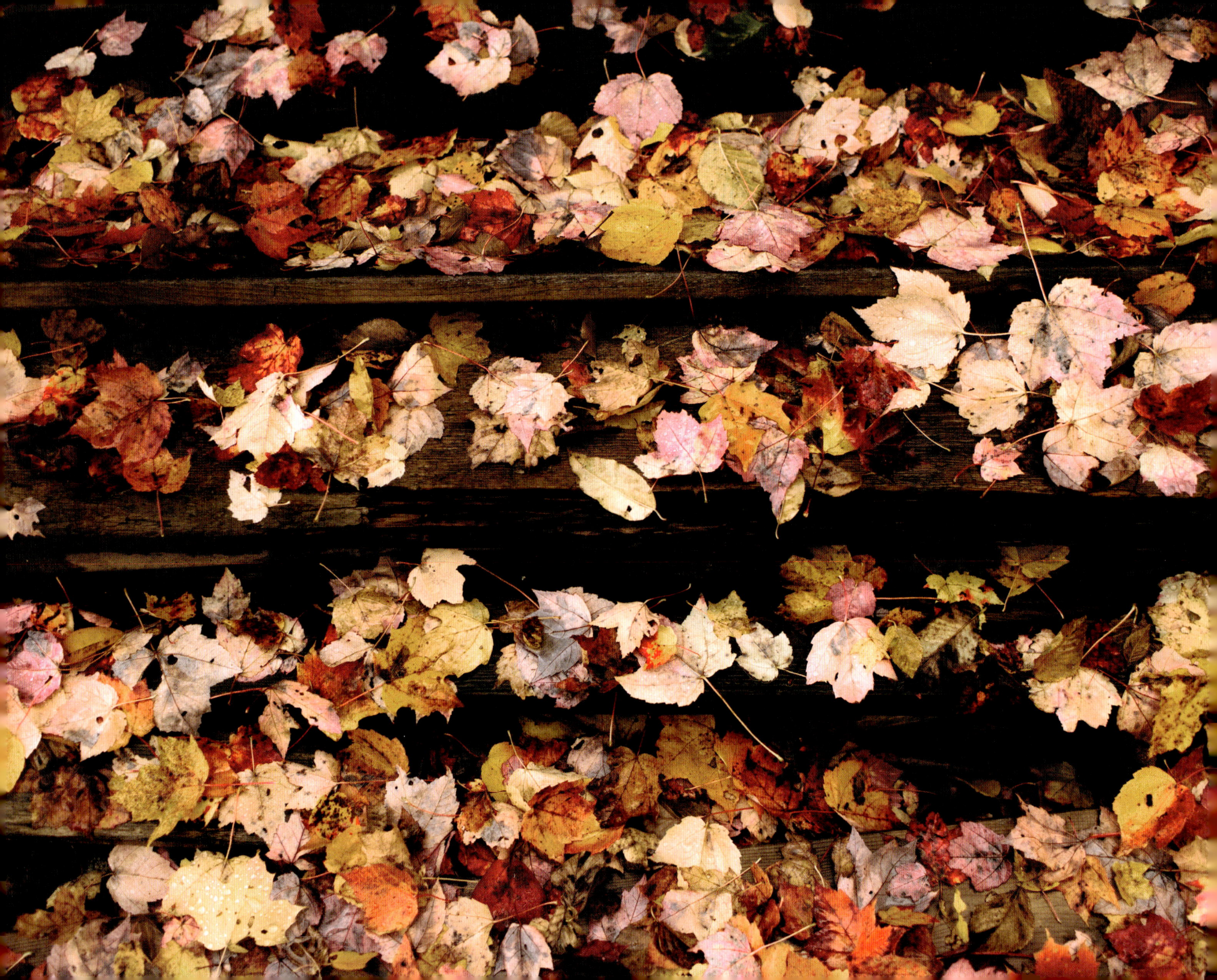

AN AUTUMN FIRE, MUSKOKA, ONTARIO, OCTOBER 2012.

DEER IN THE CANOLA FIELDS, MOOSE JAW, SASKATCHEWAN, JULY 2017.

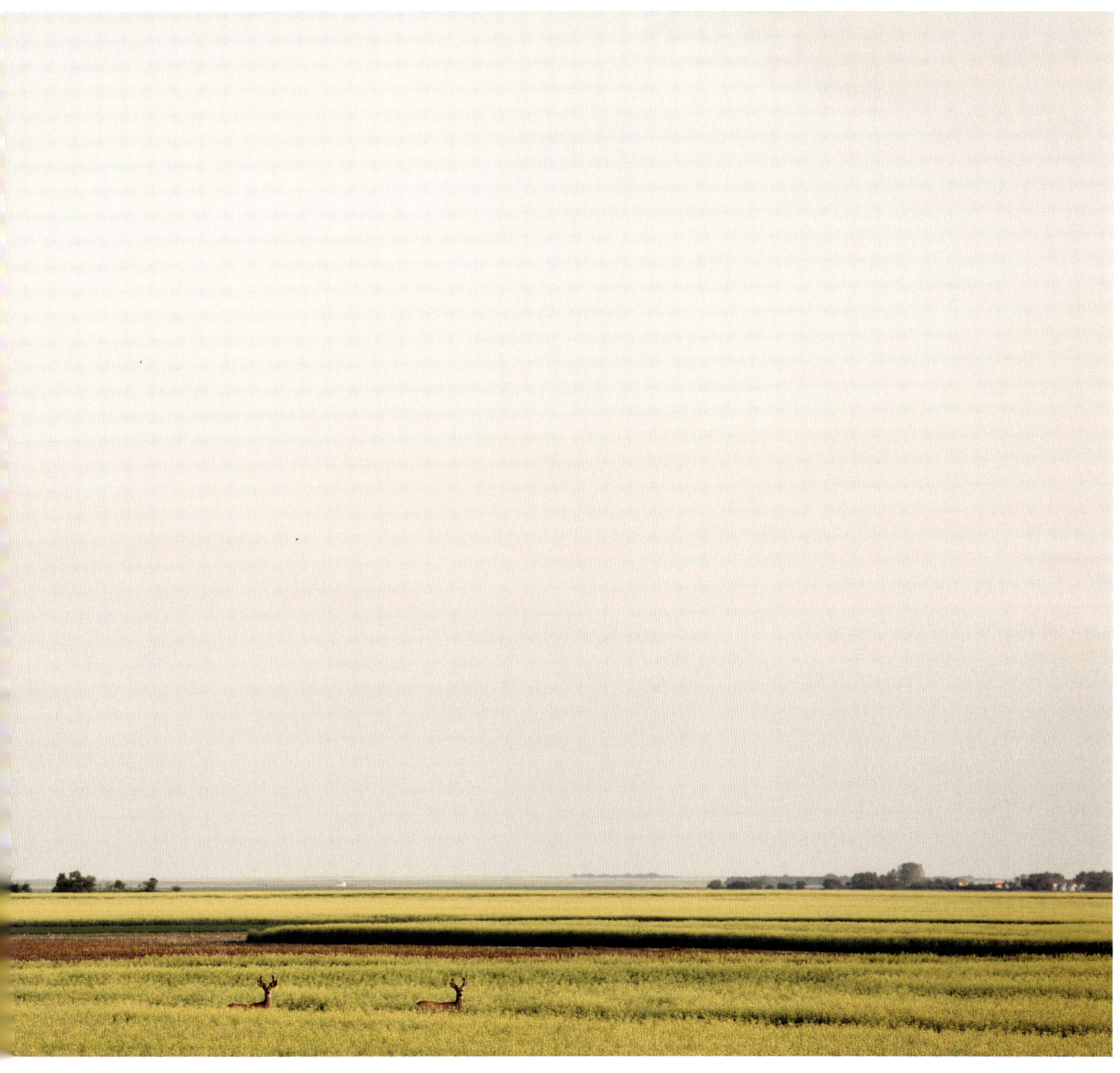

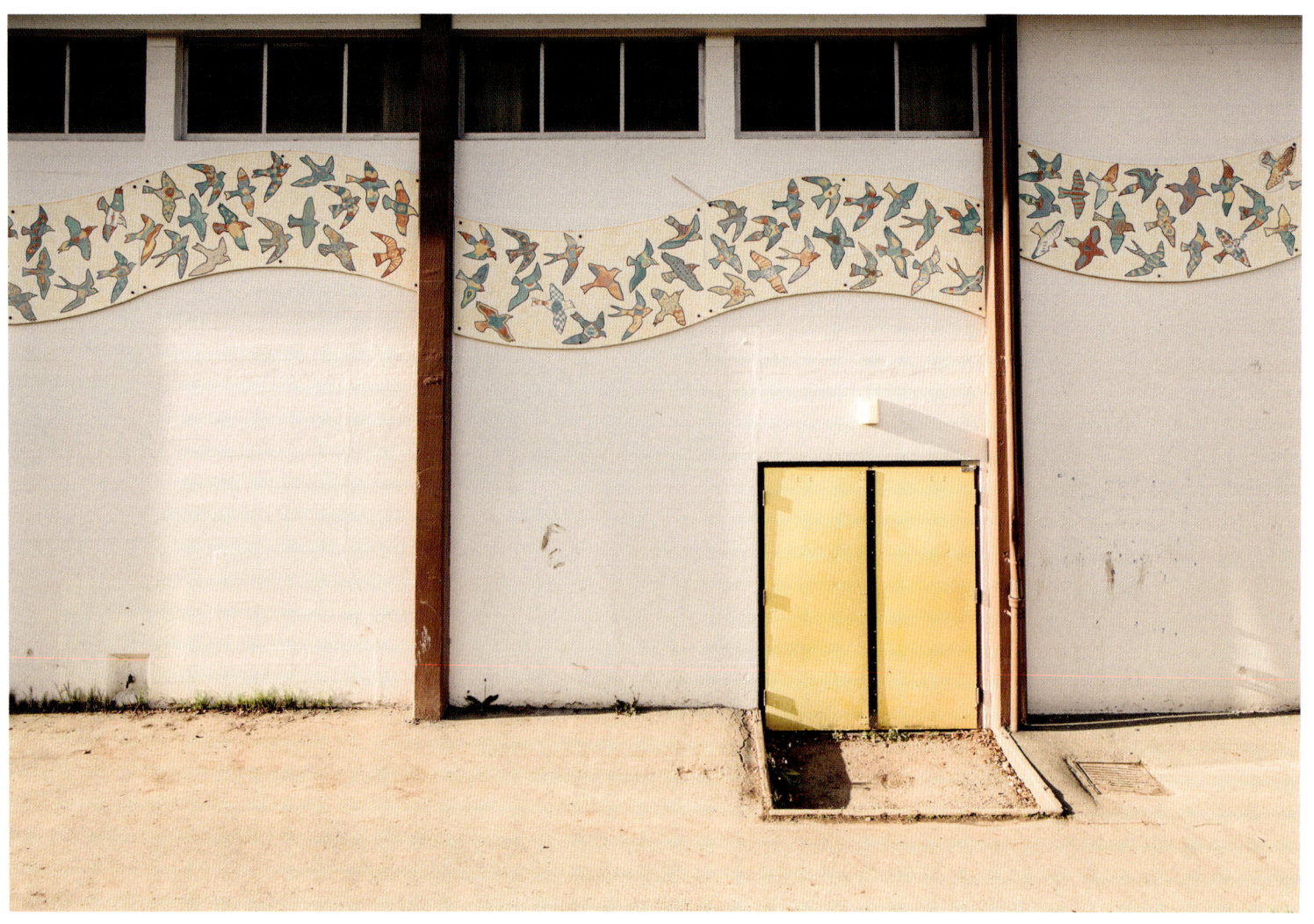

↑ ELEMENTARY SCHOOL, VANCOUVER, BRITISH COLUMBIA, APRIL 2017.

→ BIRDS FLOCK OVER SLAVE LAKE, ALBERTA, JULY 2012.

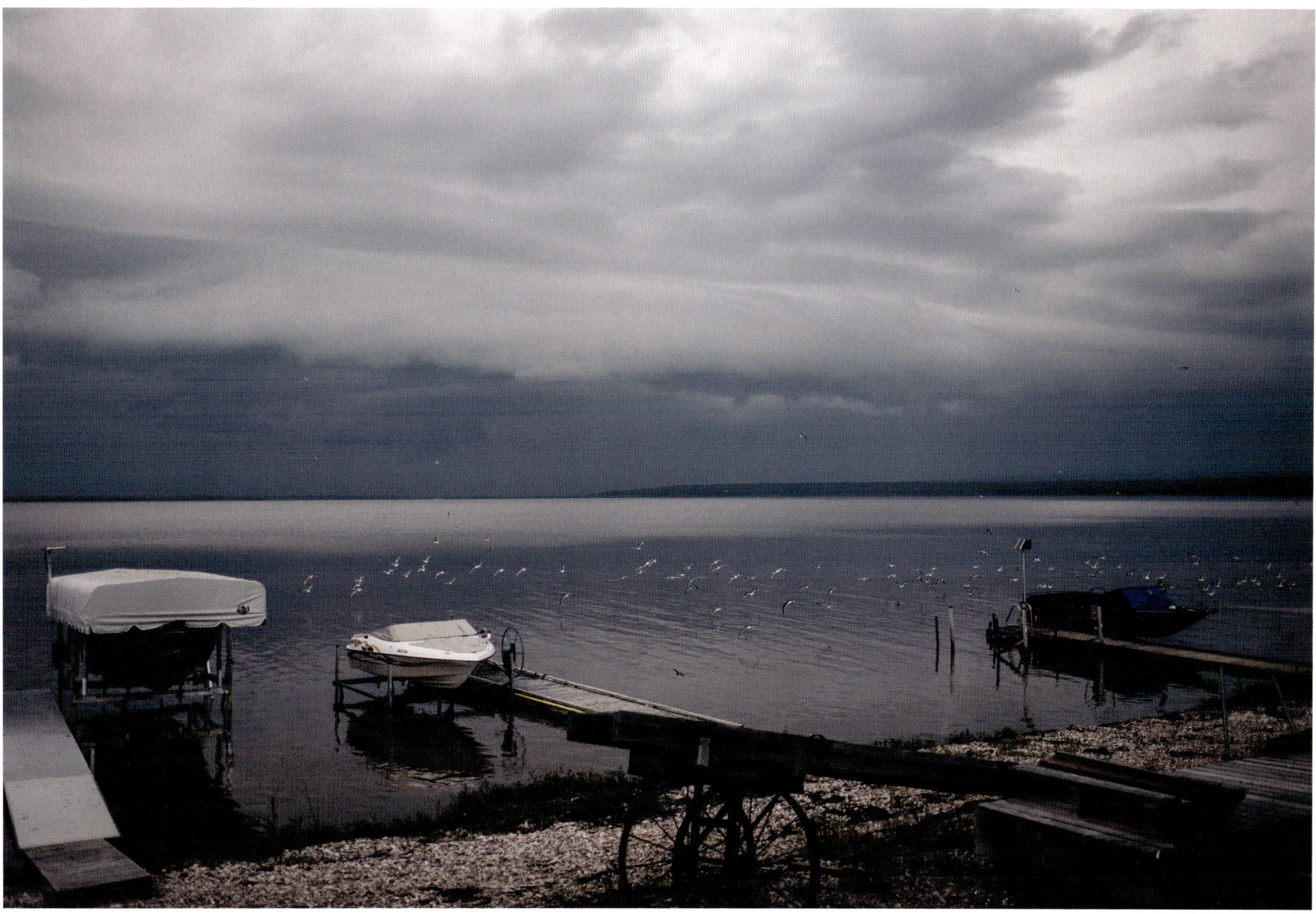

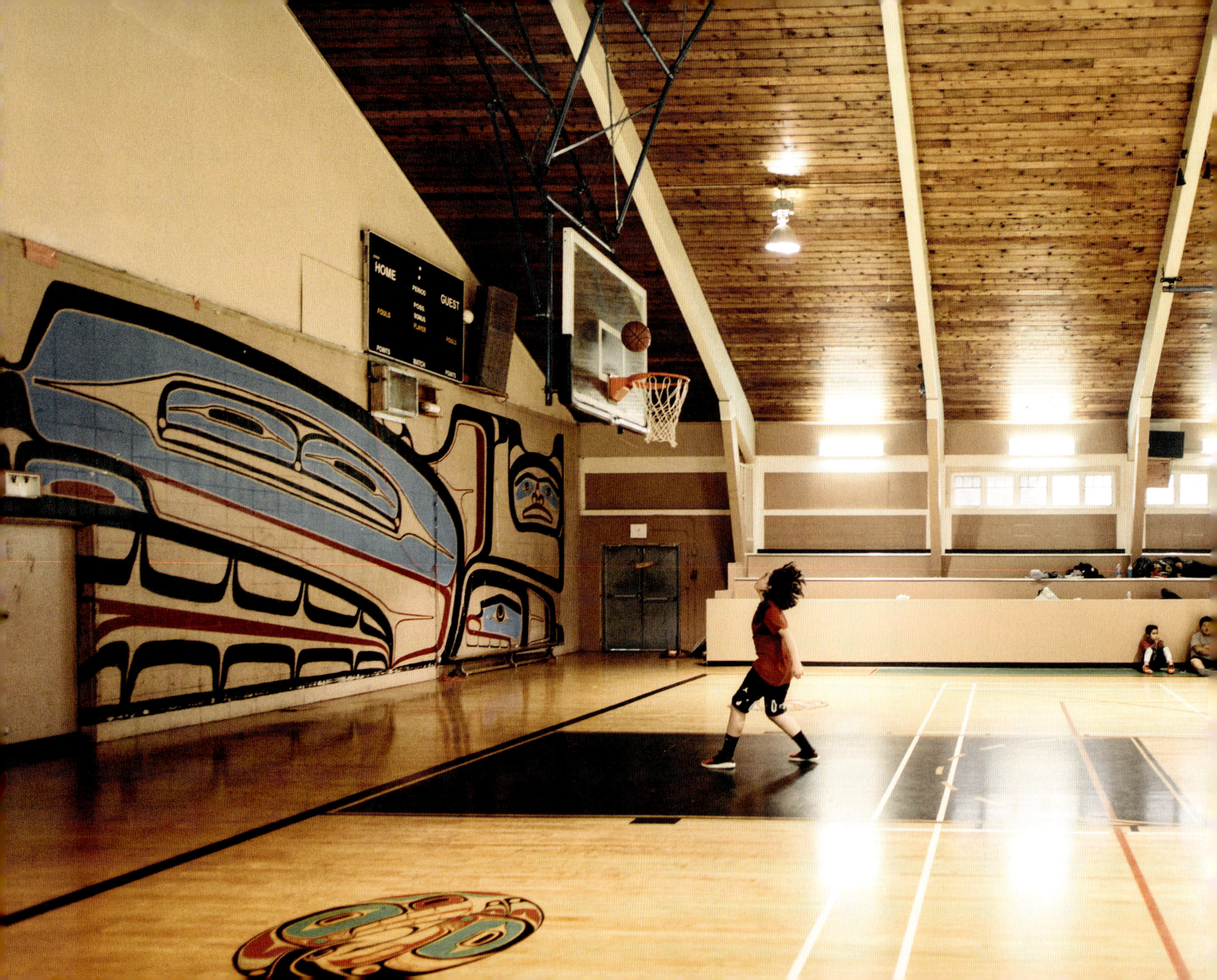

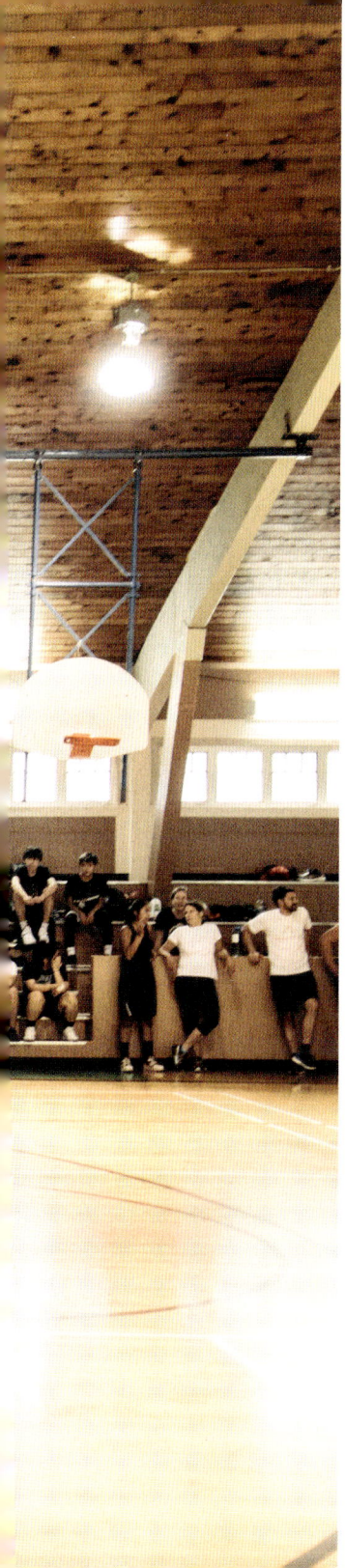

SHOOTING HOOPS IN BELLA BELLA, ALSO KNOWN AS WAGLISLA, WHICH IS THE HOME TO THE HEILTSUK NATION. BASKETBALL IS PARTICULARLY POPULAR IN NORTHERN BC. BELLA BELLA, BRITISH COLUMBIA, OCTOBER 2017.

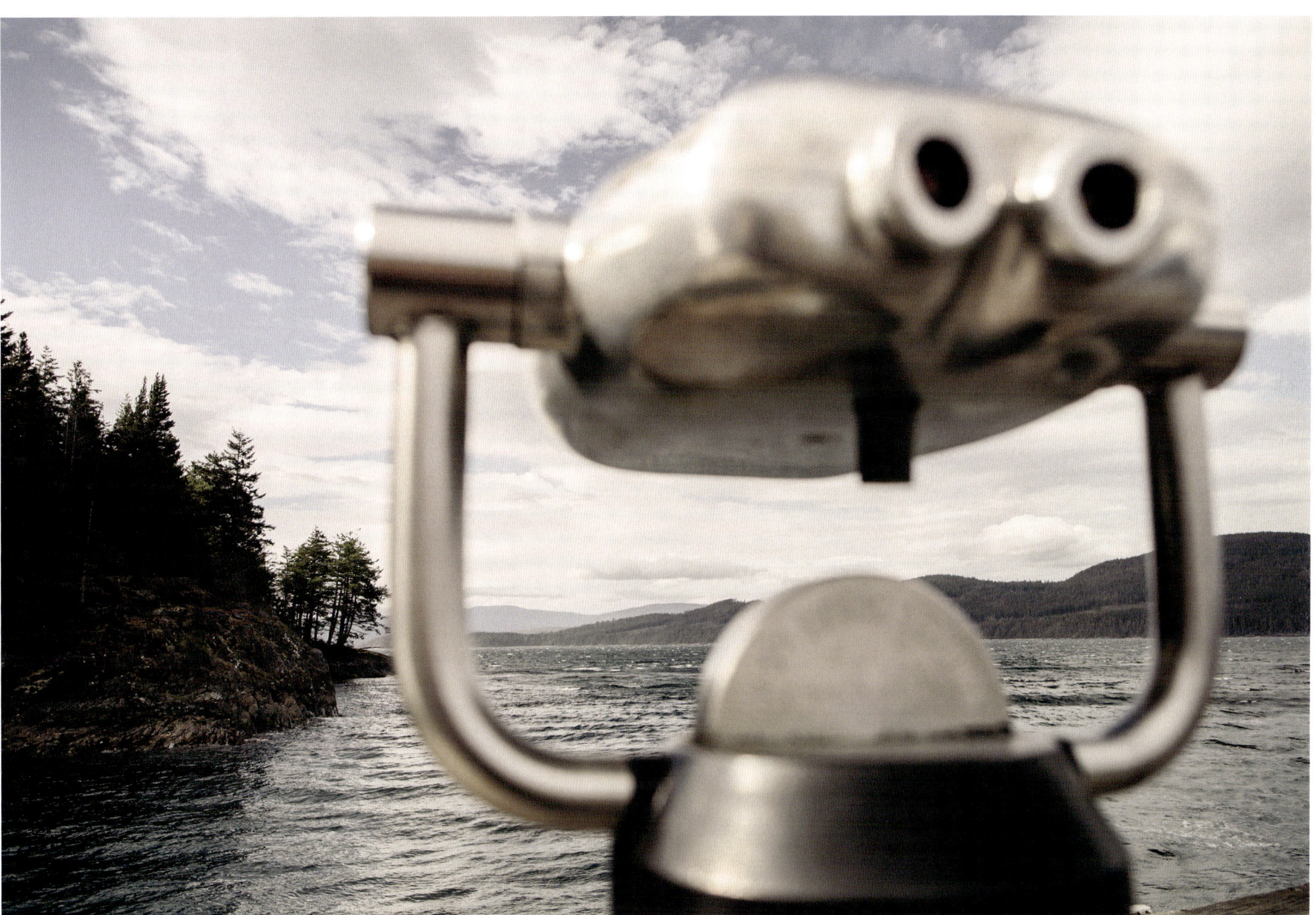

↓ FISHING BOAT MURAL IN PORT HARDY, VANCOUVER ISLAND, BRITISH COLUMBIA, OCTOBER 2017.

→ FISHING BOAT, CAPE BRETON ISLAND, NOVA SCOTIA, AUGUST 2017.

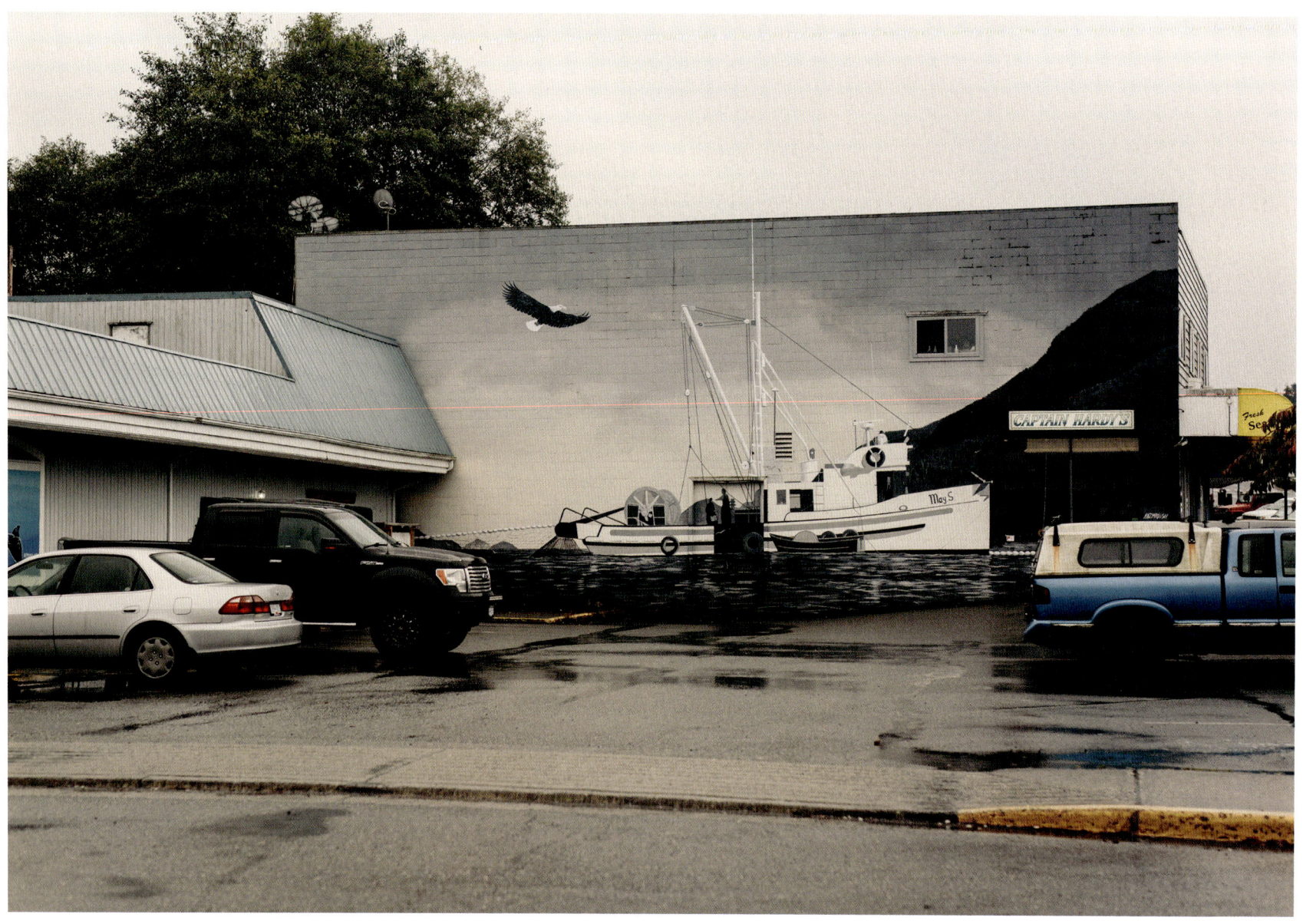

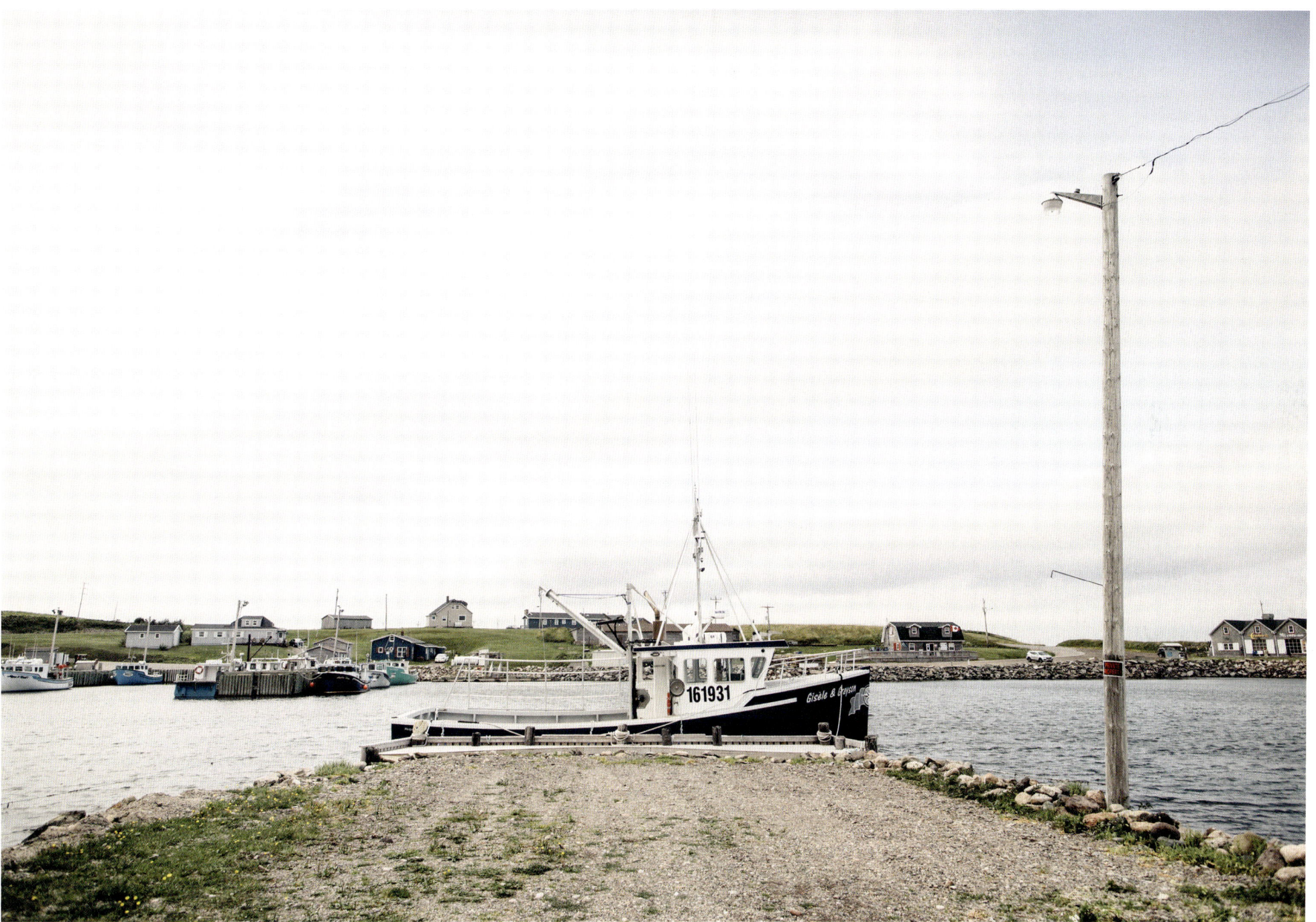

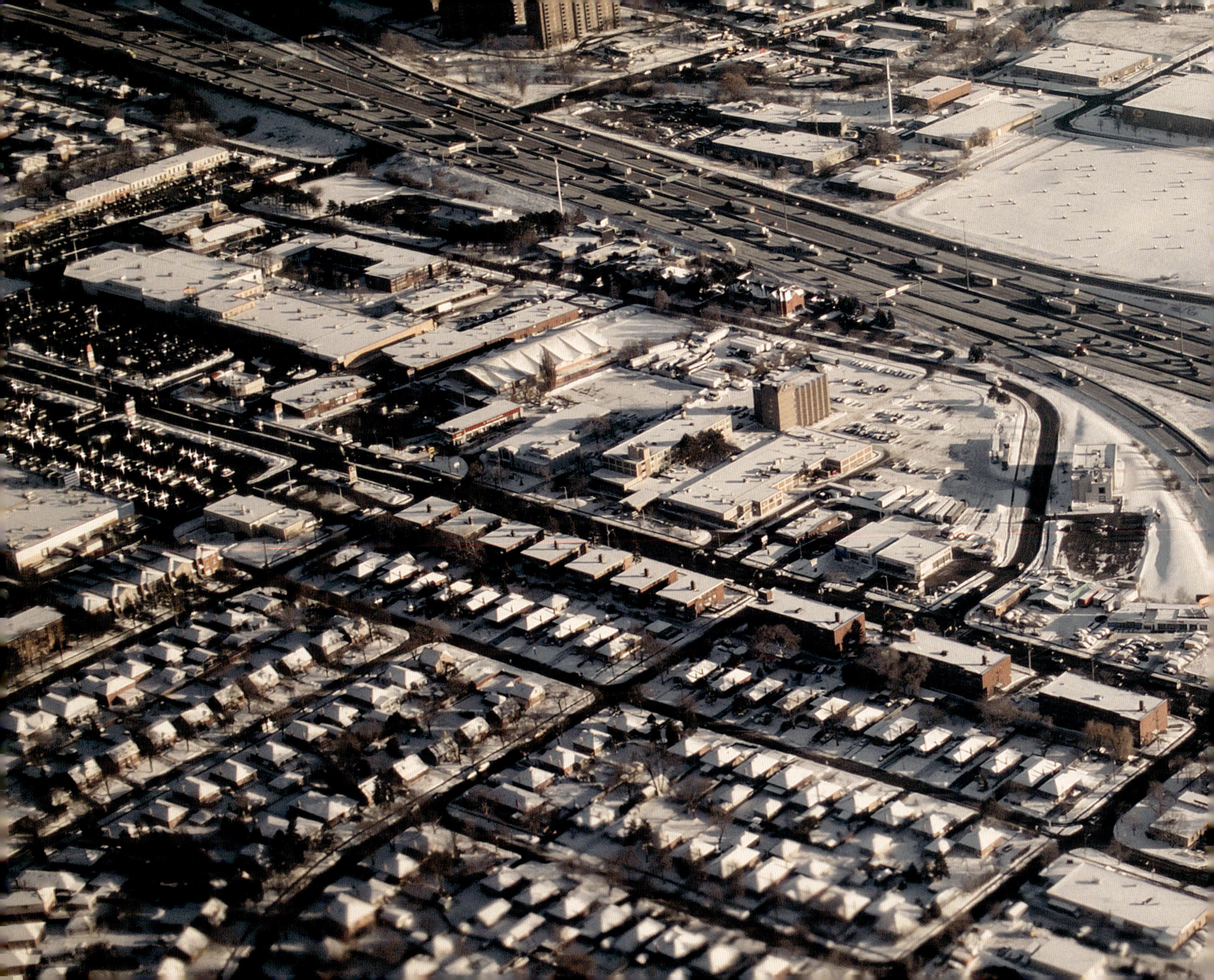

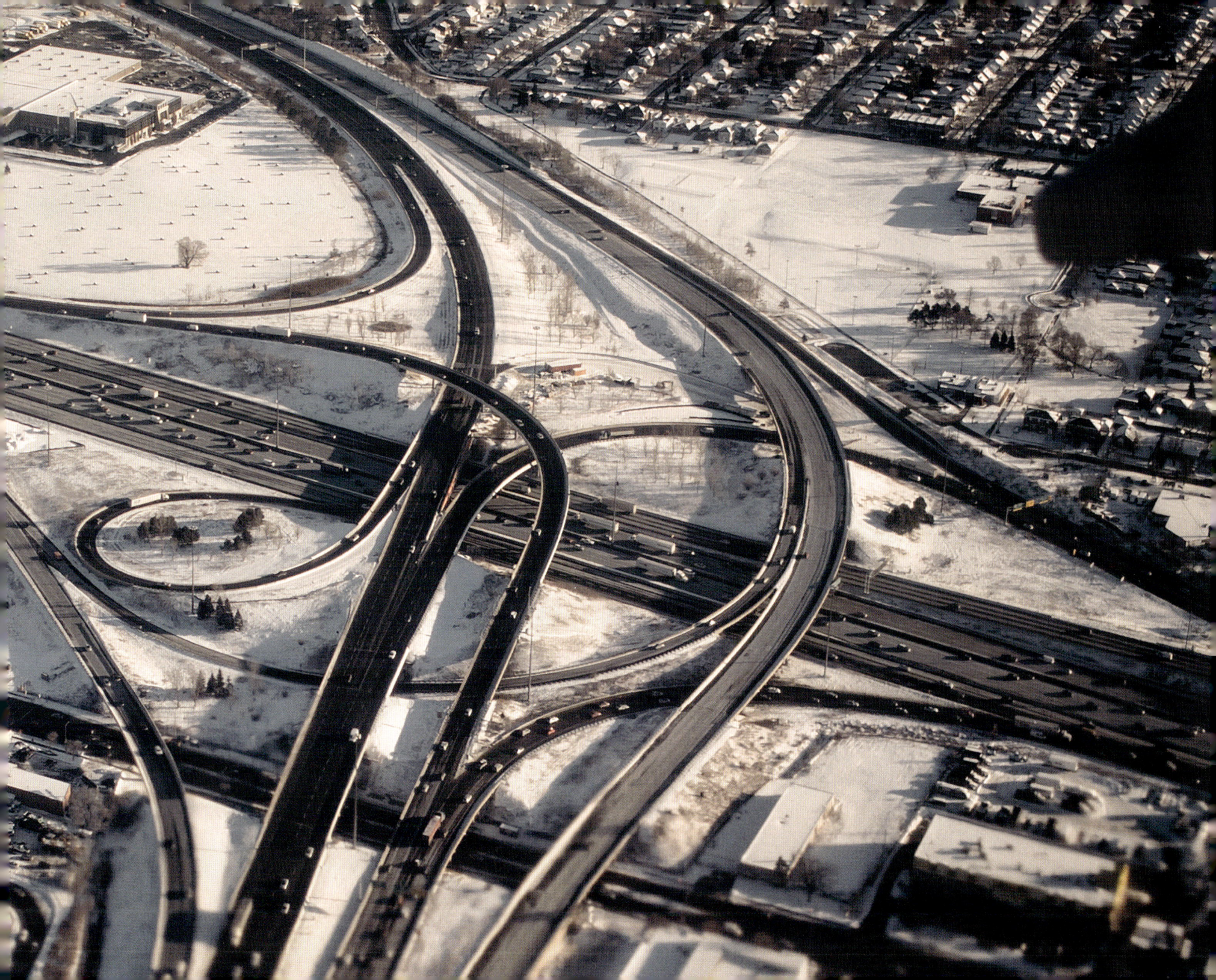

46

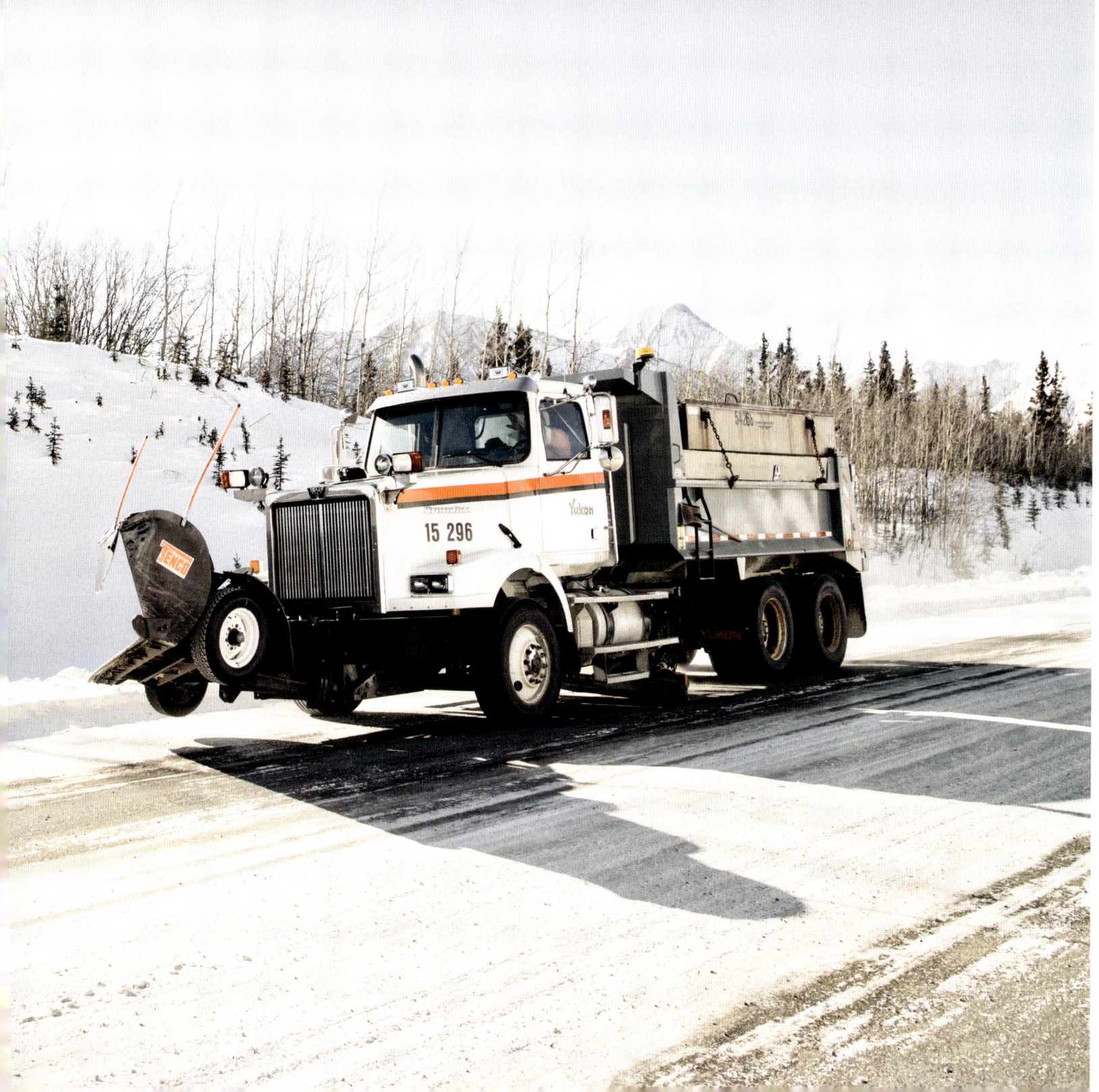

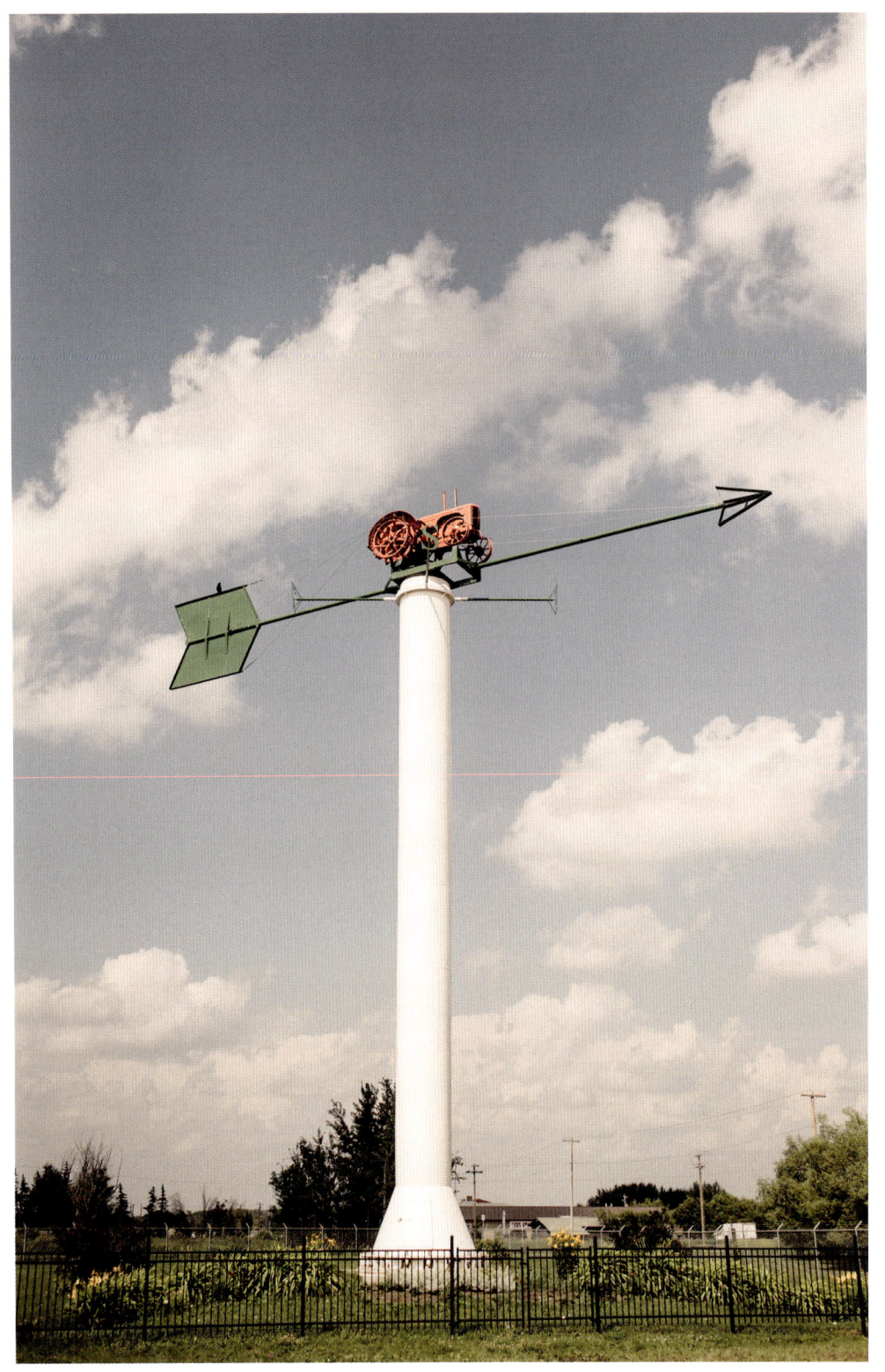

→ MAIN STREET CHRISTMAS TRACTOR
PARADE, SCHOMBERG, ONTARIO,
DECEMBER 2018.

← WEATHERVANE AT THE CANADIAN
TRACTOR MUSEUM, WESTLOCK,
ALBERTA, JULY 2012.

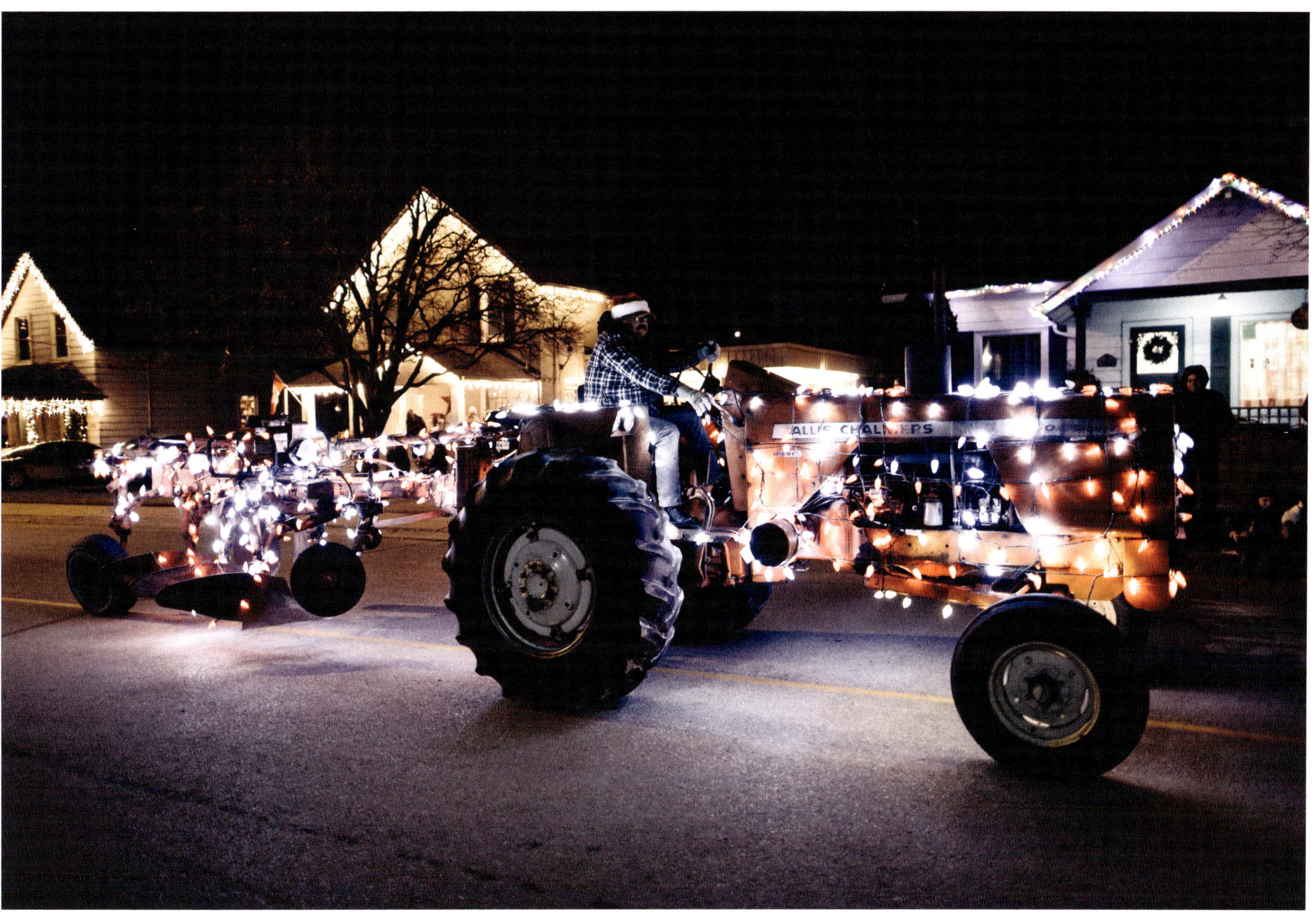

CLEARWATER COUNTY, ALBERTA, JANUARY 2019.

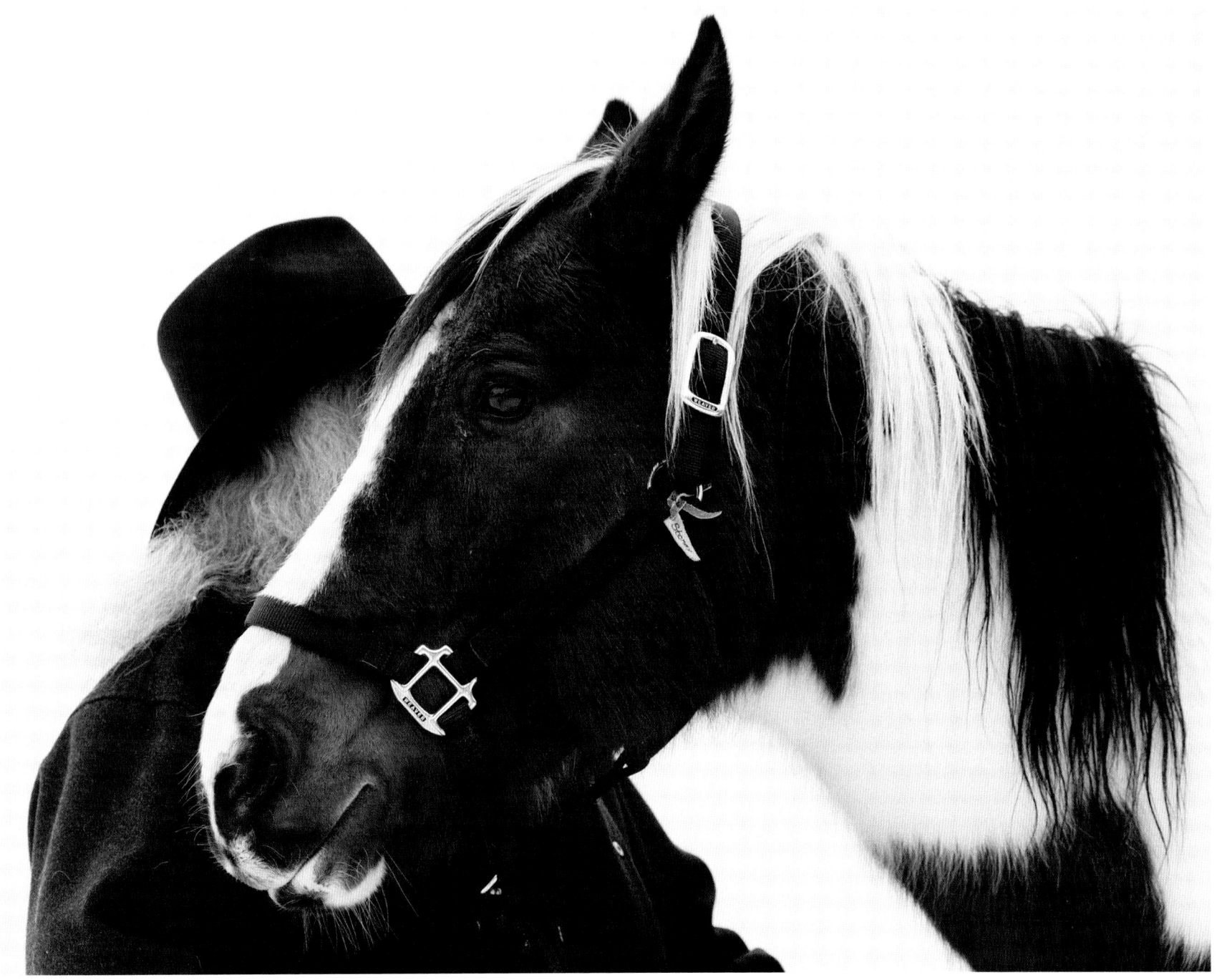

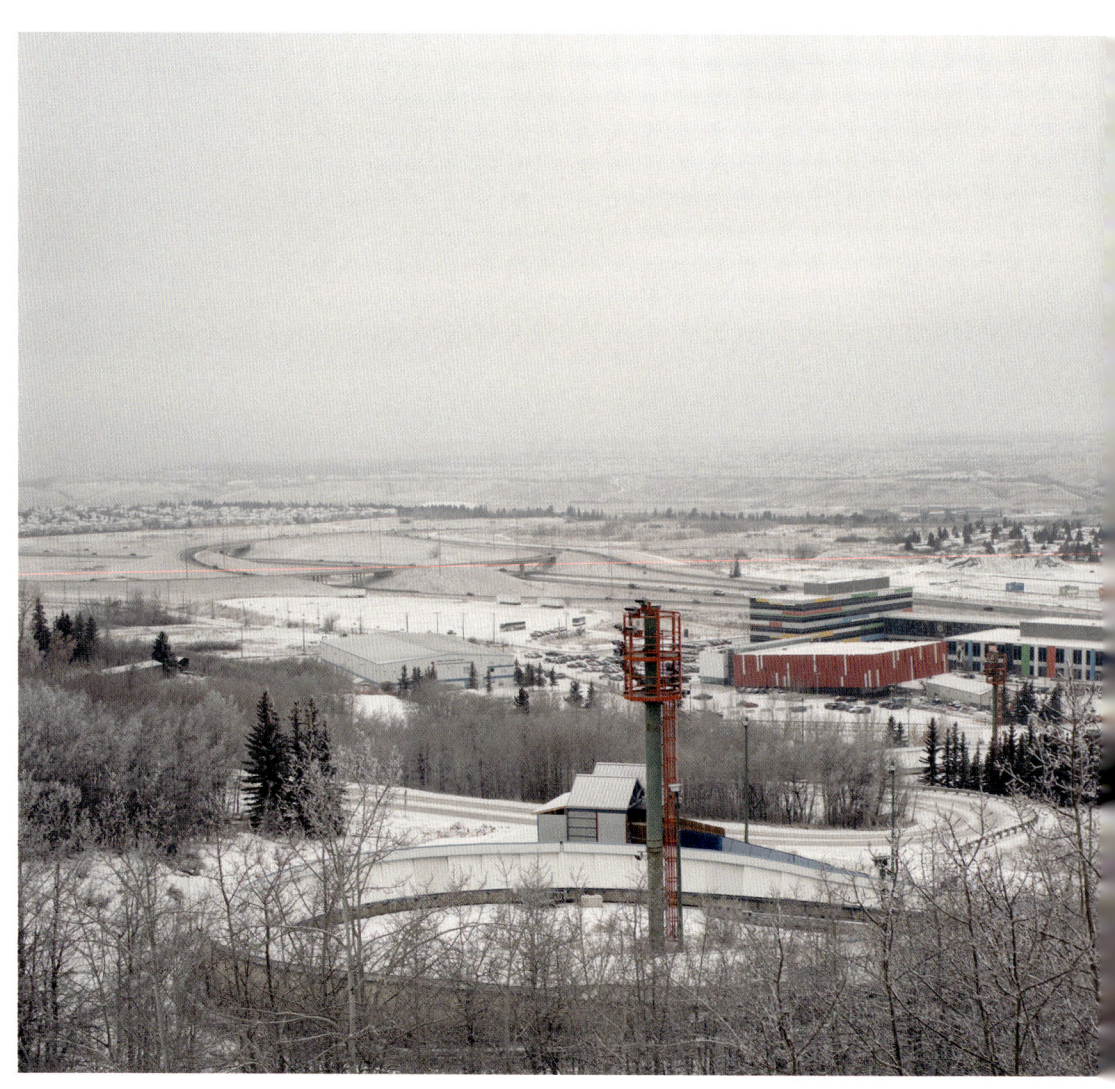

SPREAD BOBSLED TRACK AT WINSPORT,
WHERE THE WINTER OLYMPICS WERE HELD
IN 1988. CALGARY, ALBERTA, FEBRUARY 2019.

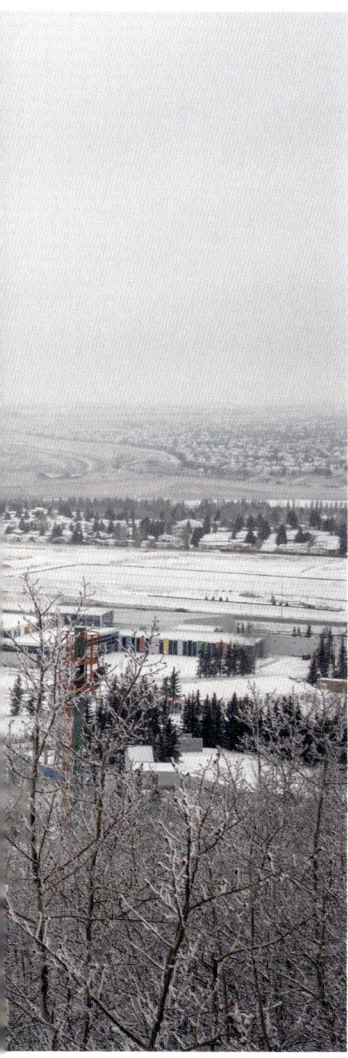

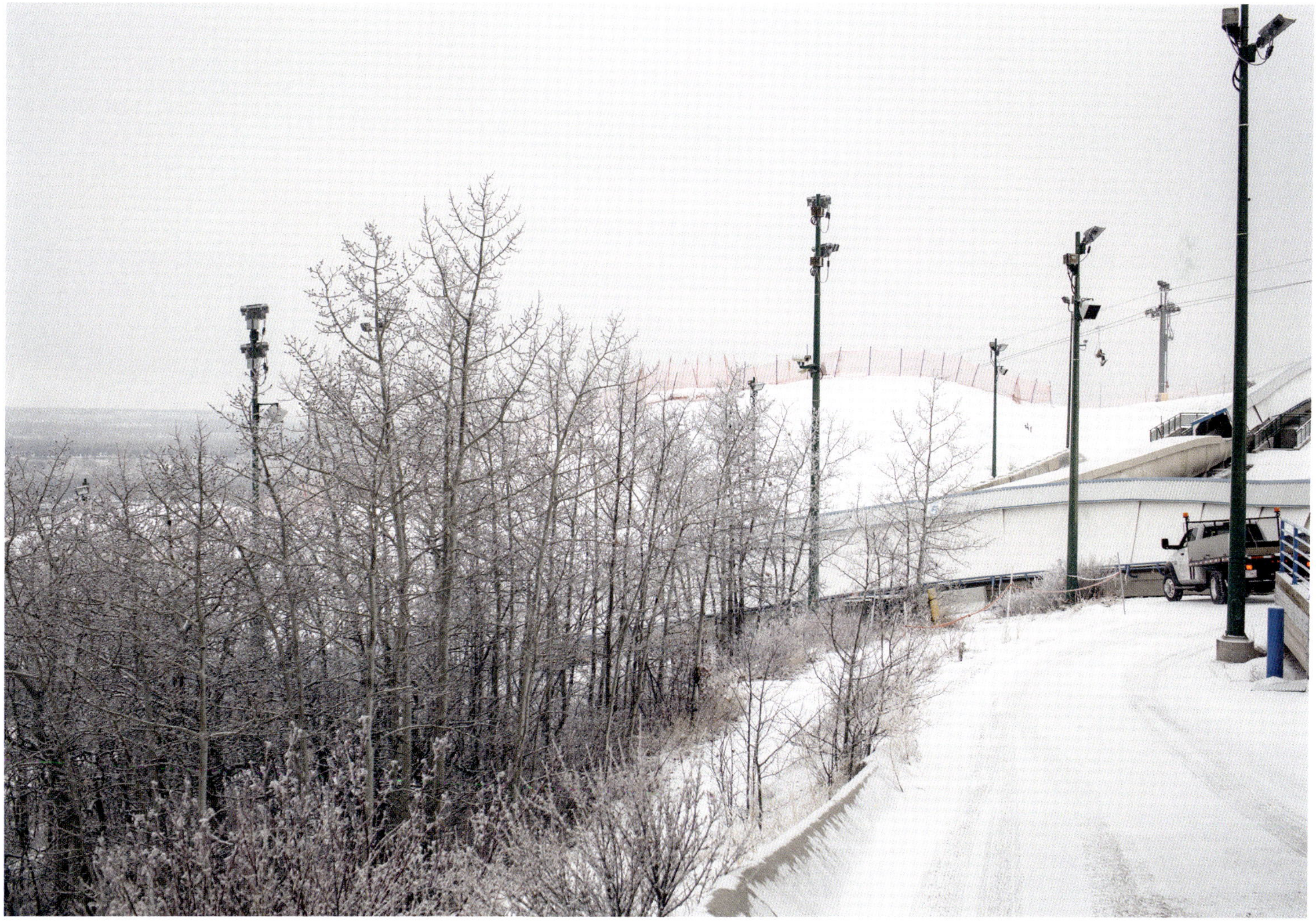

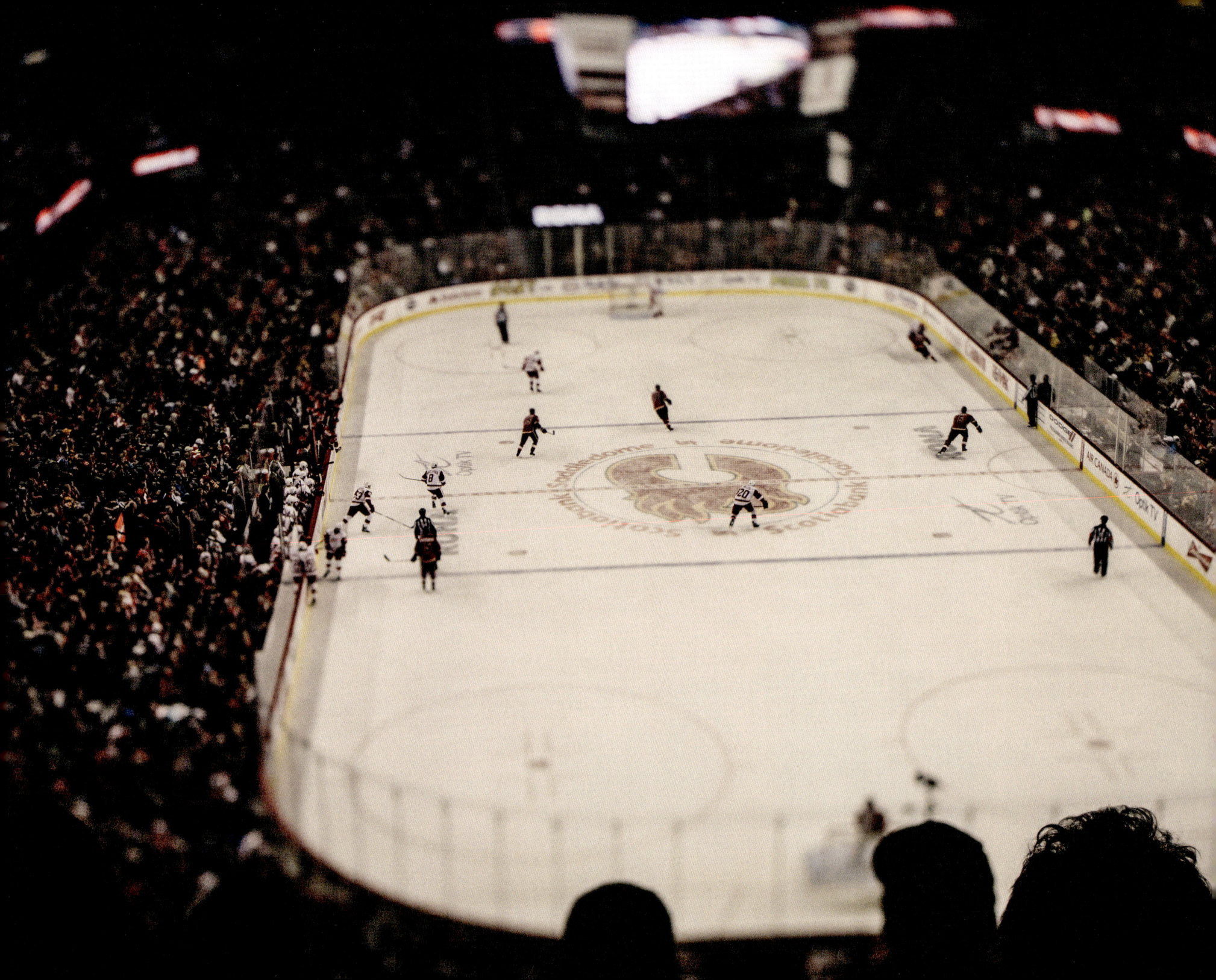

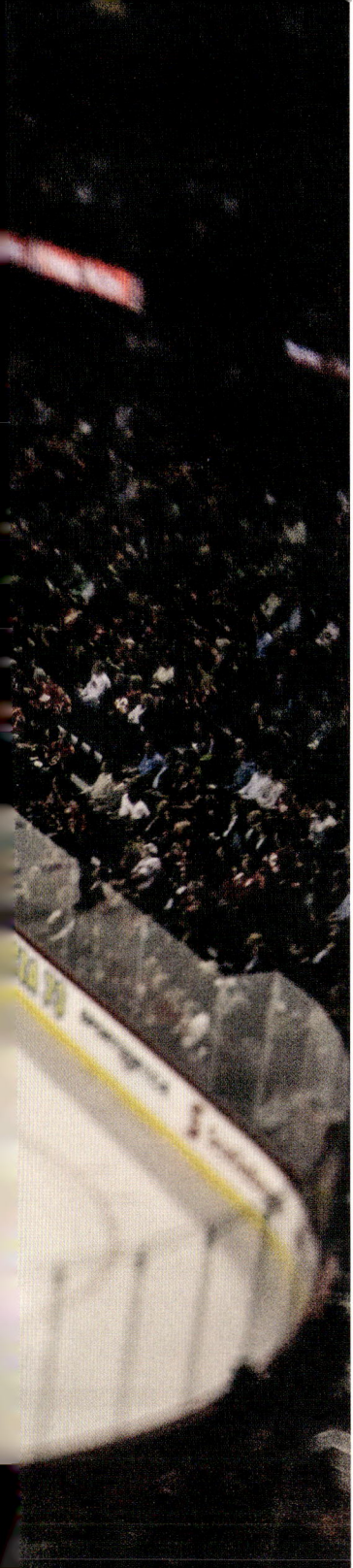

CALGARY FLAMES GAME AT THE
SADDLEDOME STADIUM IN CALGARY,
ALBERTA, APRIL 2013.

→ CANADA DAY FIREWORKS IN HONEY HARBOUR, ONTARIO, JULY 2011.

← WELDING A HOPPER CONE TO FIT OVER A GRAIN BIN IN BRIERCREST, SASKATCHEWAN, APRIL 2013.

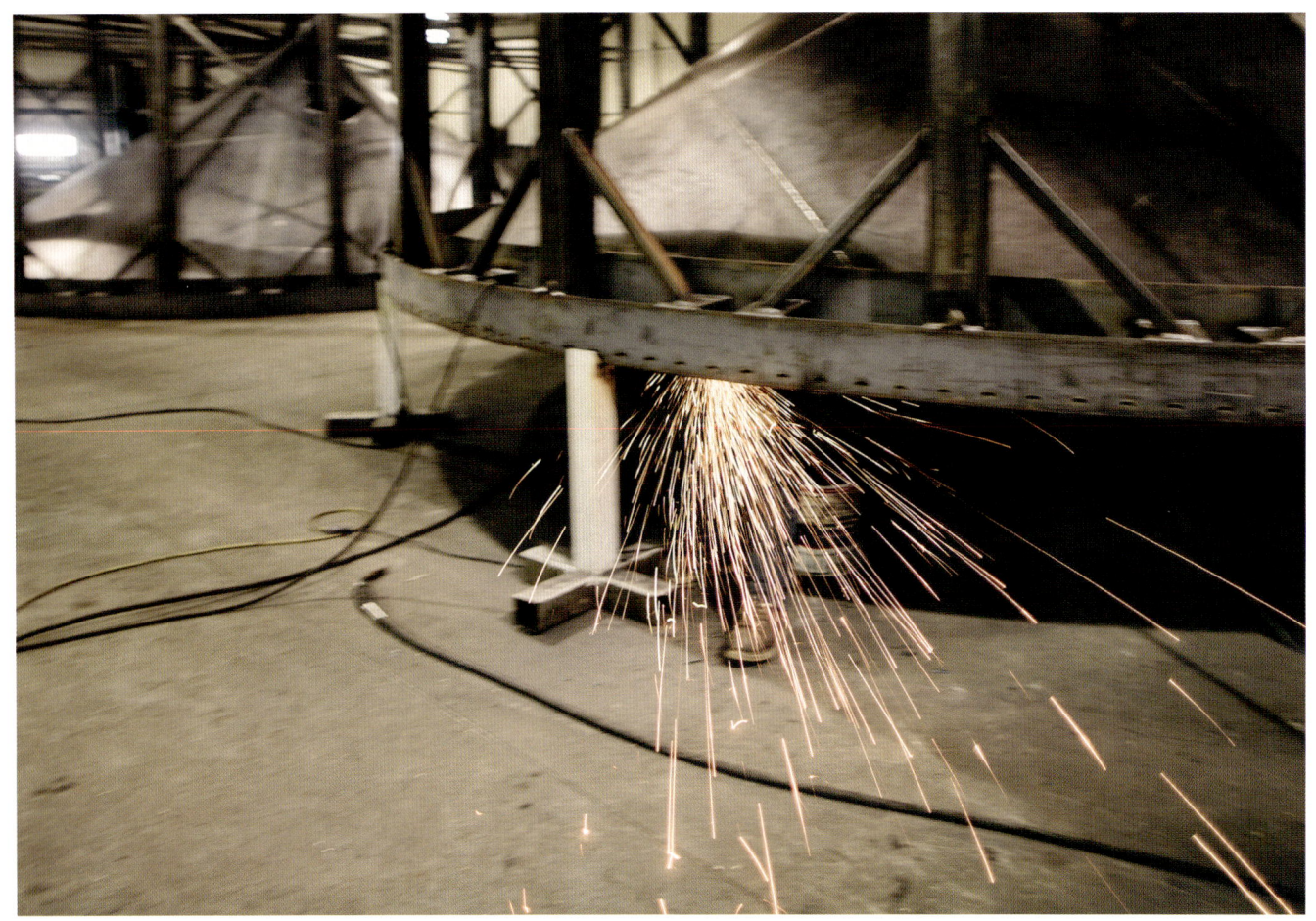

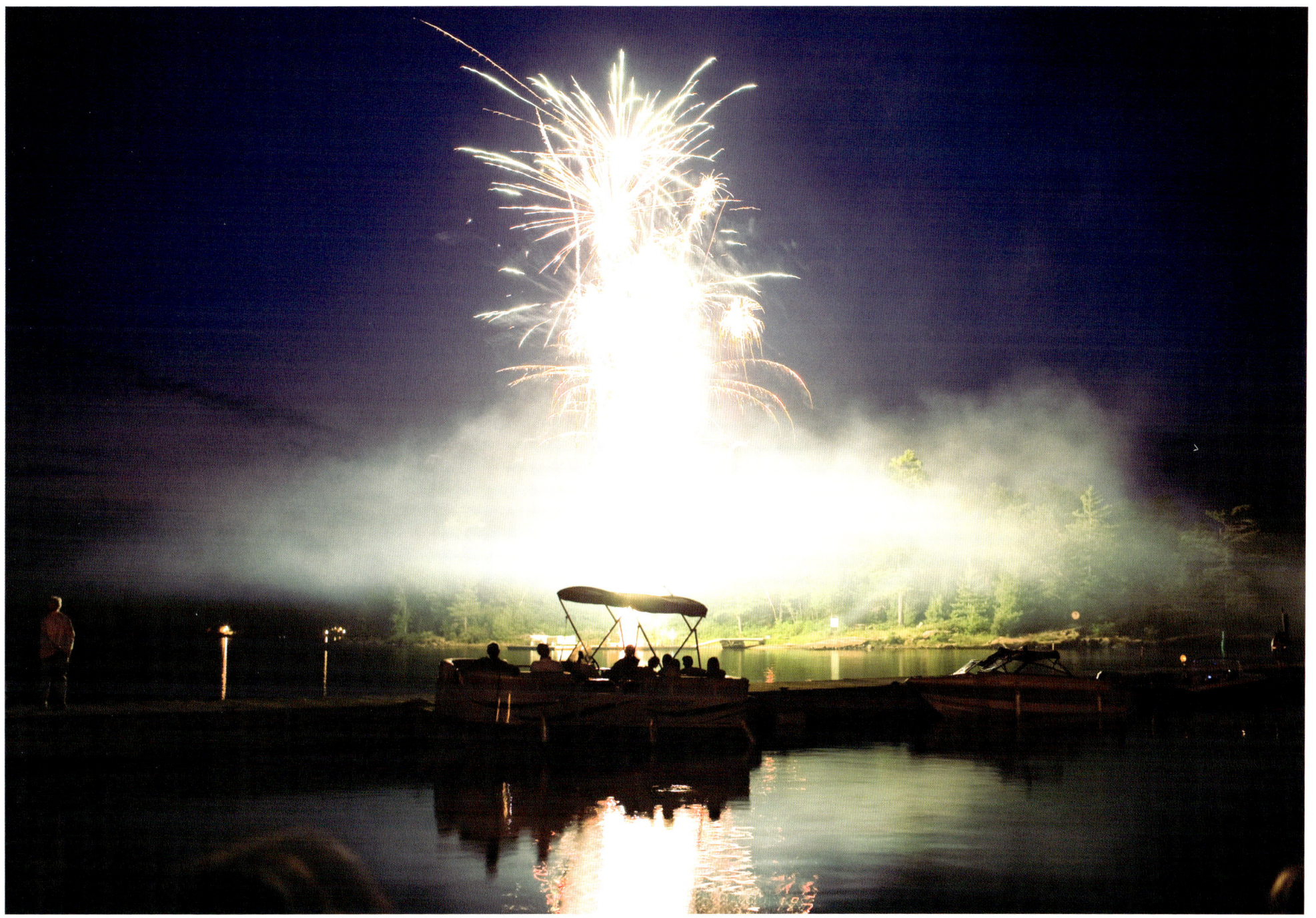

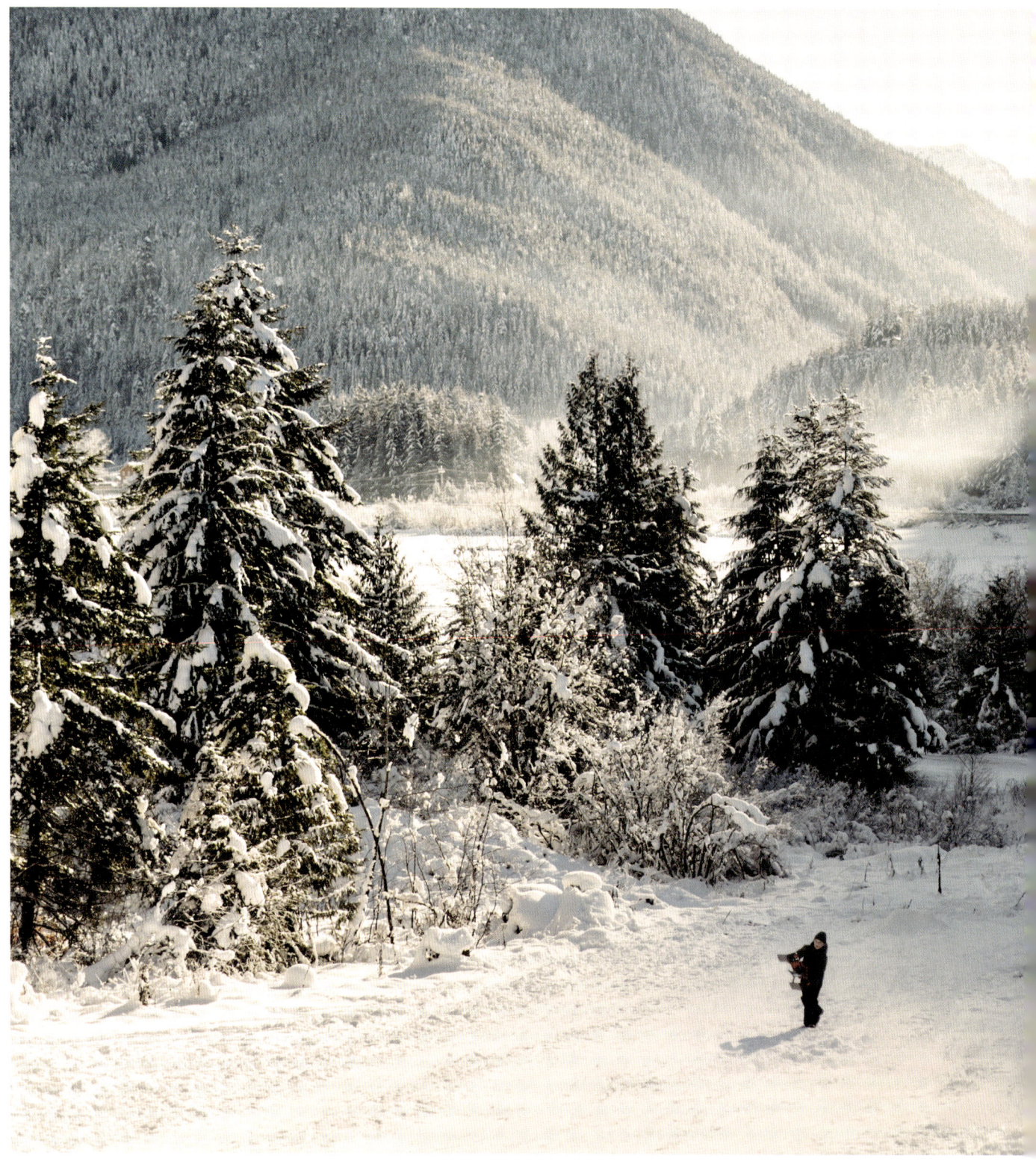

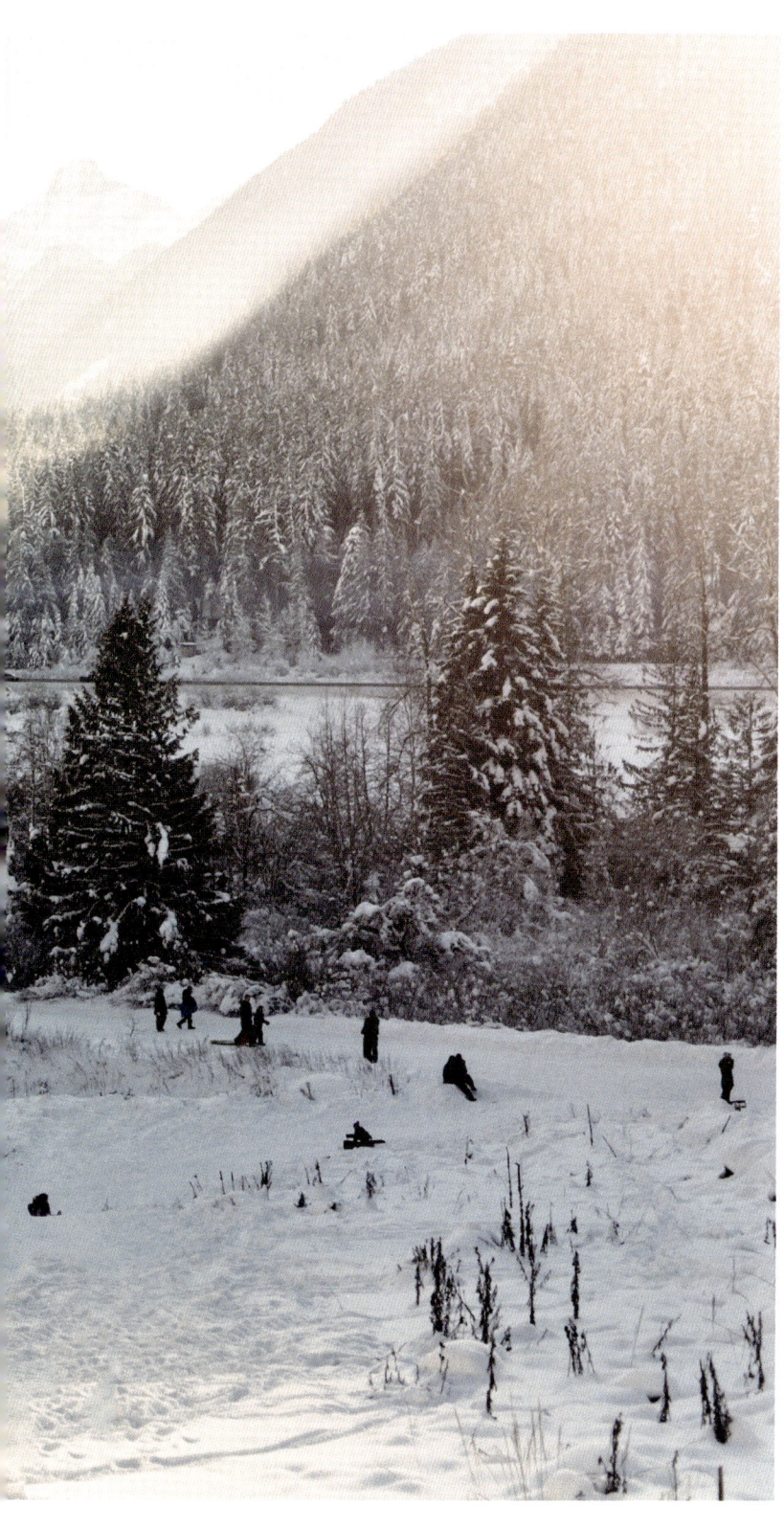

GT SNOW RACER AT THE BOTTOM OF THE TOBOGGAN HILL
IN SUNSHINE VALLEY, BRITISH COLUMBIA, JANUARY 2016.

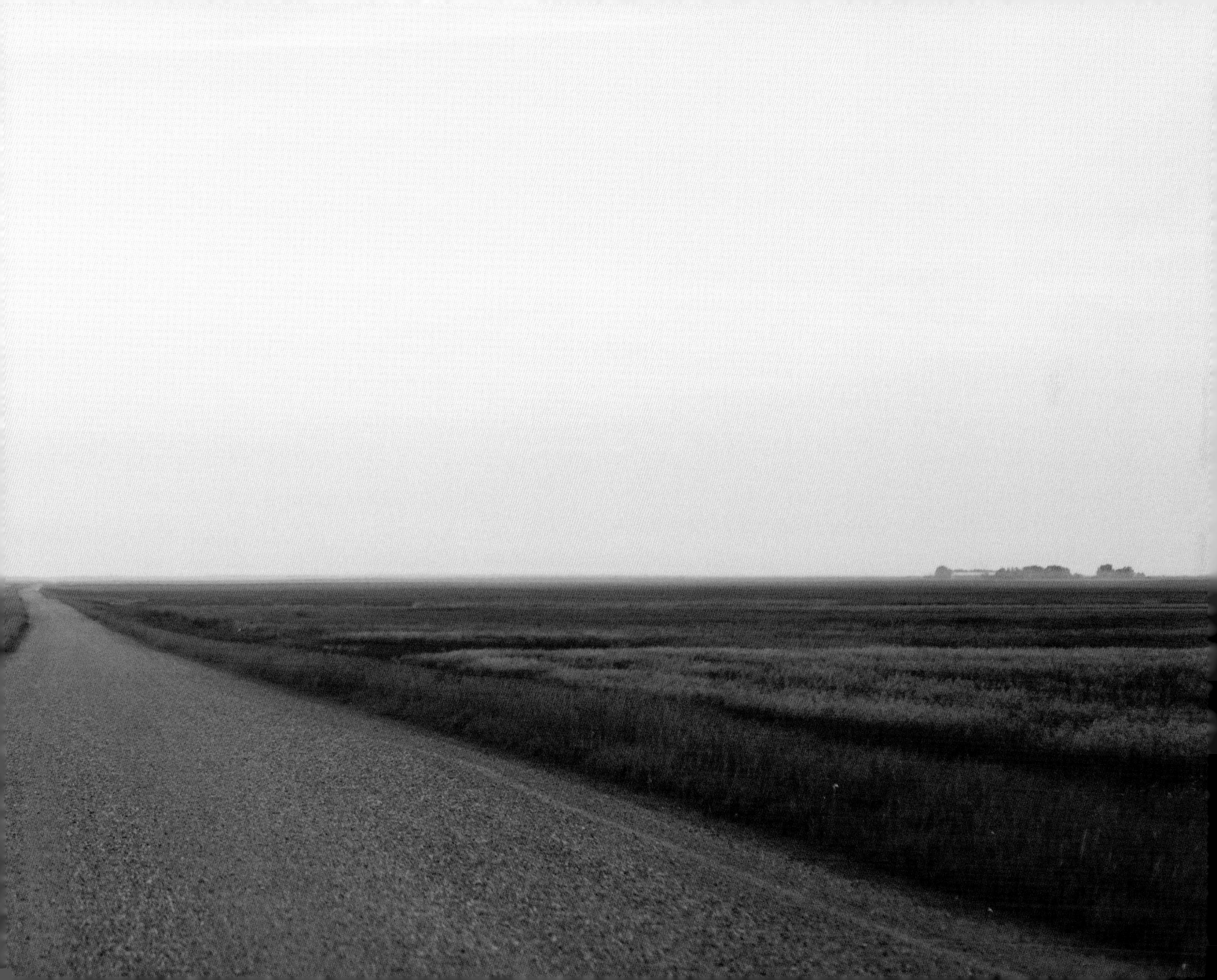

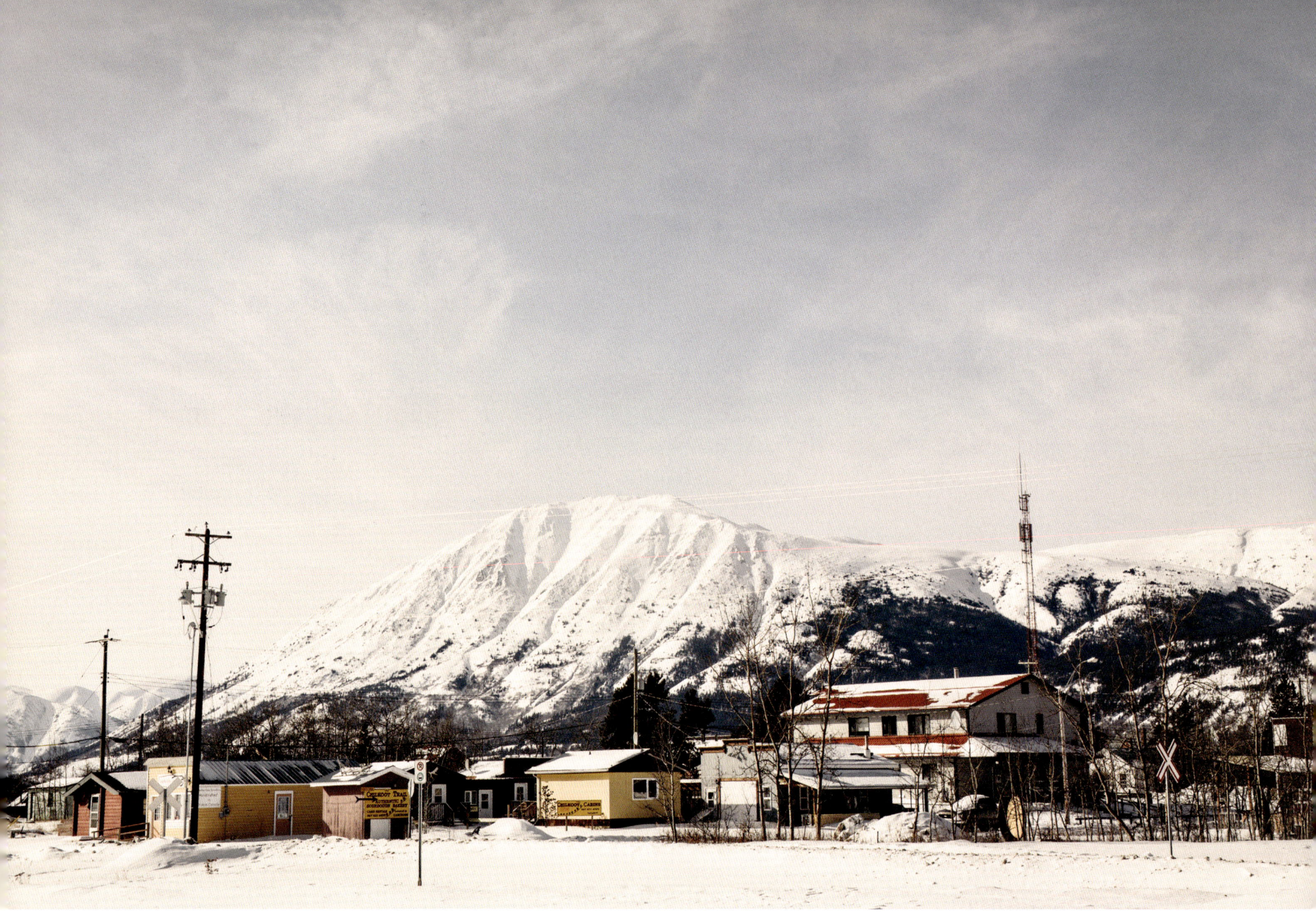

PREVIOUS SPREAD GRAVEL ROADS WEST
OF SASKATOON, SASKATCHEWAN, JULY 2017.

THE COLOURS REMINDED ME OF A TED HARRISON PAINTING.
CARCROSS, YUKON, FEBRUARY 2016.

SUNSET OVER THE ATLANTIC OCEAN ON CEDAR DUNES BEACH
ON PRINCE EDWARD ISLAND, AUGUST 2017.

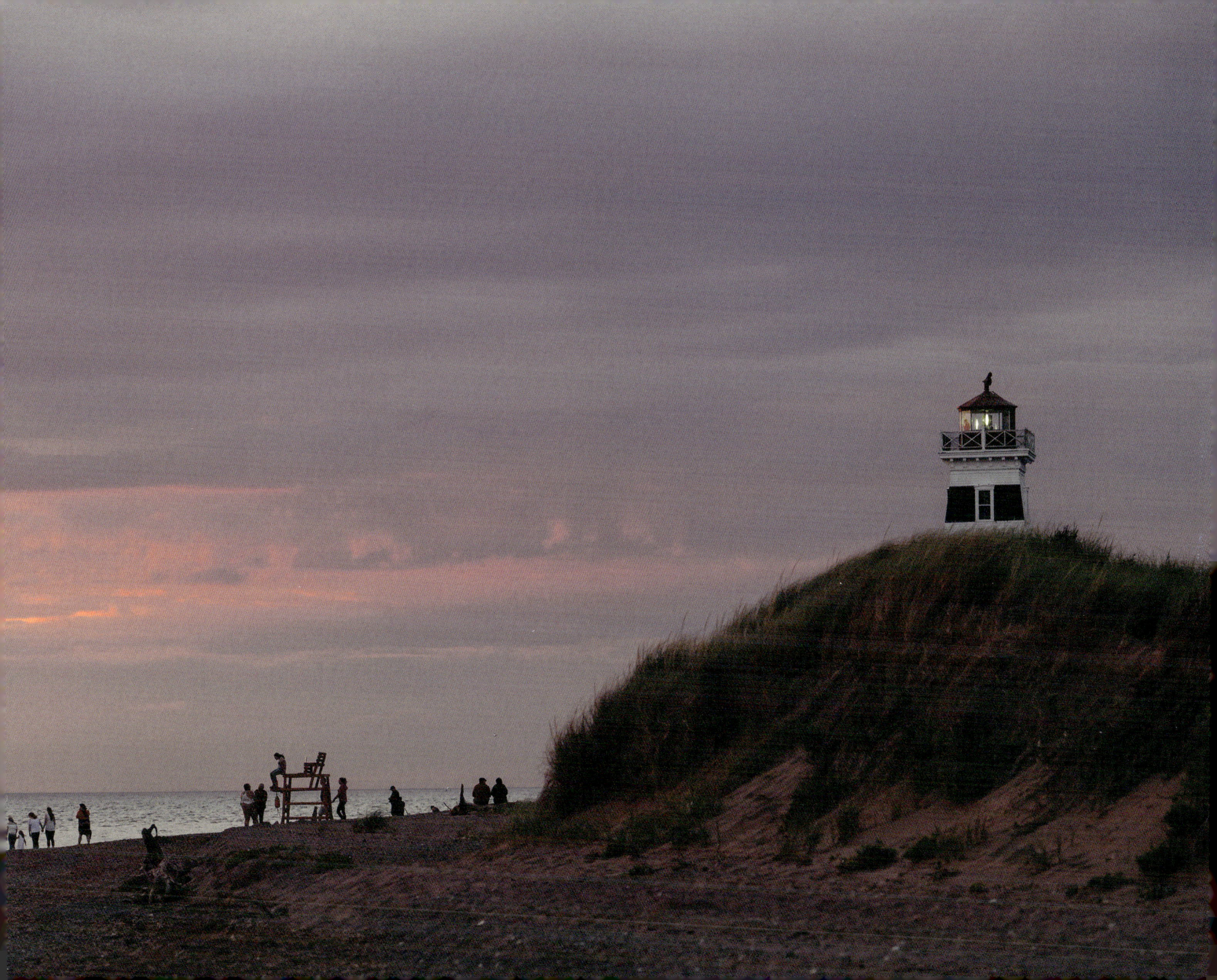

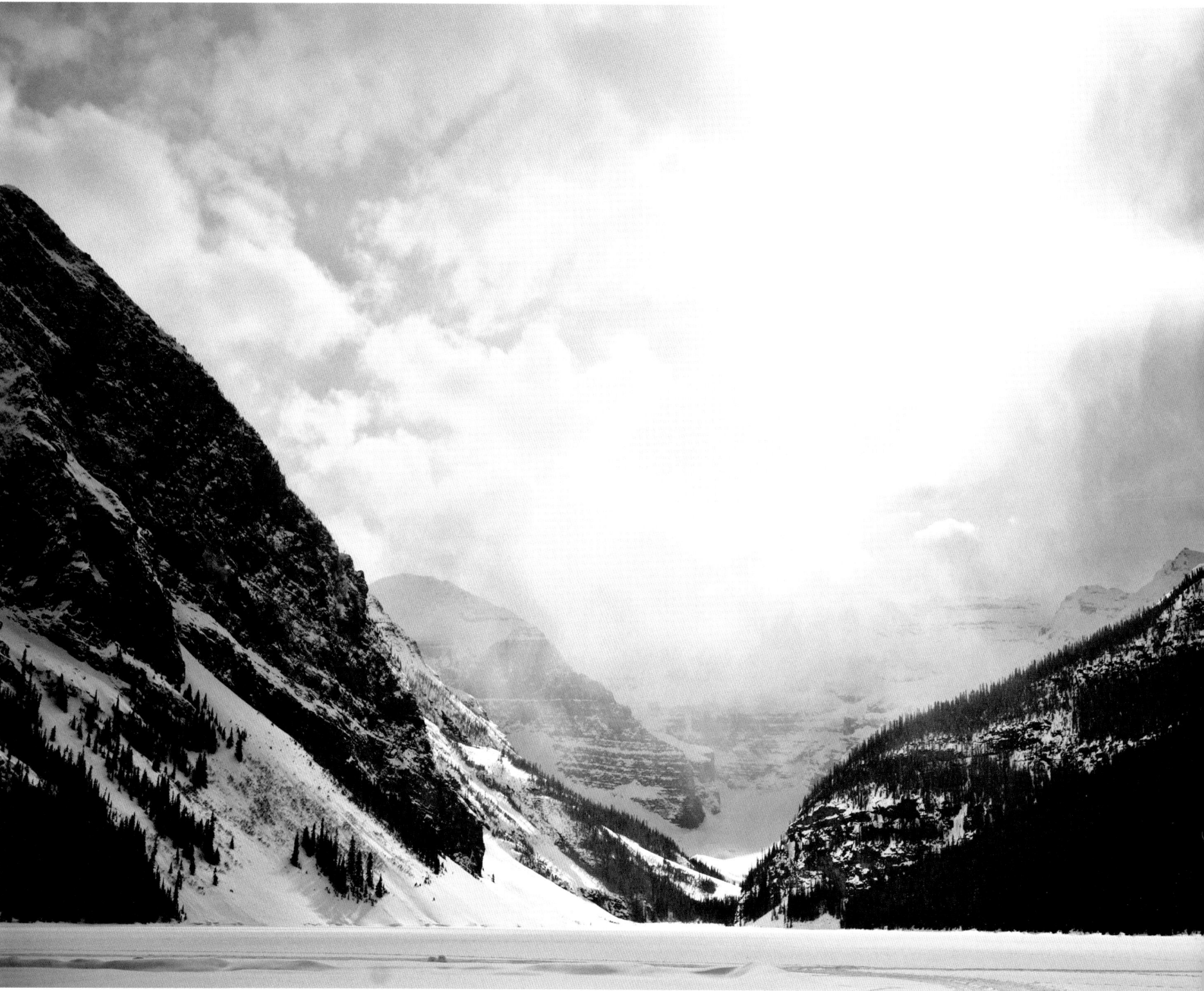

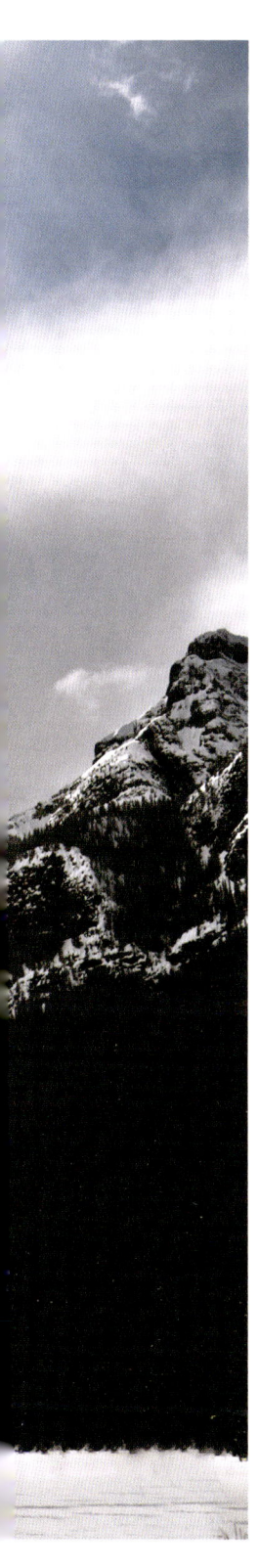

LAKE LOUISE, ALBERTA, APRIL 2012.

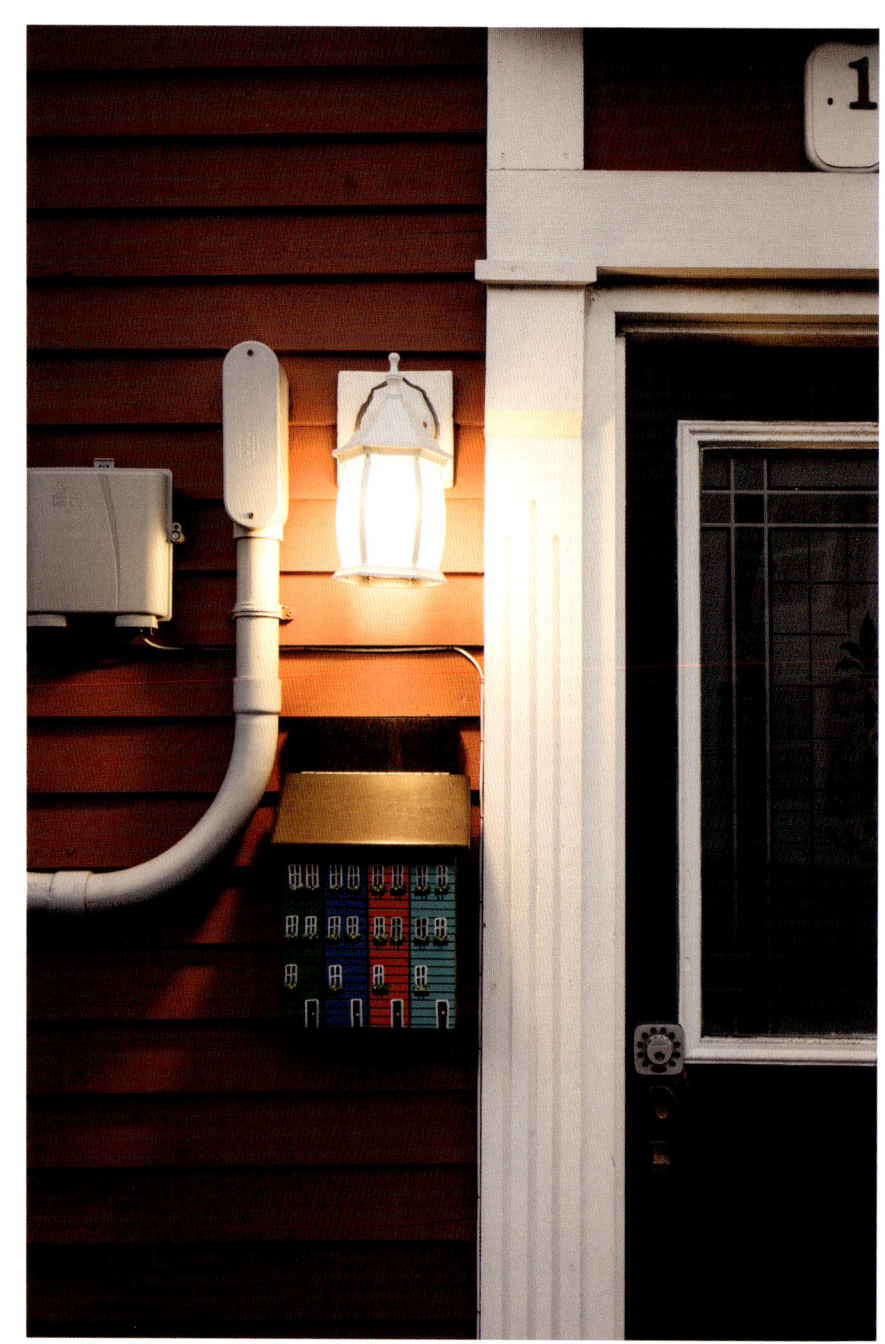

SPREAD ST. JOHN'S, NEWFOUNDLAND, MAY 2022.

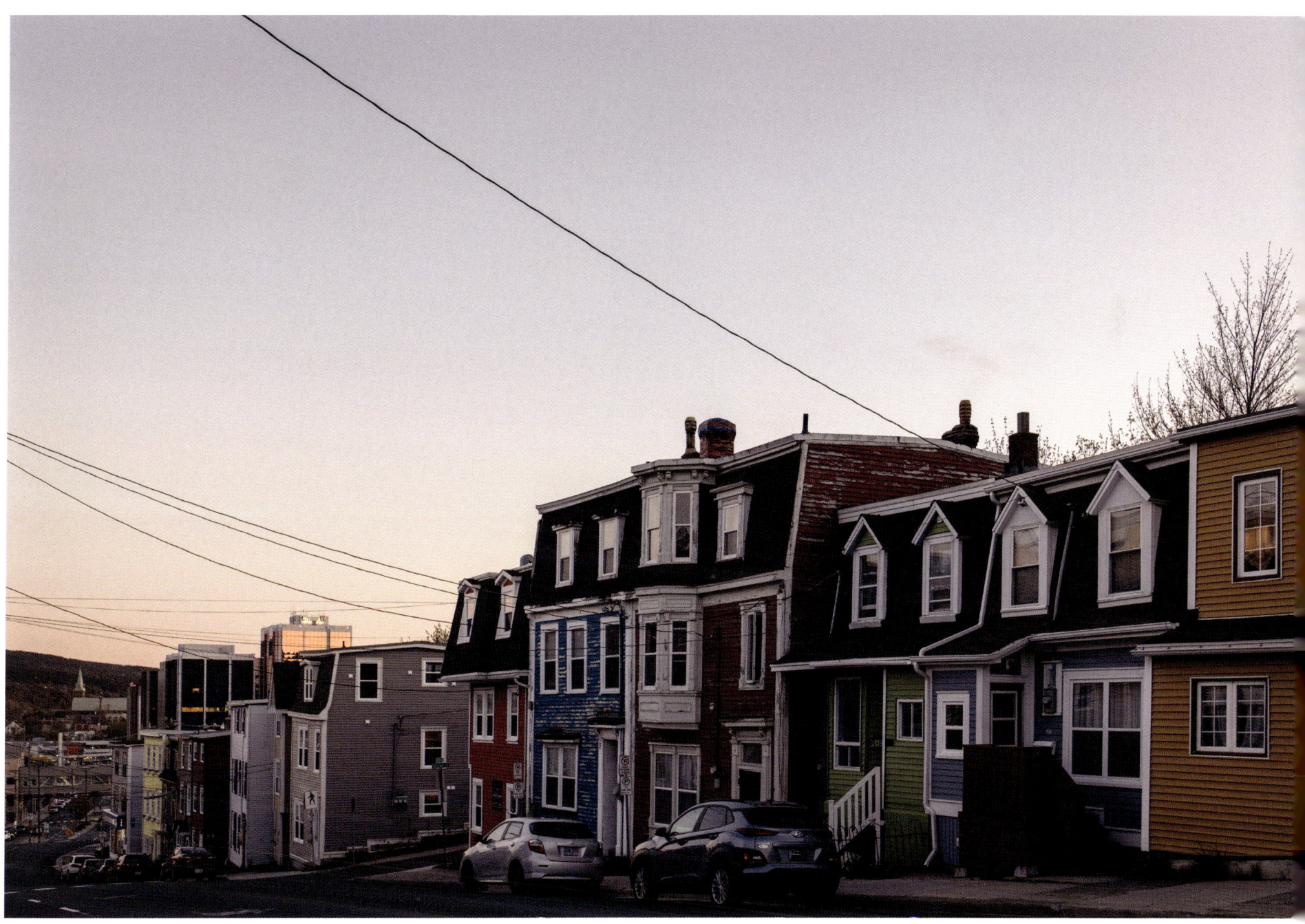

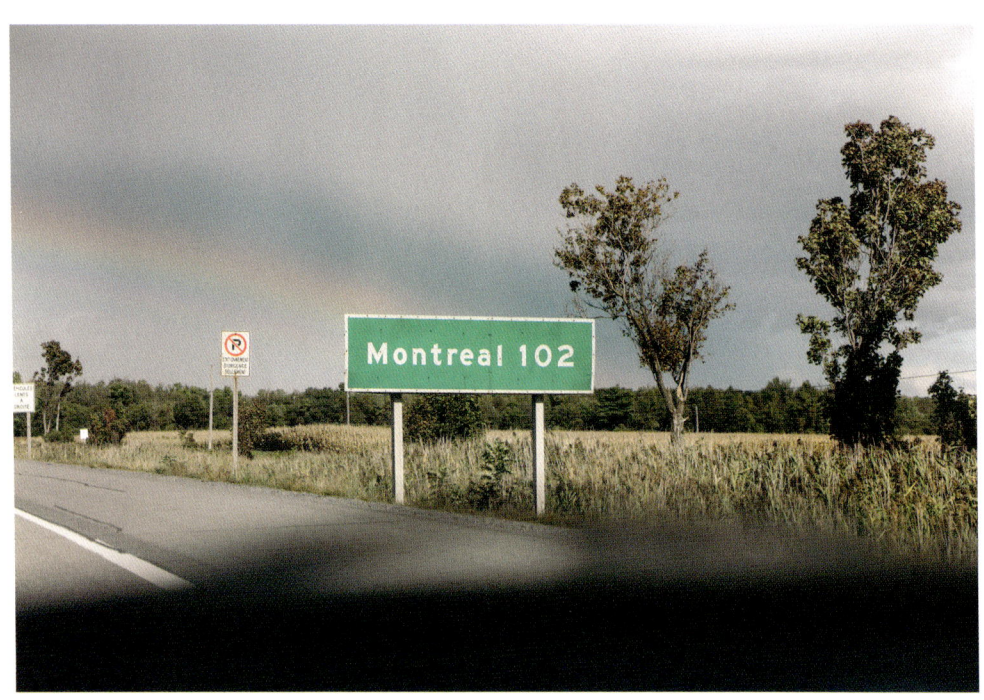

→ PRIDE PARADE, TORONTO, ONTARIO, JULY 2011. ON JULY 20, 2005, CANADA PASSED THE CIVIL MARRIAGE ACT, ALLOWING SAME-SEX COUPLES TO MARRY.

There are few nations whose citizens cannot look to Canada and see their own reflection. For generations, men, women and families from the four corners of the globe have made the decision to choose Canada as their home. Many have come here seeking freedom of thought, religion and belief, seeking the freedom simply to be...

...The people of Canada have worked hard to build a country that opens its doors to include all, regardless of their differences; a country that respects all, regardless of their differences; and a country that demands equality for all, regardless of their differences.

—PRIME MINISTER PAUL MARTIN, *speaking to Parliament, February 2005*

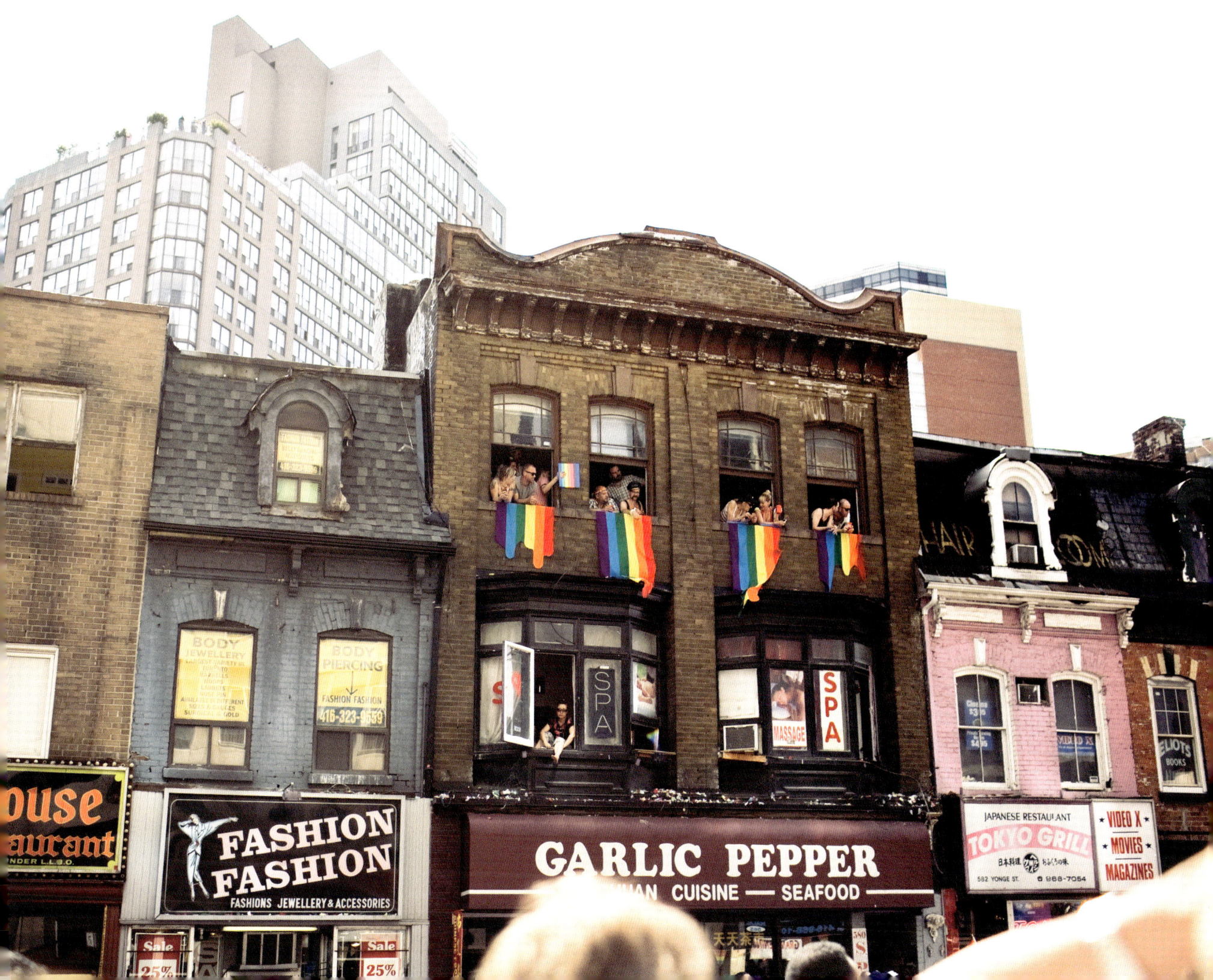

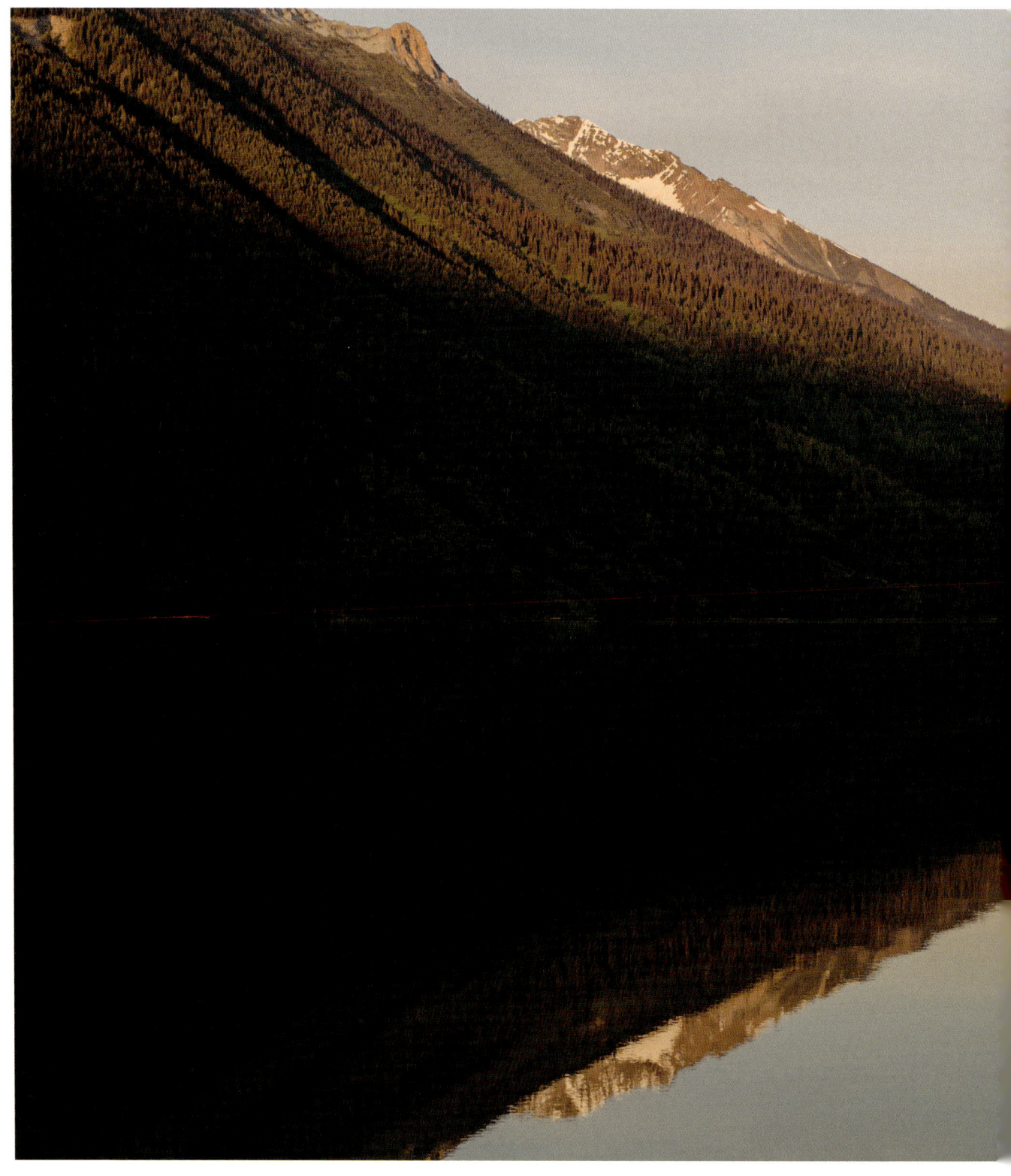

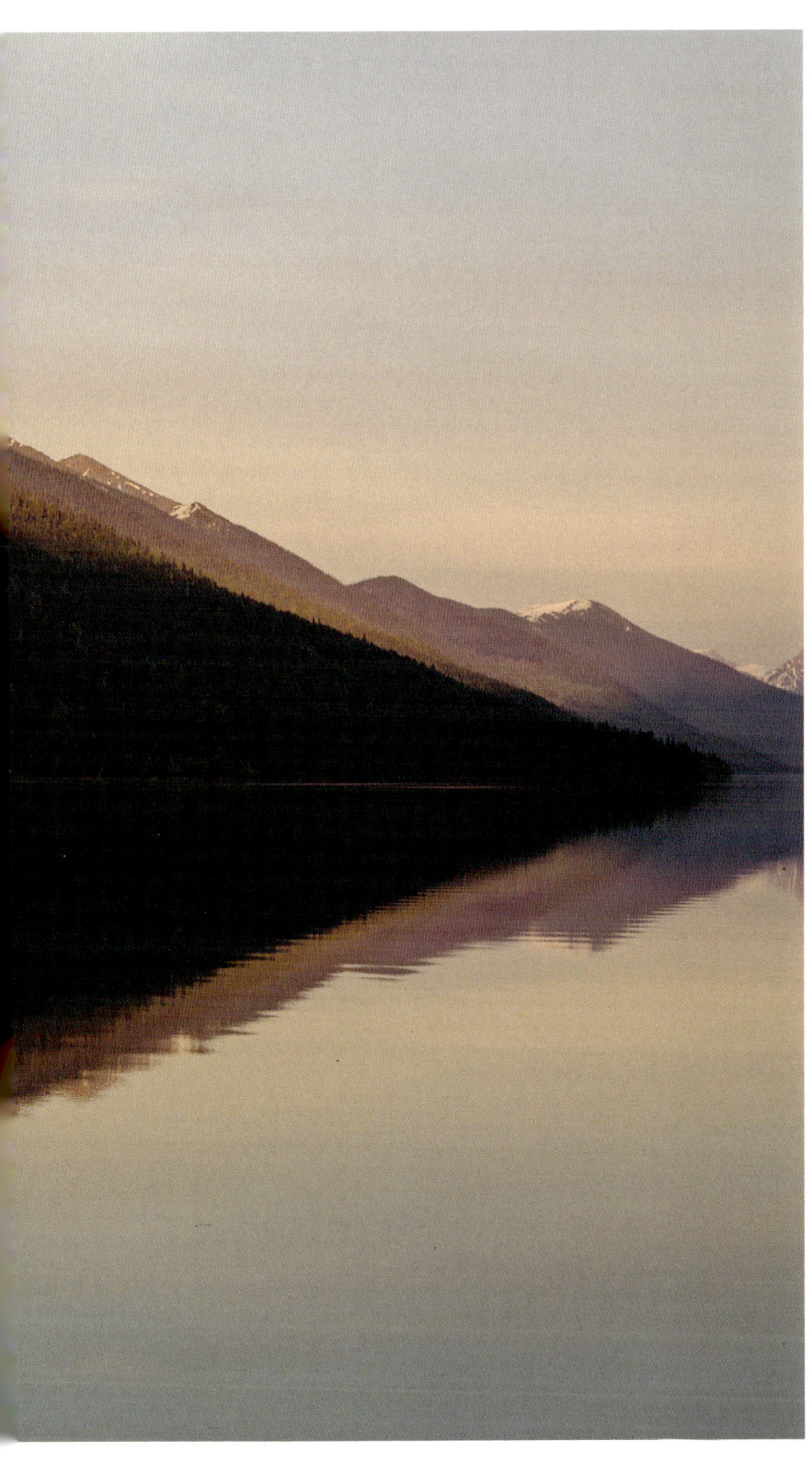

BOWRON LAKE PROVINCIAL PARK, JUST OUTSIDE OF WELLS,
BRITISH COLUMBIA, JUNE 2017.

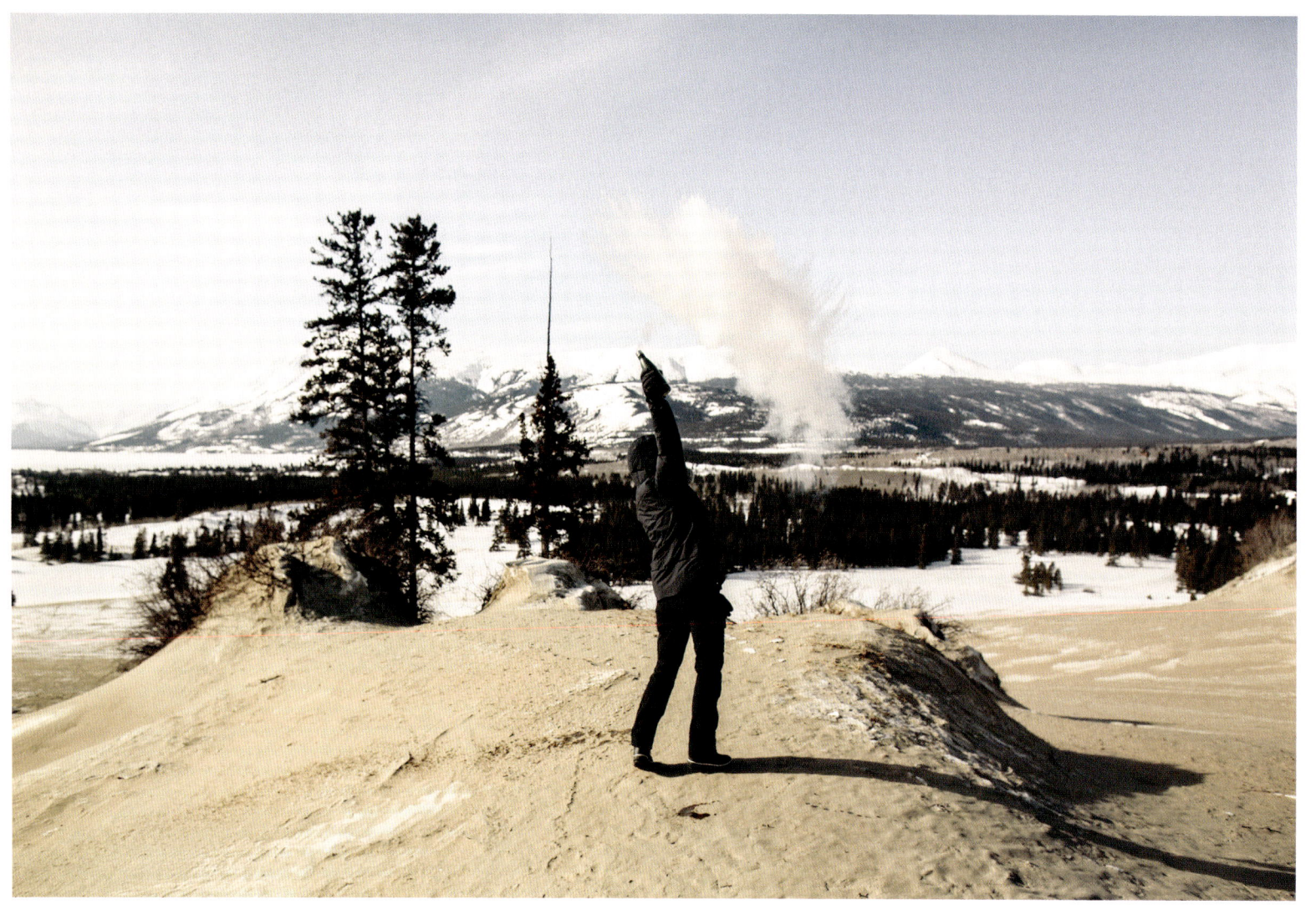

↑ LIQUID WATER BEING THROWN INTO THE AIR AT -30°C AND FREEZING IMMEDIATELY IN THE CARCROSS DESERT, YUKON, MARCH 2017.

→ WAVE CRASHES ALONG THE SHORE ON THE WEST COAST TRAIL IN PACIFIC RIM NATIONAL PARK RESERVE, BRITISH COLUMBIA, MAY 2016.

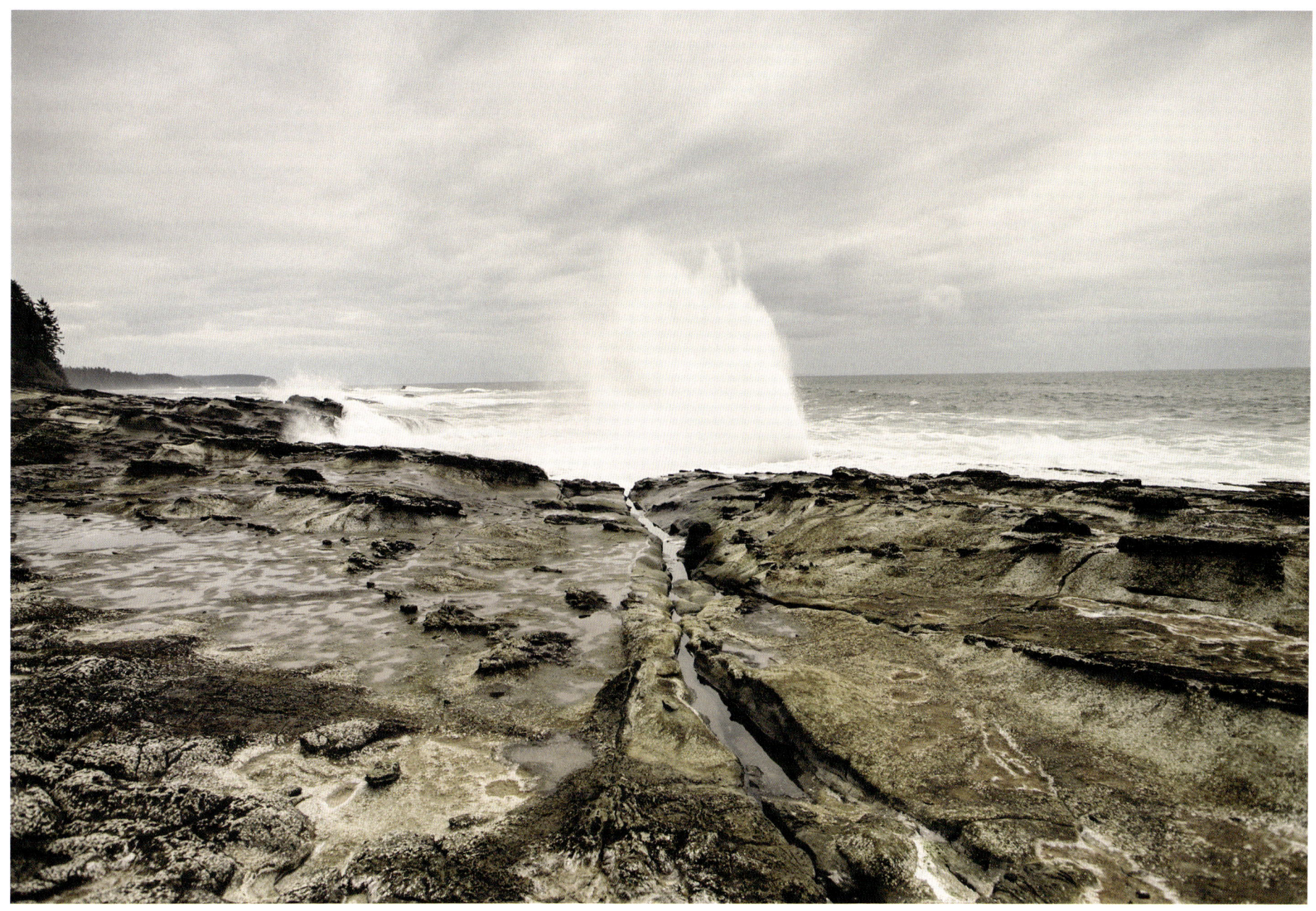

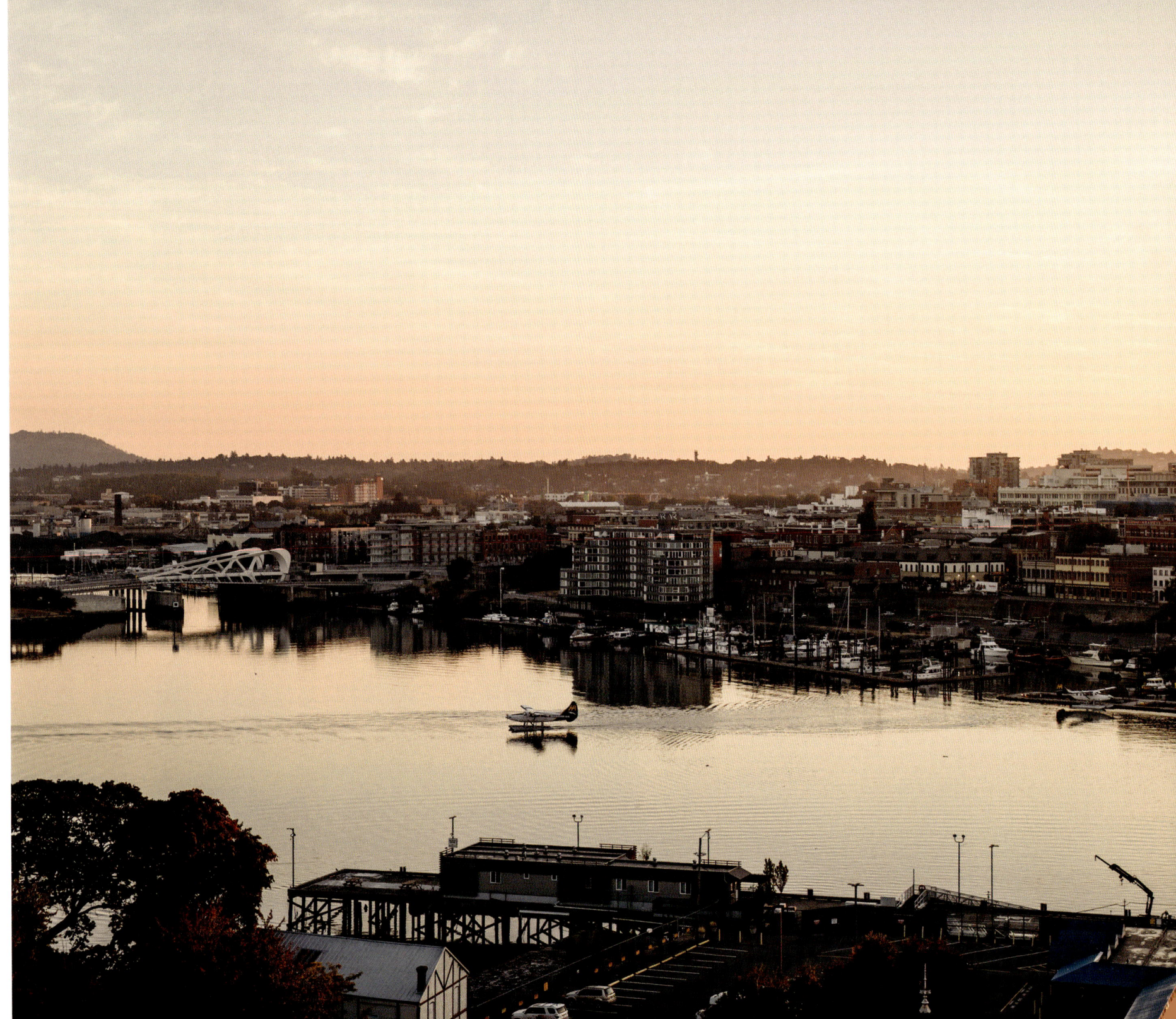

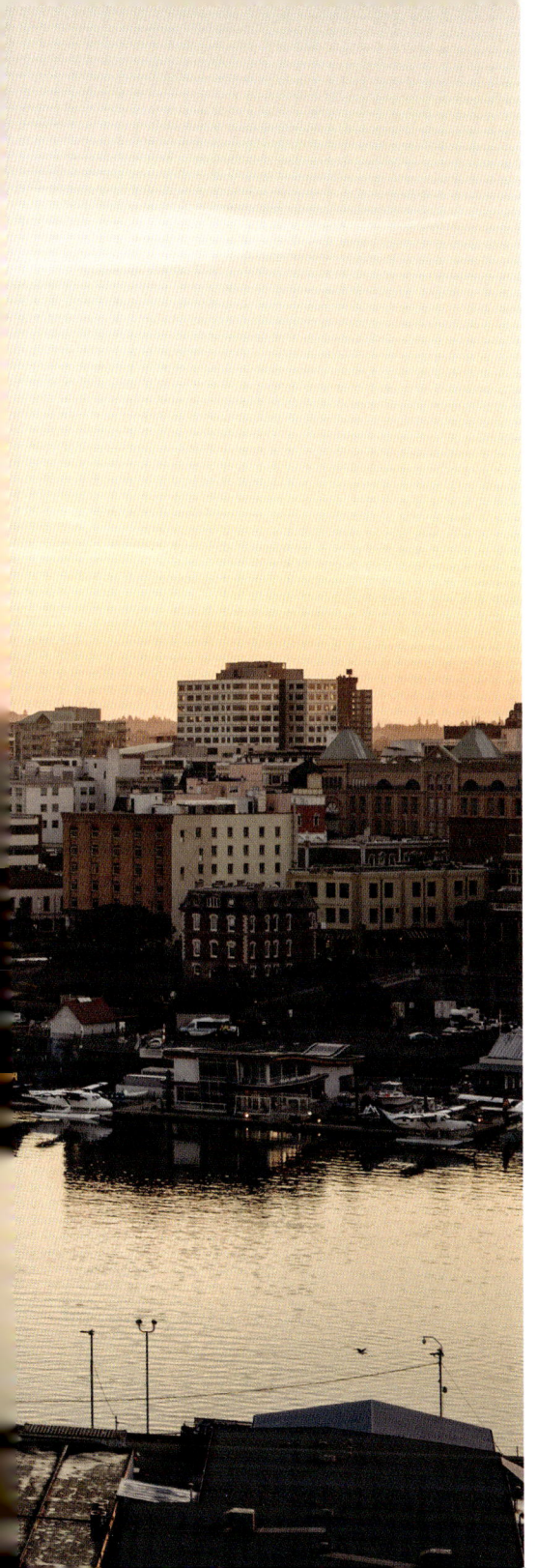

VICTORIA, BRITISH COLUMBIA, SEPTEMBER 2018.

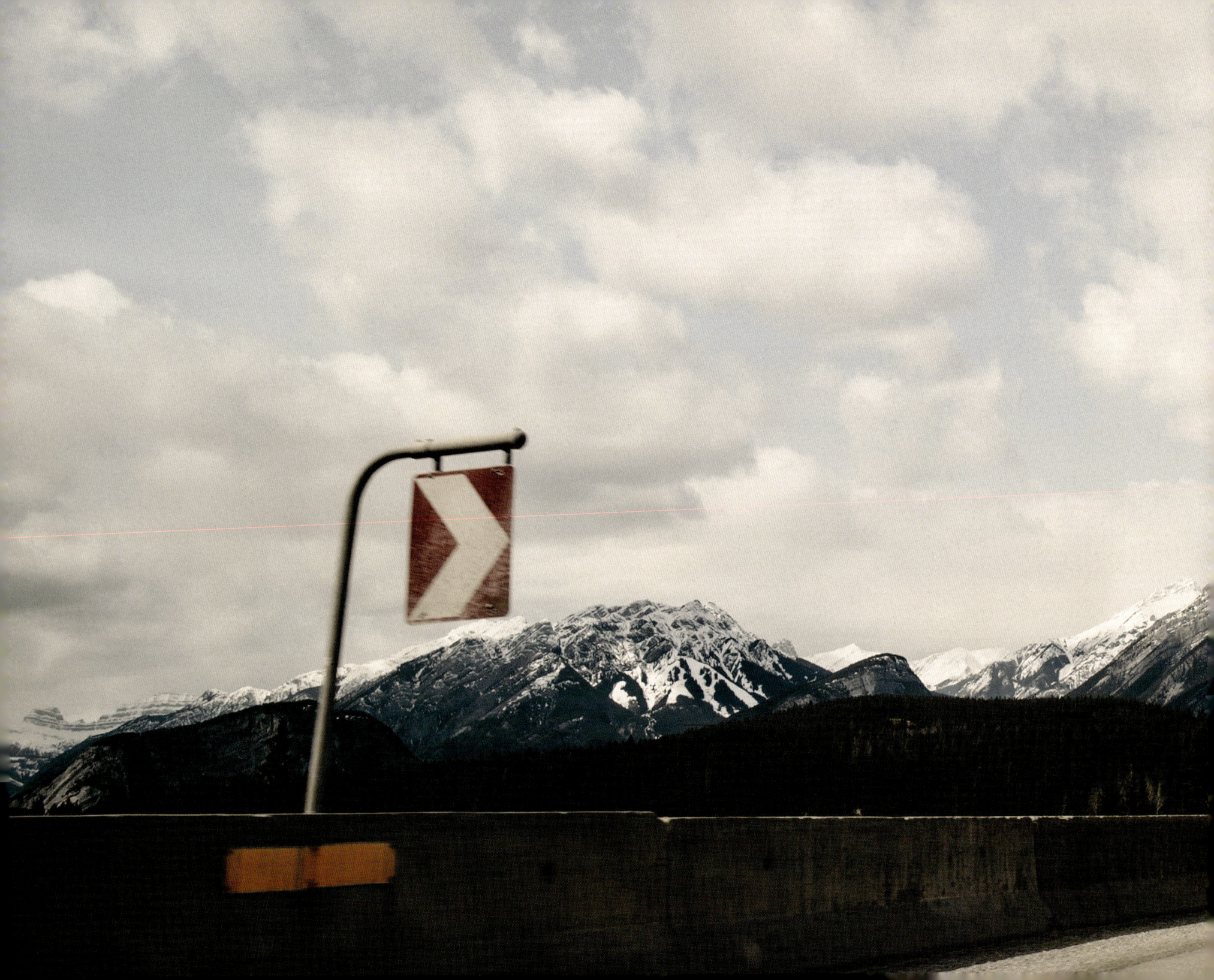

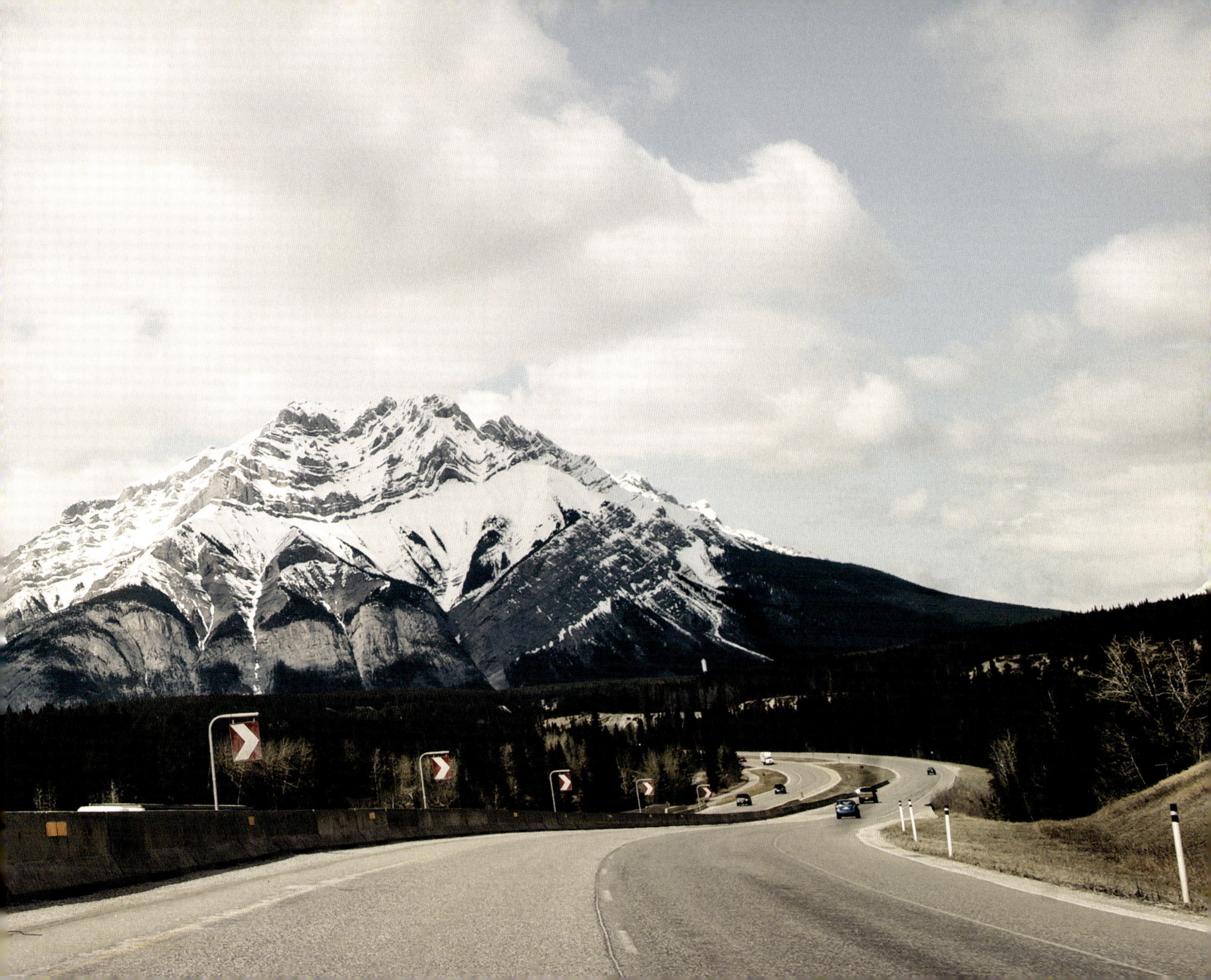

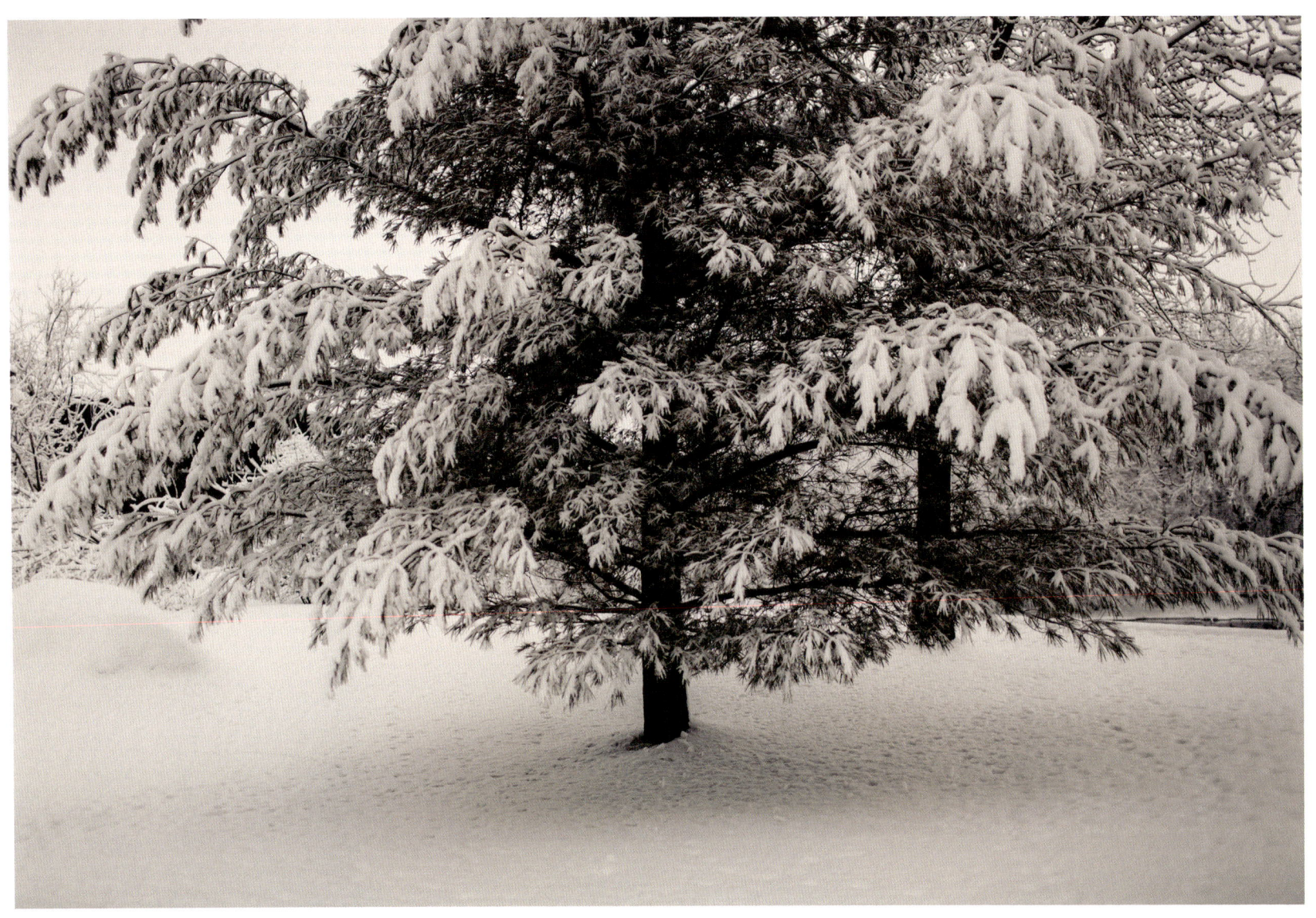

OVERLEAF TRANS-CANADA HIGHWAY HEADING
WEST TOWARD BANFF, ALBERTA, APRIL 2013.

WINTER TREE, GUELPH, ONTARIO, FEBRUARY 2013.

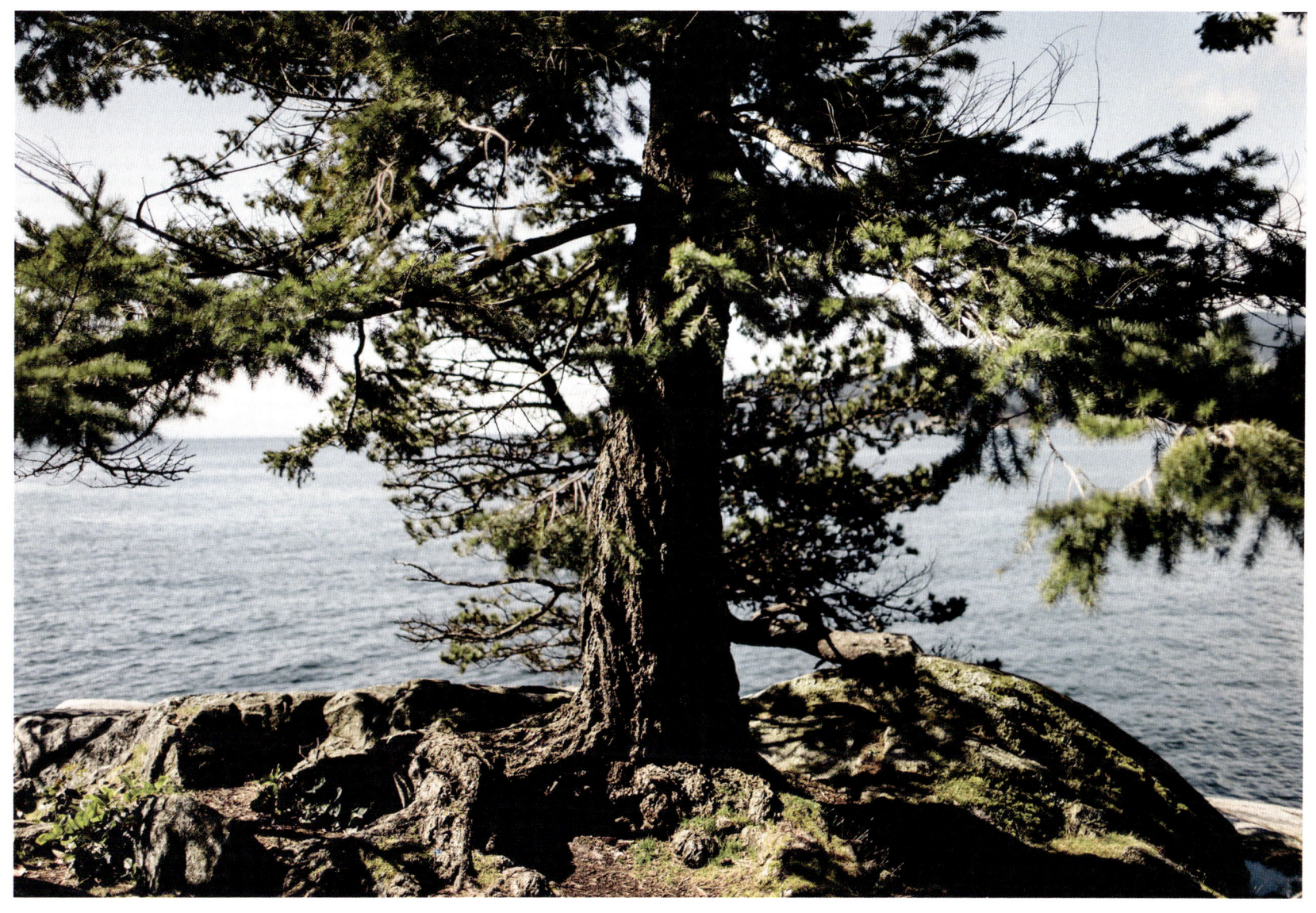

SUMMER TREE, LIGHTHOUSE PARK, VANCOUVER,
BRITISH COLUMBIA, APRIL 2012.

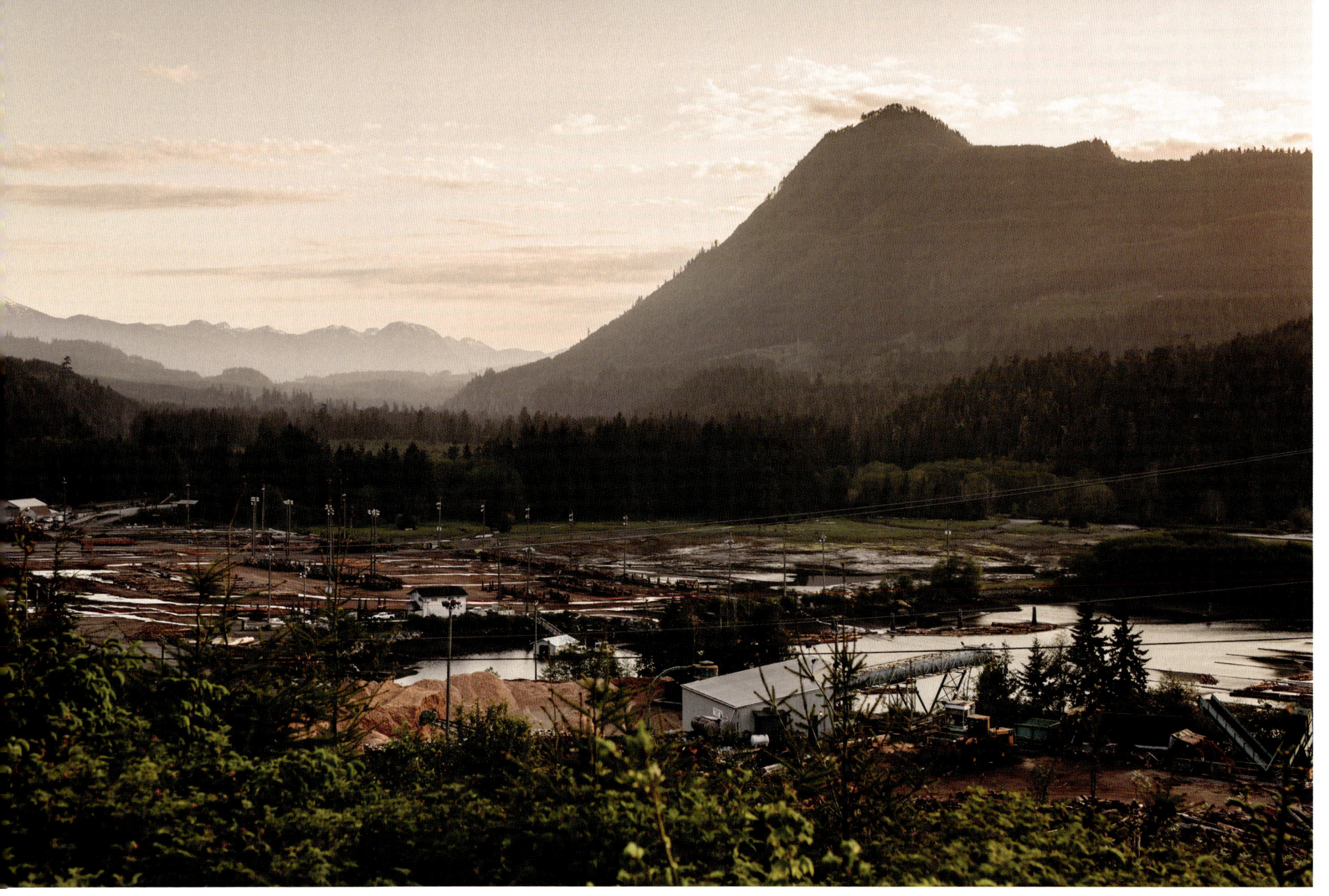

SAWMILL IN TELEGRAPH COVE, VANCOUVER ISLAND, BRITISH COLUMBIA, MAY 2018.

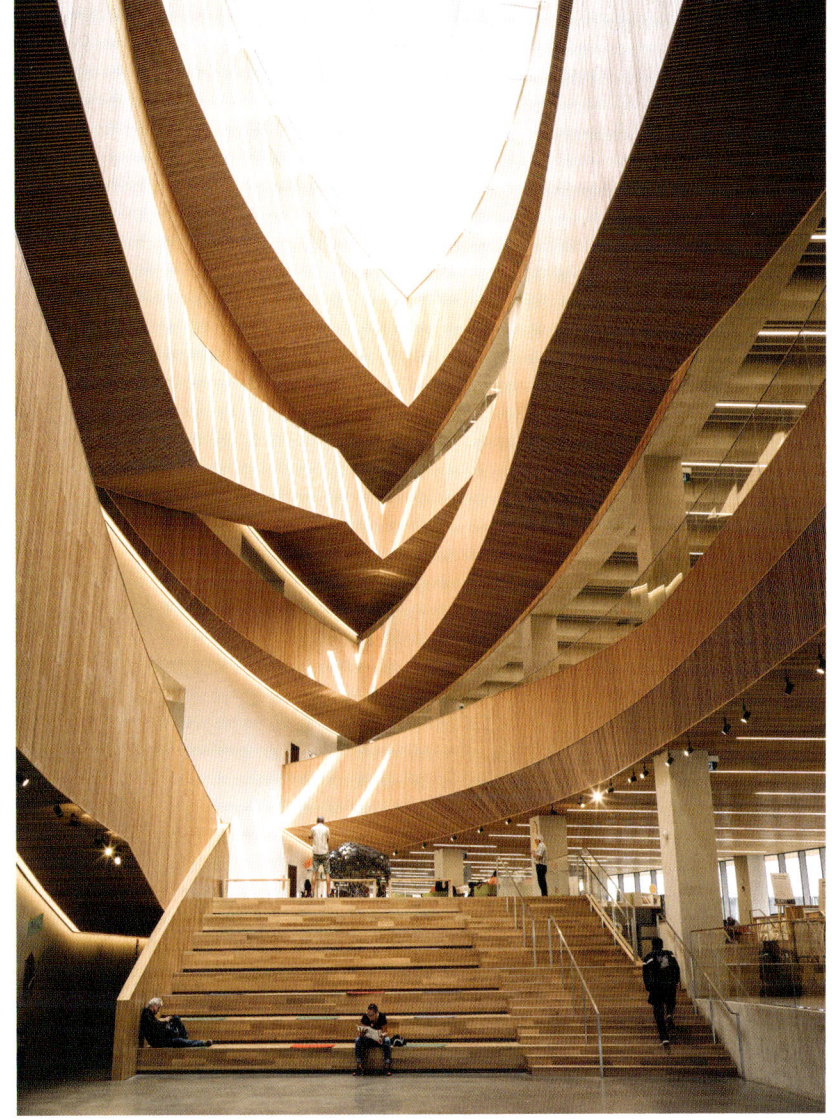

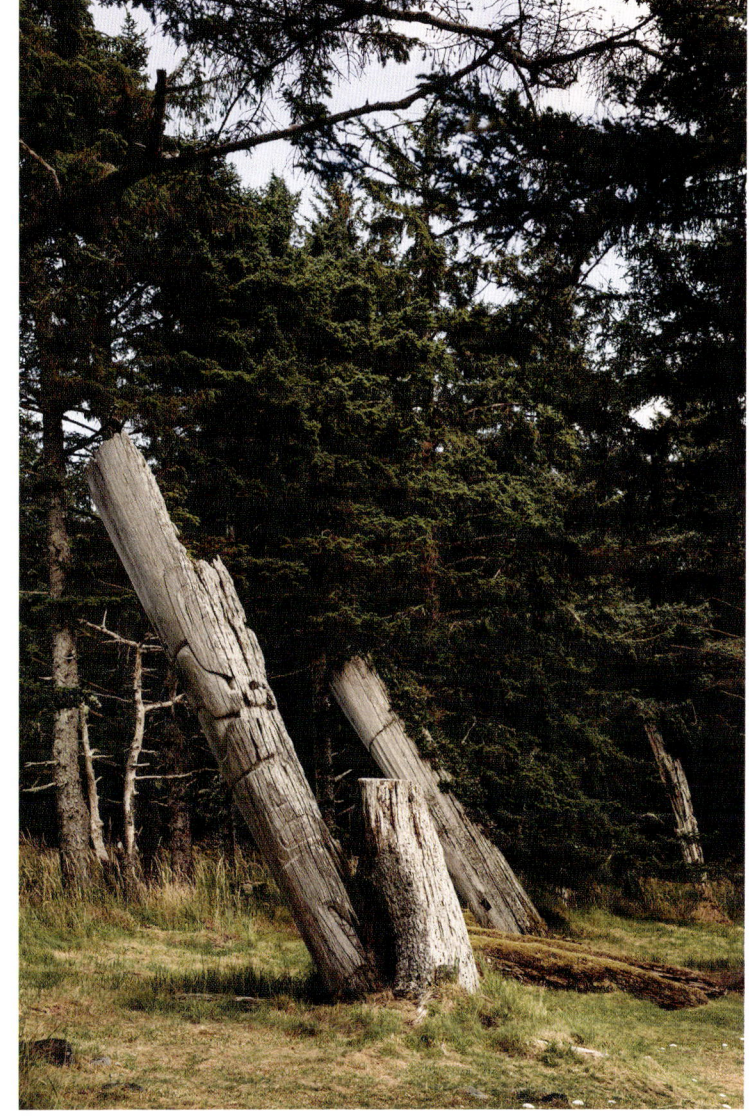

PUBLIC LIBRARY, CALGARY, ALBERTA, SEPTEMBER 2019.

MORTUARY POLE IN GWAII HAANAS NATIONAL PARK RESERVE. THIS POLE WOULD HAVE BEEN ERECTED UPON THE DEATH OF A HIGH-RANKING PERSON, AND OVER TIME ALLOWED TO RETURN TO THE EARTH. HAIDA GWAII, BRITISH COLUMBIA, AUGUST 2017.

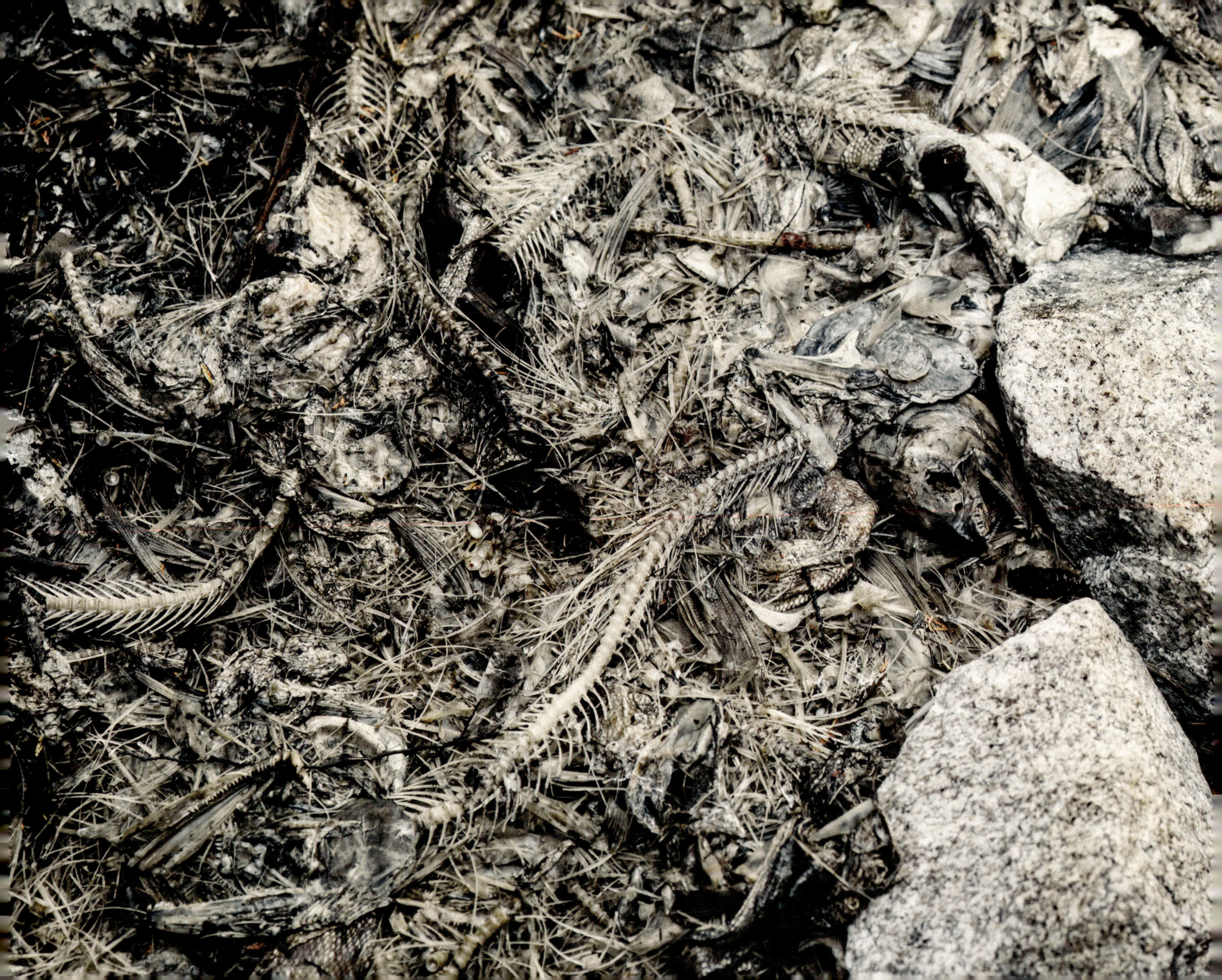

SALMON BONES AFTER THE SALMON RUN IN BELLA BELLA,
BRITISH COLUMBIA, OCTOBER 2017.

MOOSE NEAR WHITEHORSE, YUKON, MARCH 2017.

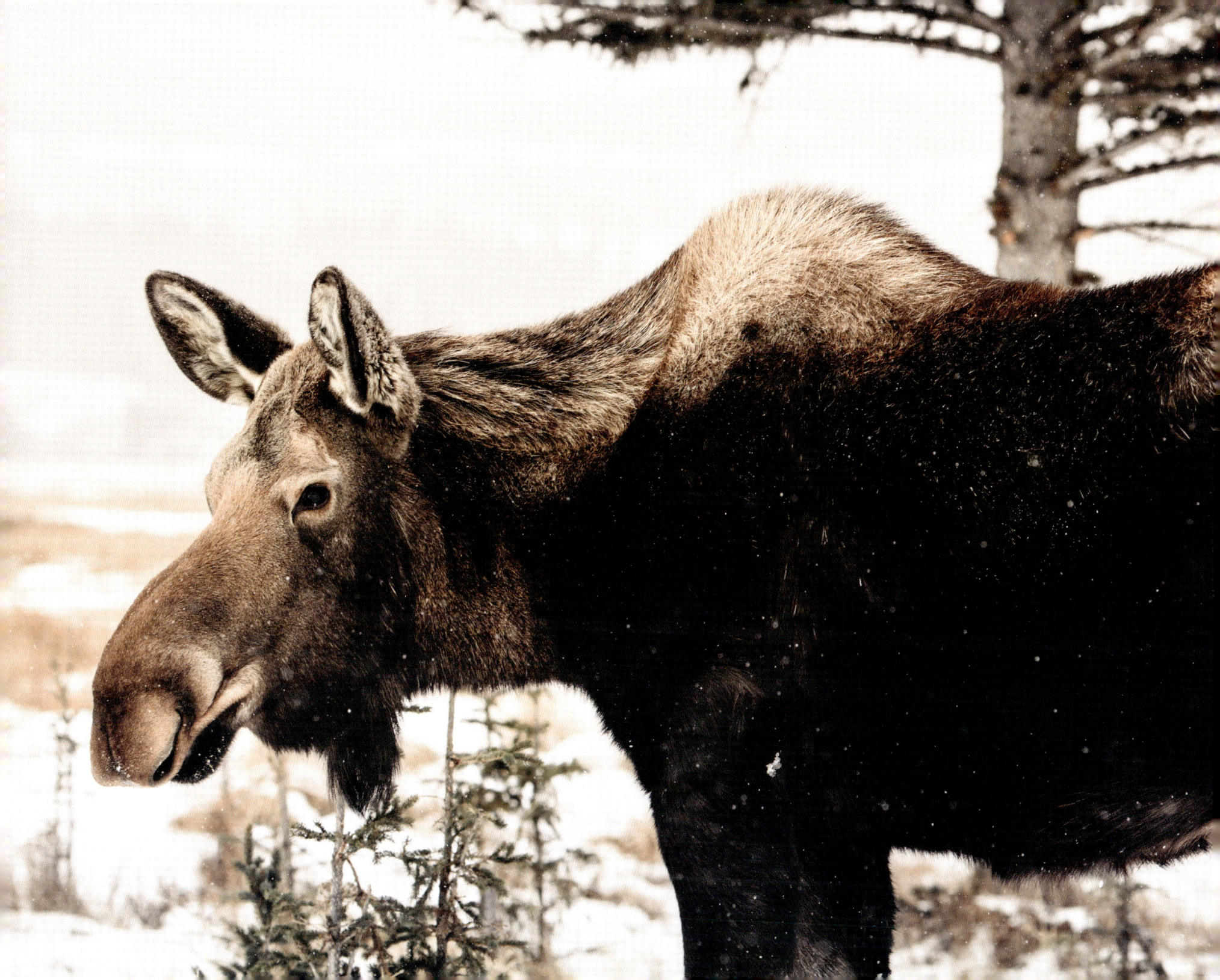

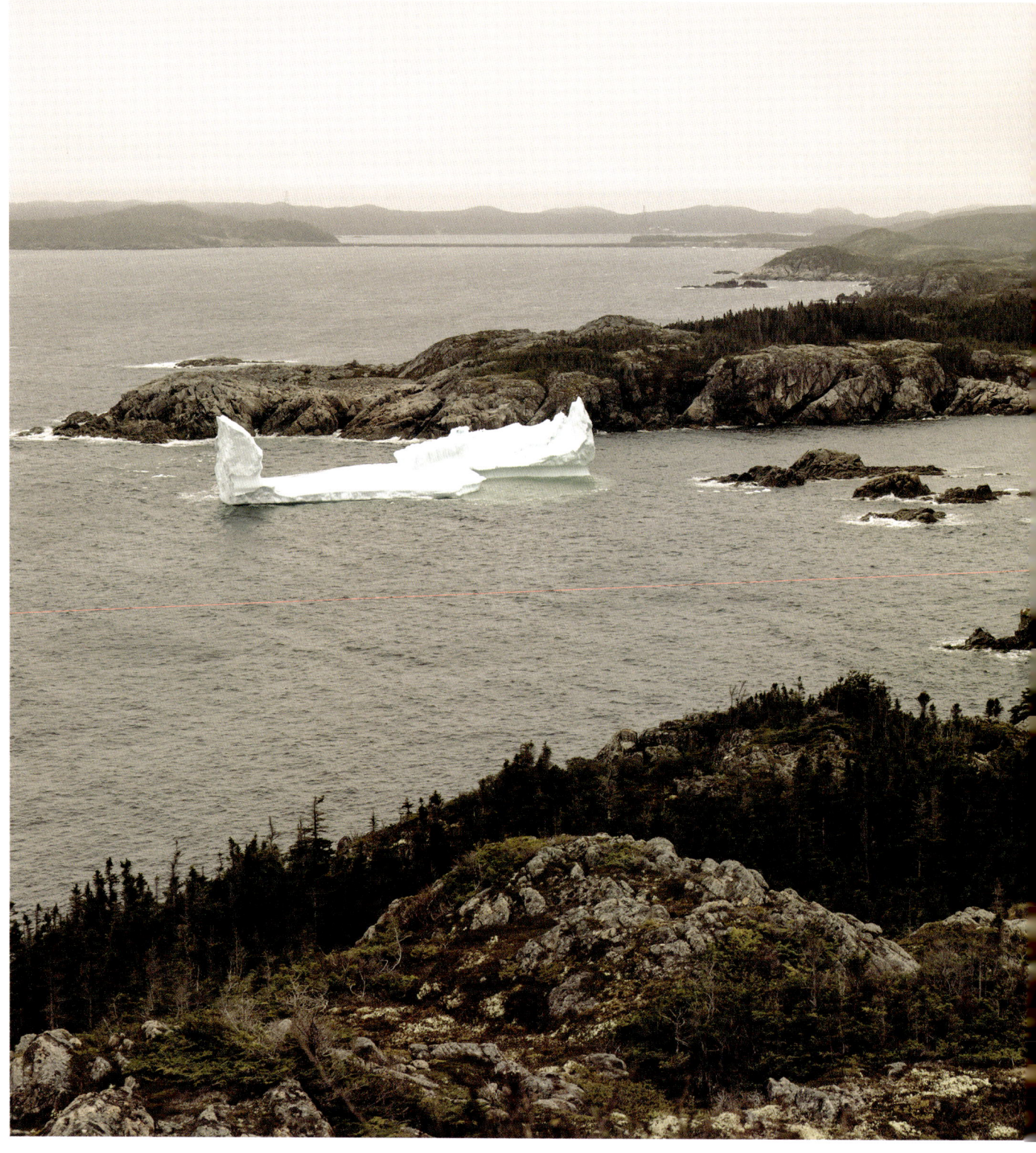

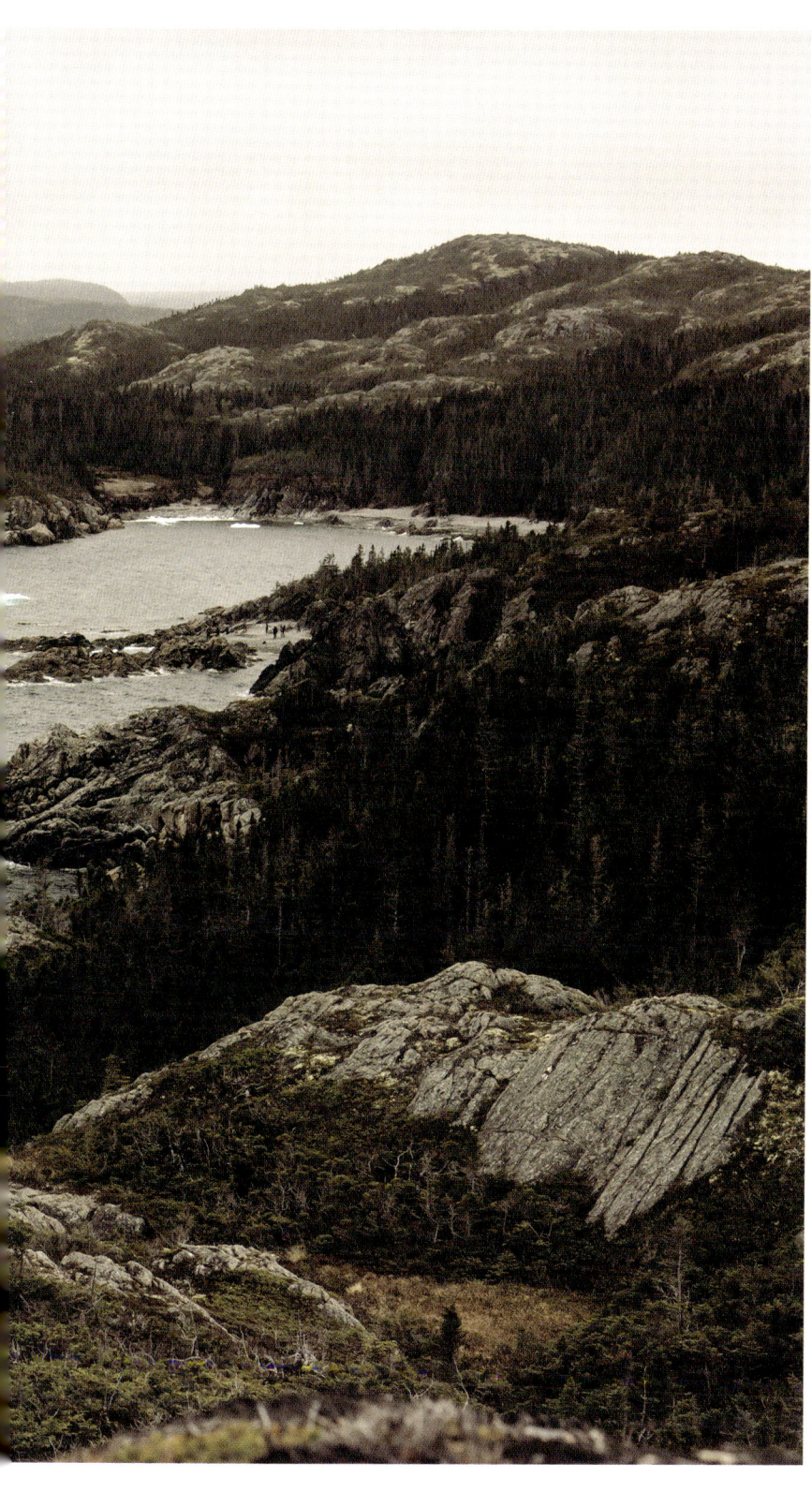

AN "ICE LICK" IS A NEWFOUNDLAND SAYING FOR A COLD WIND COMING OFF THE WATER. ICEBERG ALLEY, LITTLE HARBOUR, TWILLINGATE, NEWFOUNDLAND, MAY 2022.

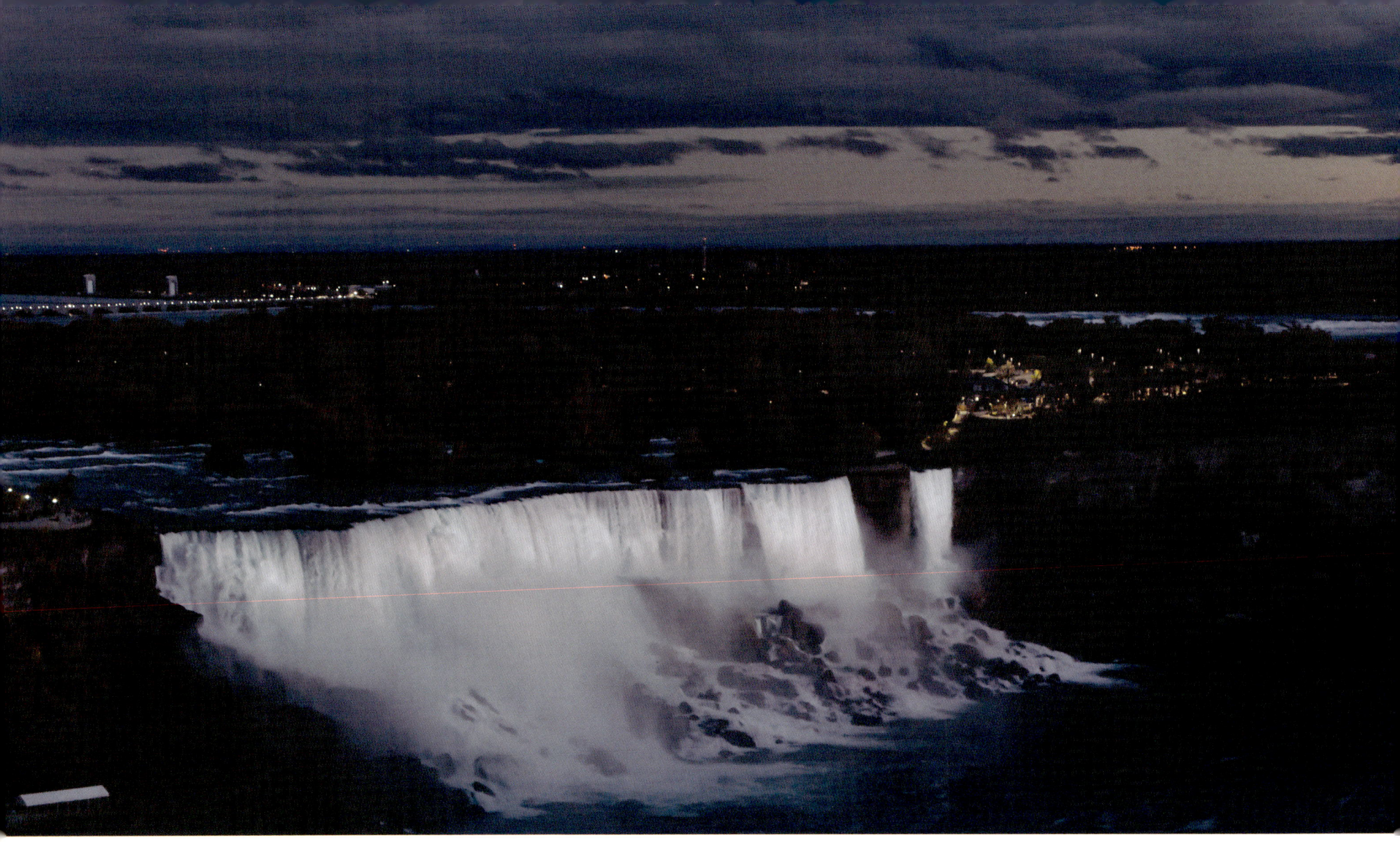

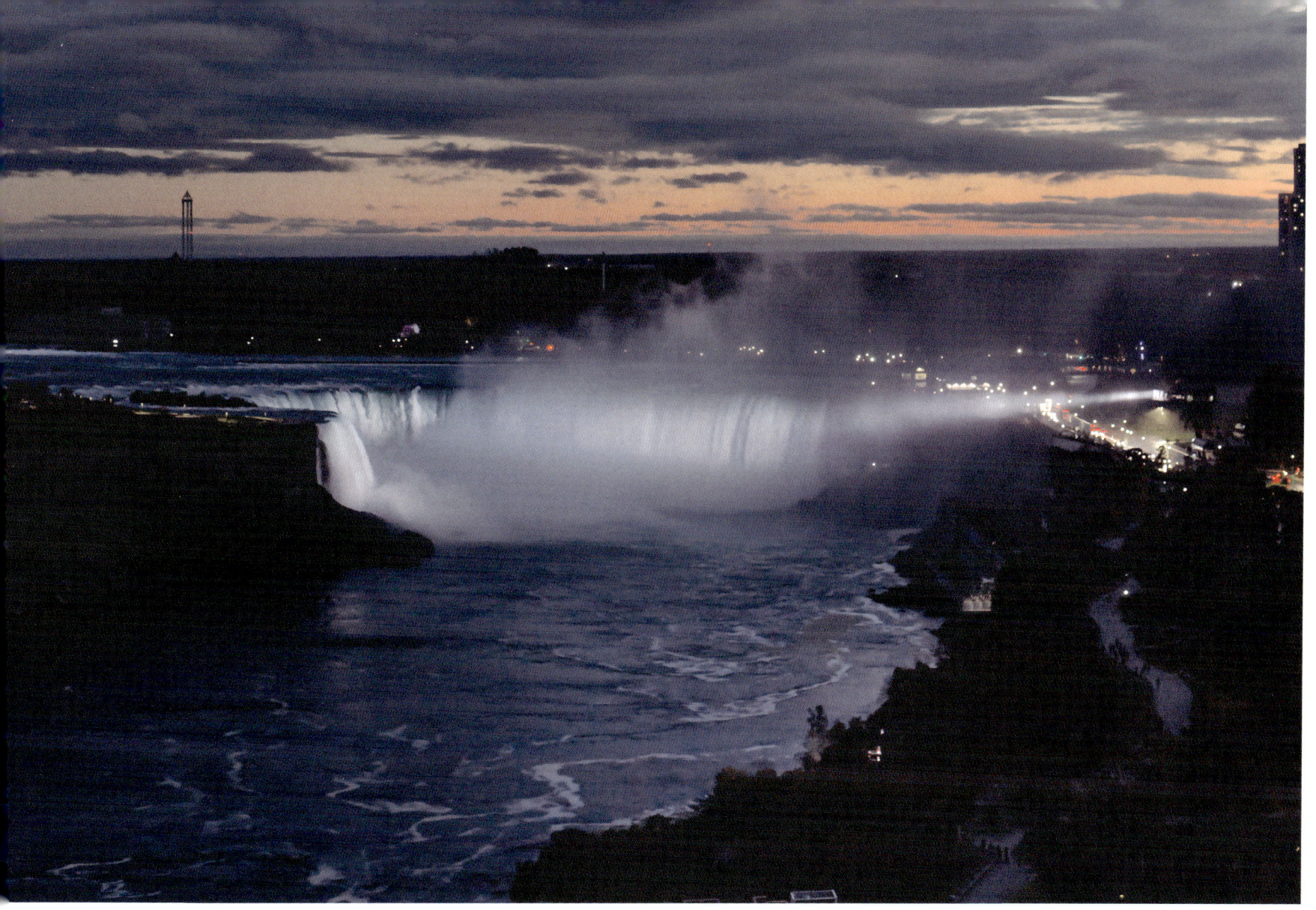

LOOKING OUT ON NIAGARA FALLS ALONG
THE US BORDER. CANADA AND THE UNITED
STATES HAVE THE LONGEST DEMILITARIZED
BORDER IN THE WORLD, AND THE MAJORITY
OF THE CANADIAN POPULATION LIVES WITHIN
TWO HOURS OF IT. WE RELY ECONOMICALLY
ON THE UNITED STATES, AND THERE IS A LOT
OF CULTURAL OVERLAP. NIAGARA FALLS,
ONTARIO, OCTOBER 2020.

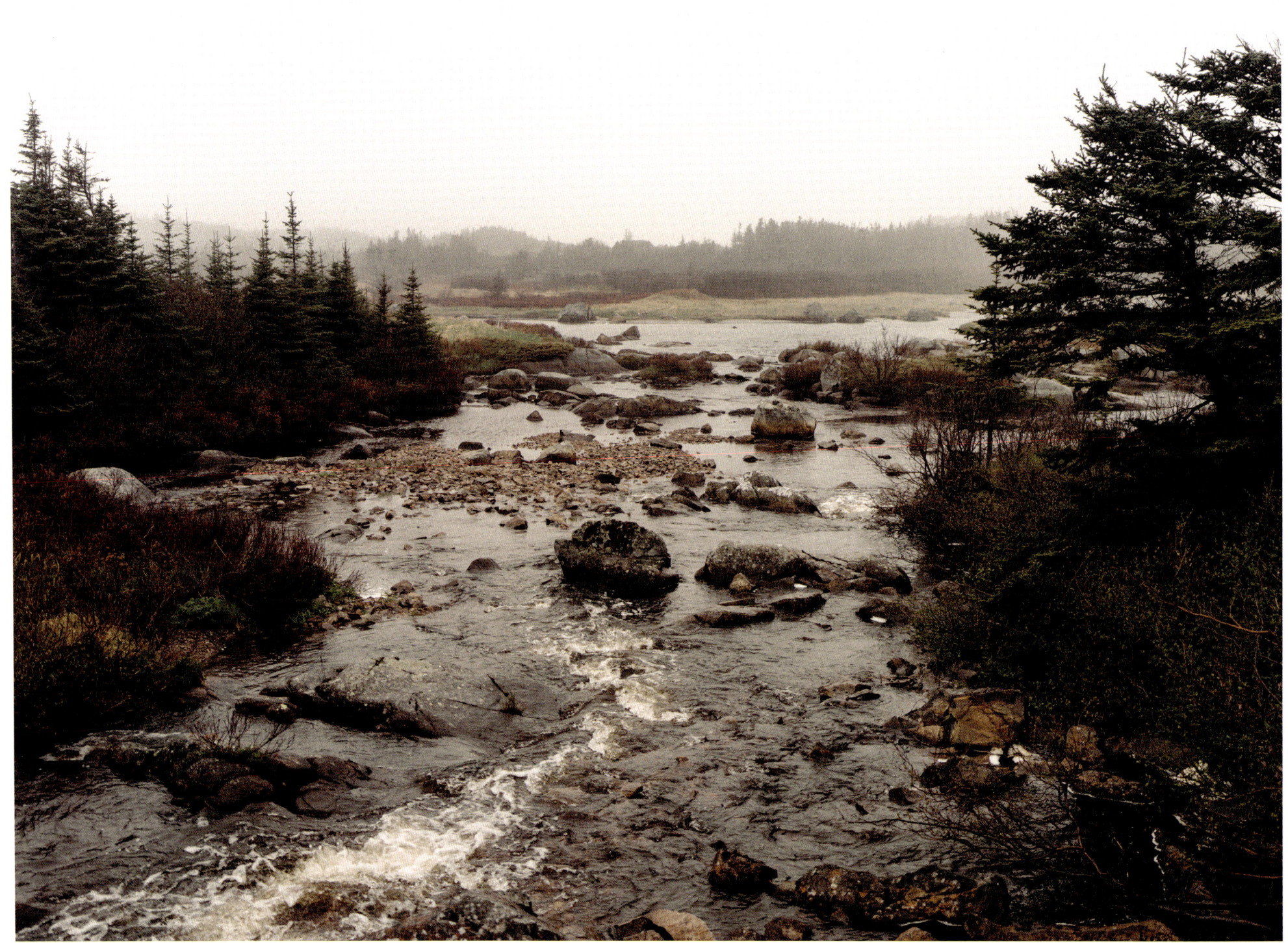

"ME MOTHER ALWAYS USED TO SAY, YOU'RE NOT MADE OF SUGAR": SAID BY A KIND STRANGER WHILE HIKING AND PHOTOGRAPHING IN THE POURING RAIN. FOGO ISLAND, NEWFOUNDLAND, MAY 2022.

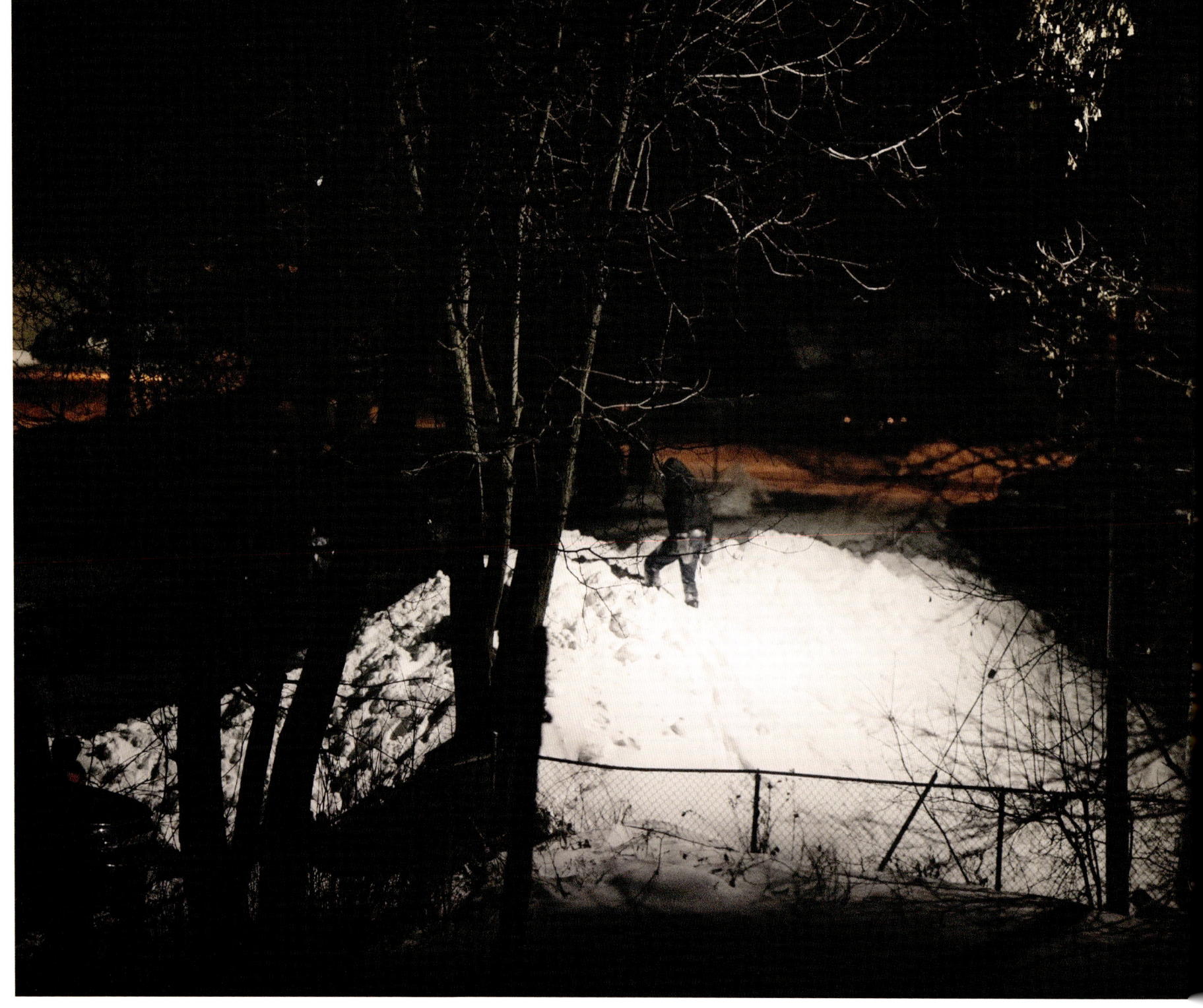

← AT THE END OF A SNOW DAY IN
GUELPH, ONTARIO, JANUARY 2012.

→ DE-ICING FLUID, A MIXTURE OF THE
CHEMICAL GLYCOL AND WATER, IS
GENERALLY HEATED AND SPRAYED
UNDER PRESSURE TO REMOVE ICE AND
SNOW FROM AN AIRCRAFT. CALGARY,
ALBERTA, NOVEMBER 2013.

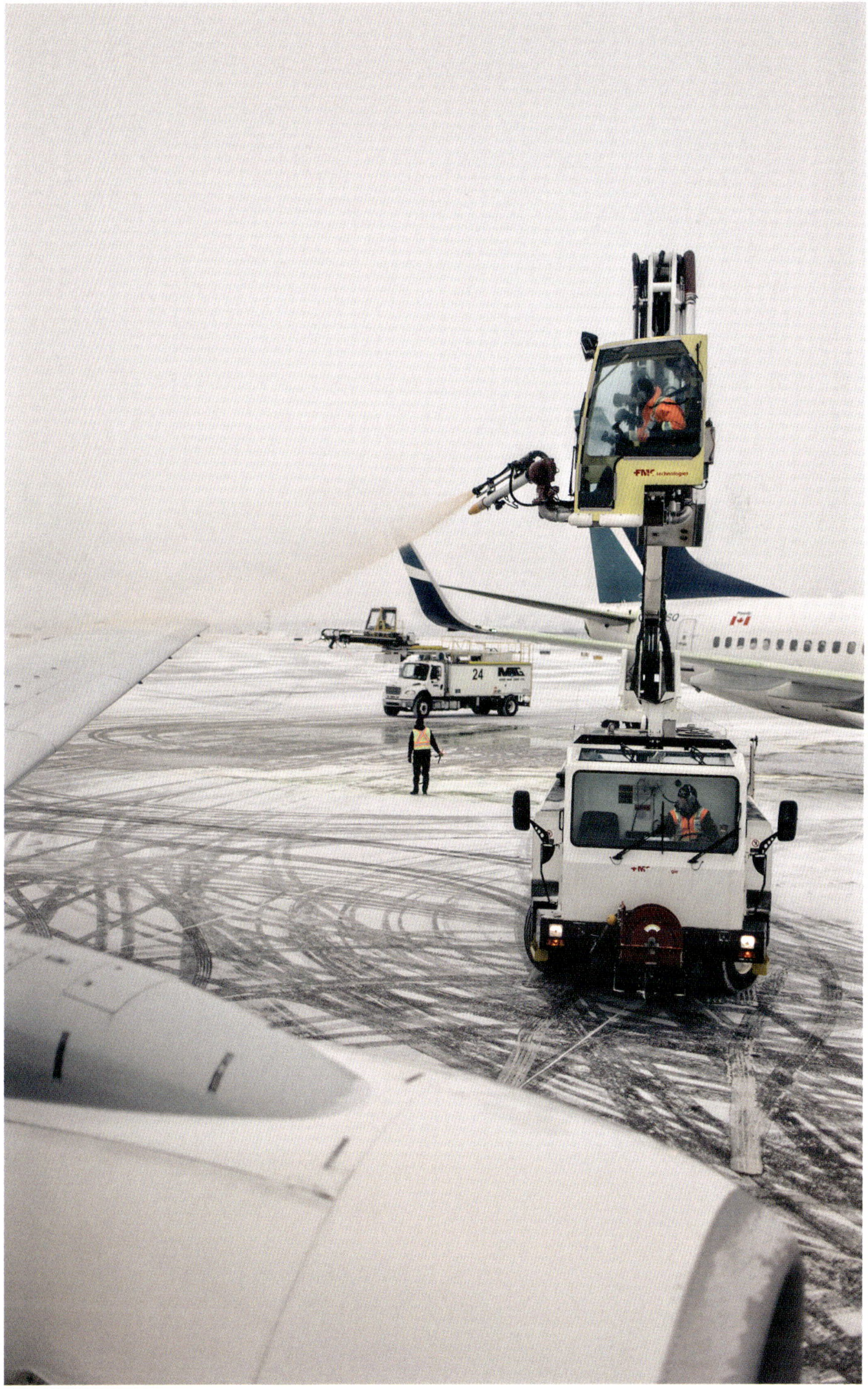

DENE FIRST NATION FROM ABOVE, YELLOWKNIFE,
NORTHWEST TERRITORIES, MARCH 2017.

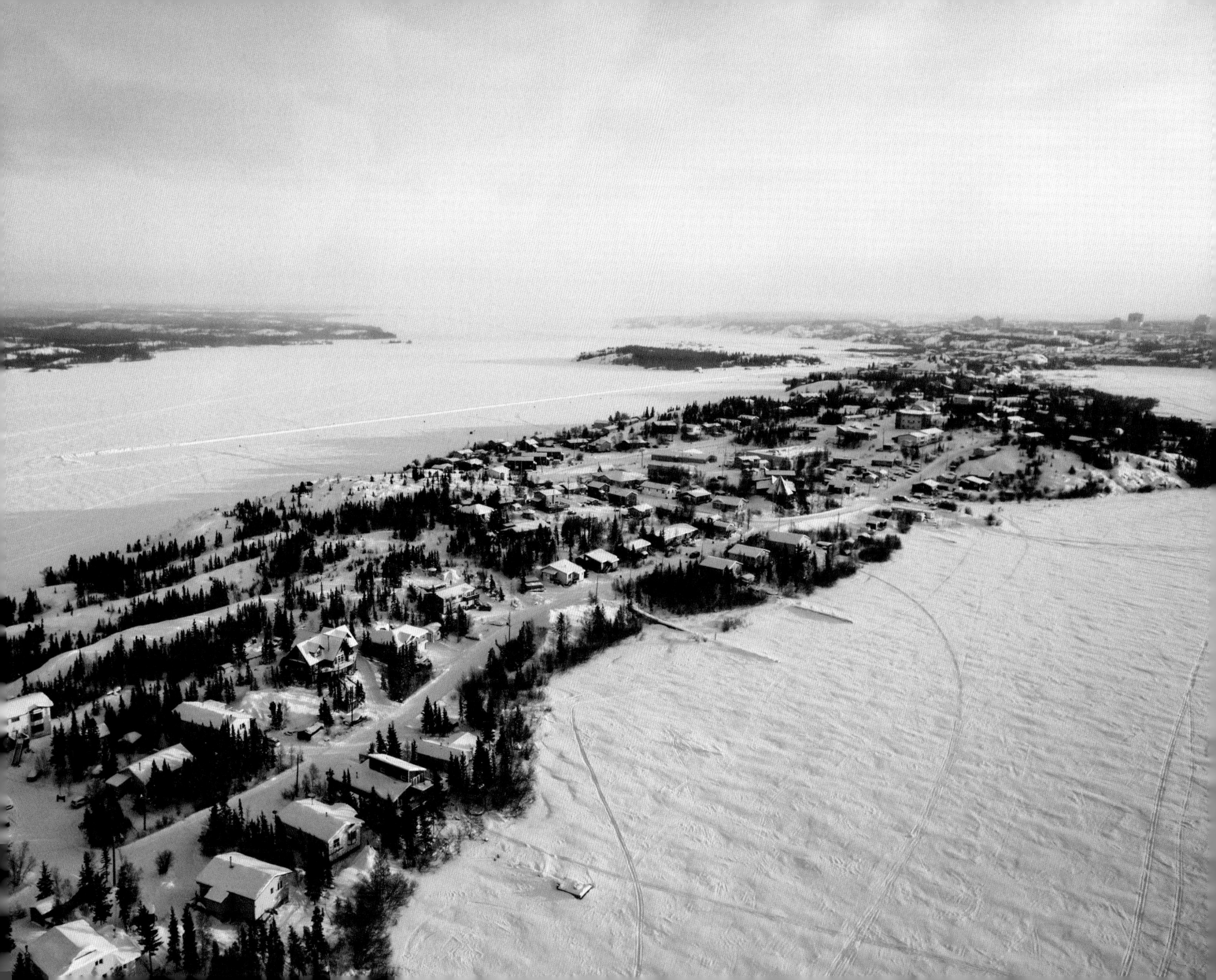

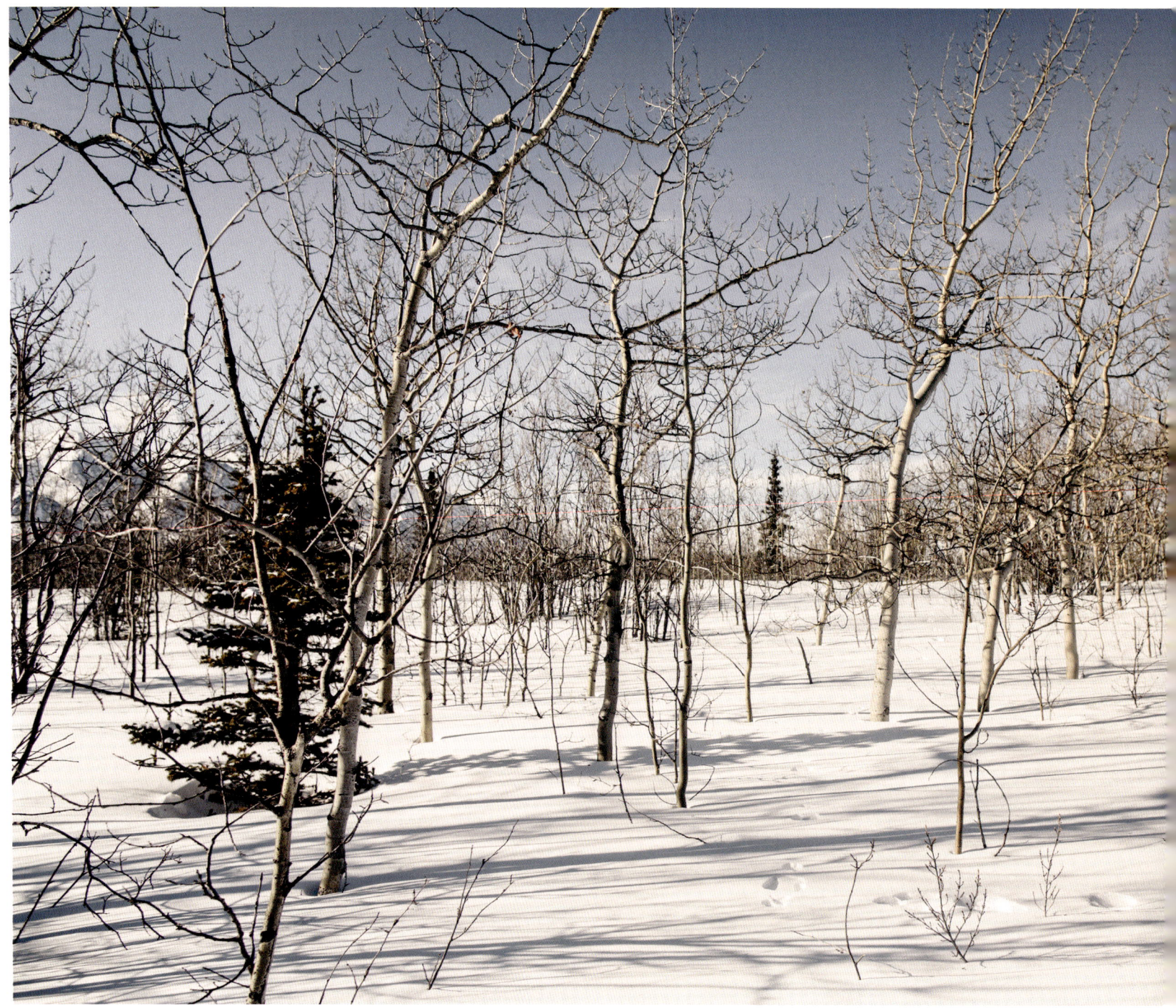

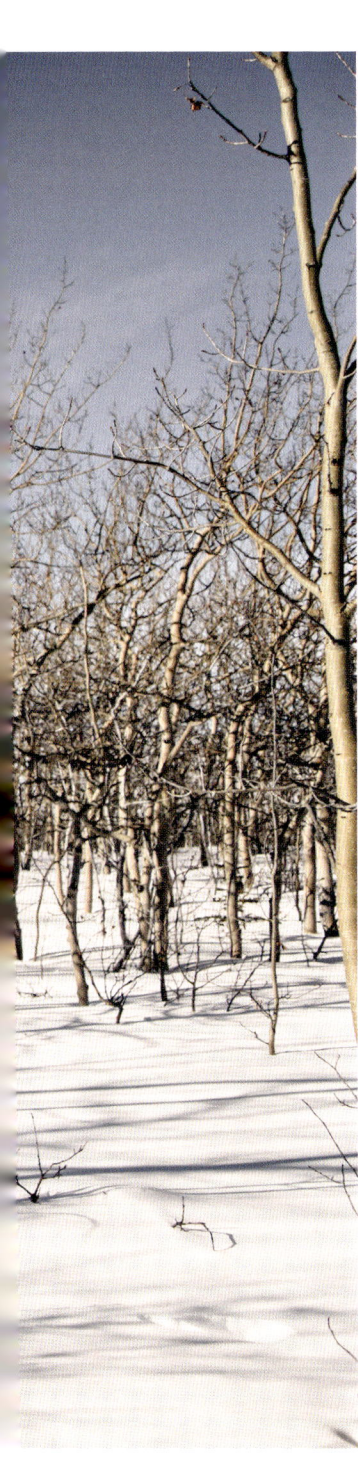

FOREST SCENE IN YUKON, MARCH 2017.

A BEAR TRACK ON A LOGGING ROAD.
PRINCE GEORGE, BRITISH COLUMBIA,
JULY 2019.

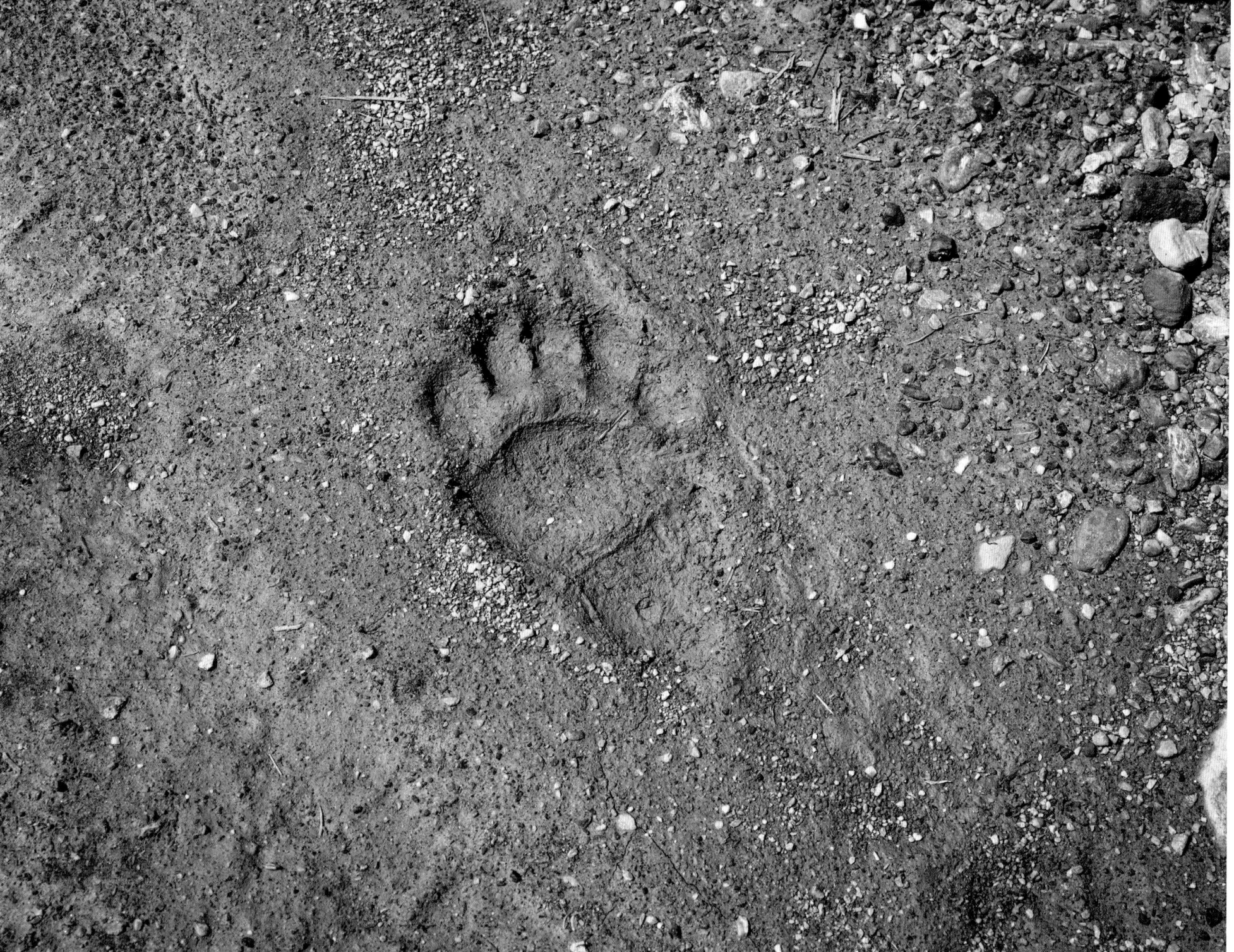

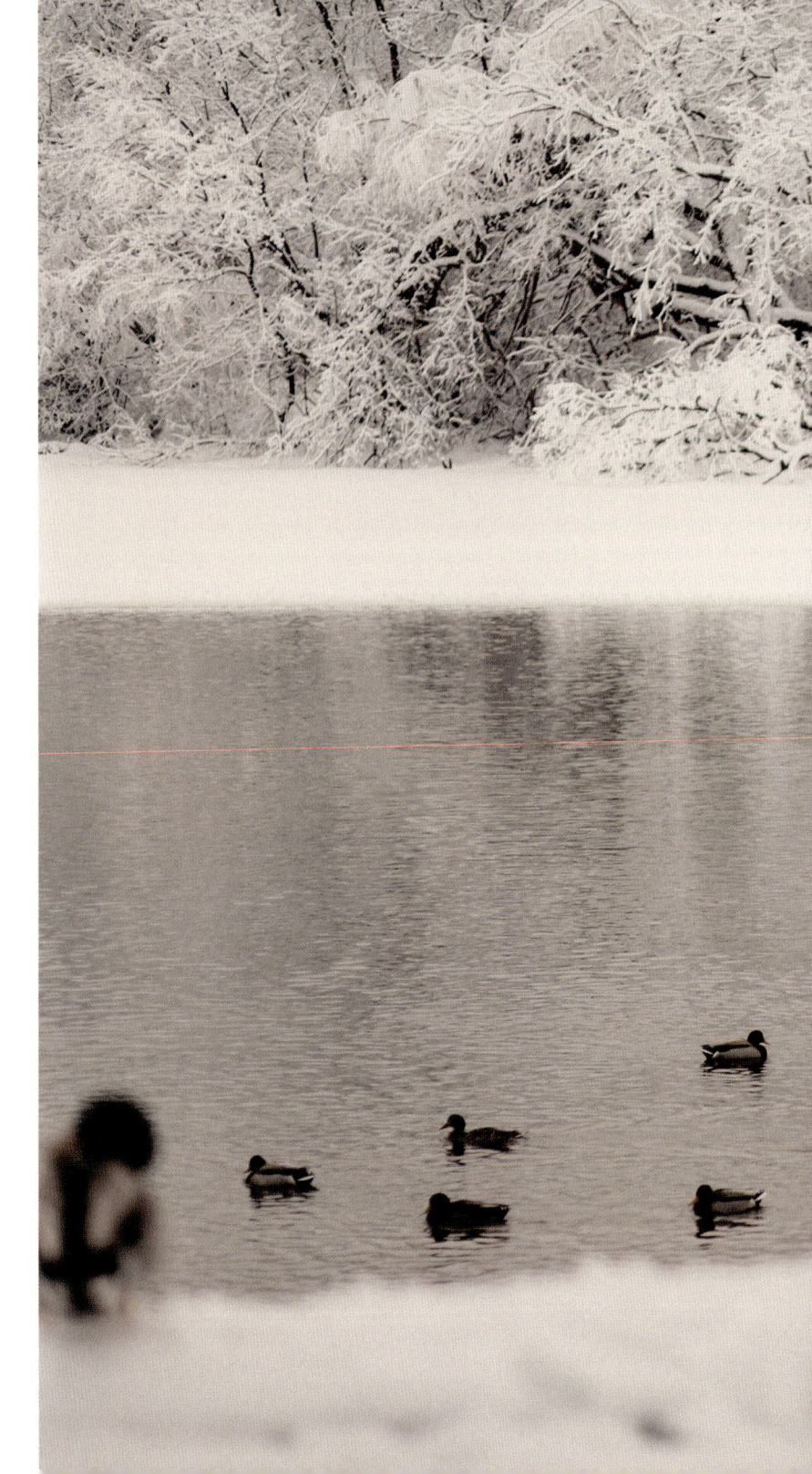

A GANDER OF CANADA GEESE AFTER A SNOWFALL
IN GUELPH, ONTARIO, FEBRUARY 2013.

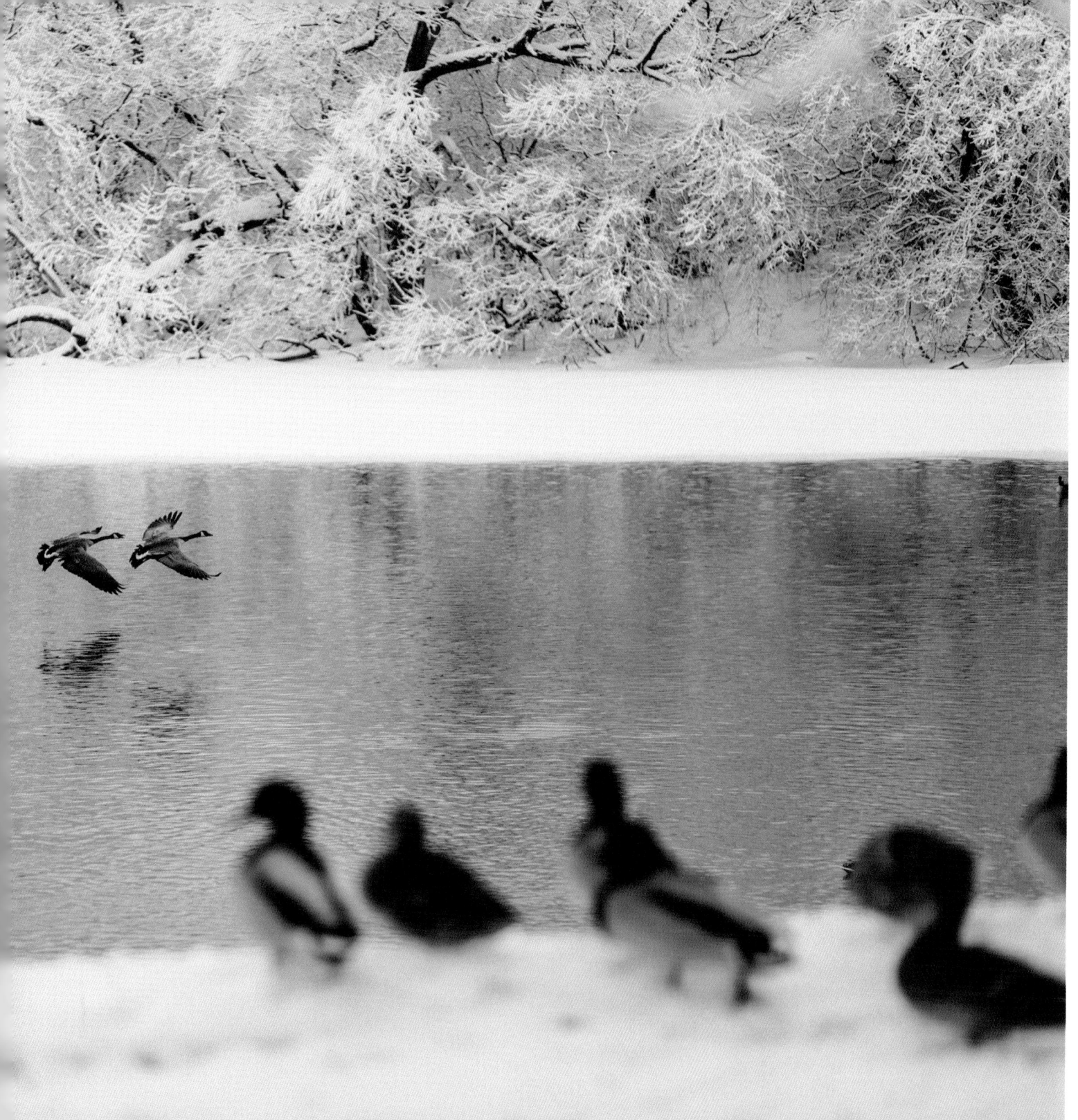

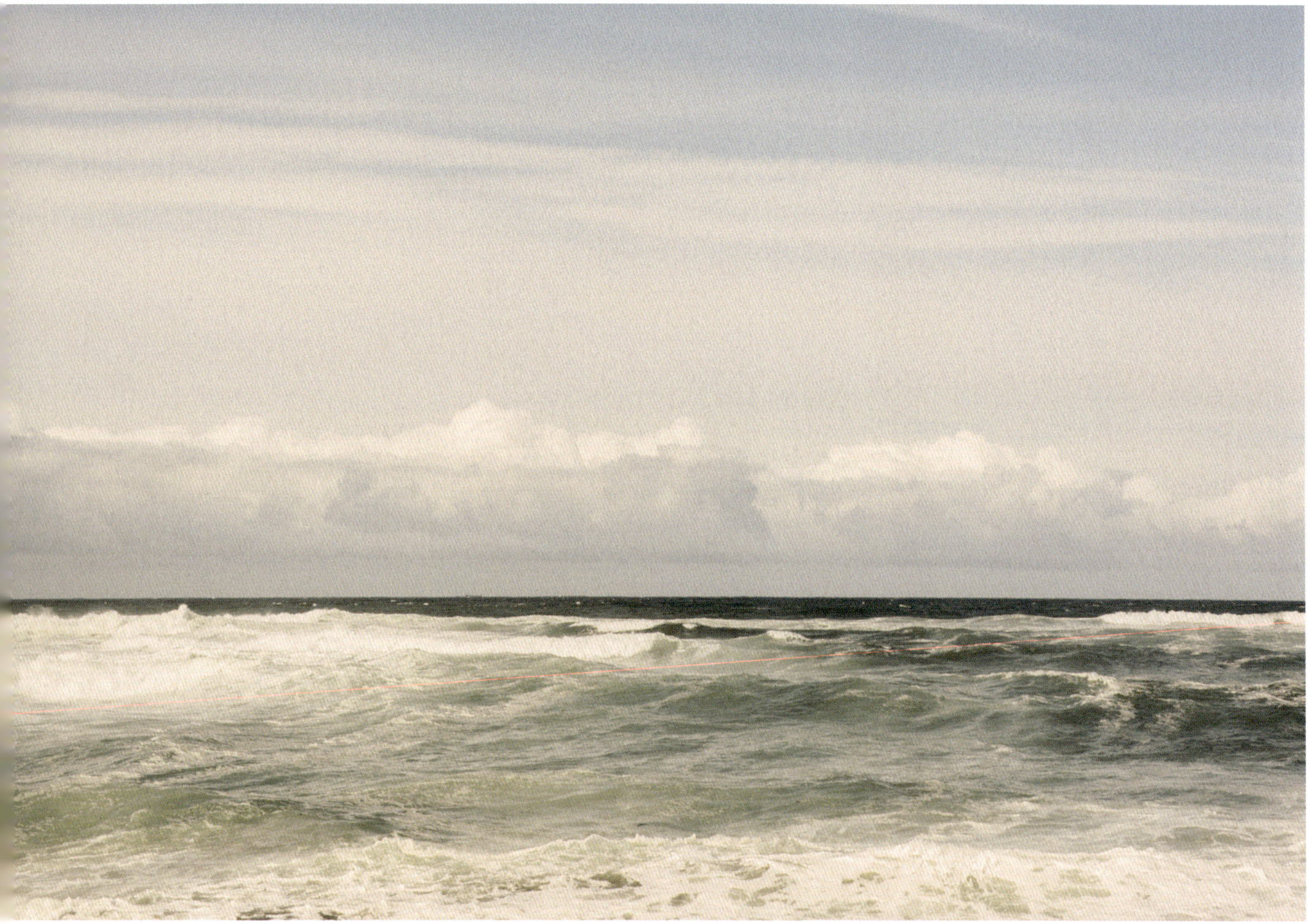

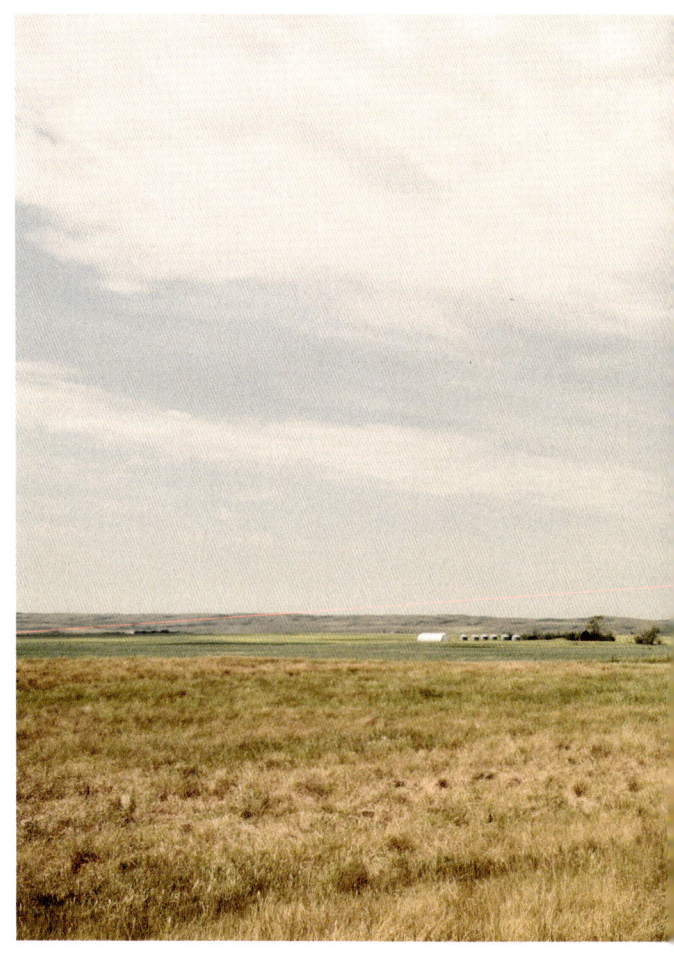

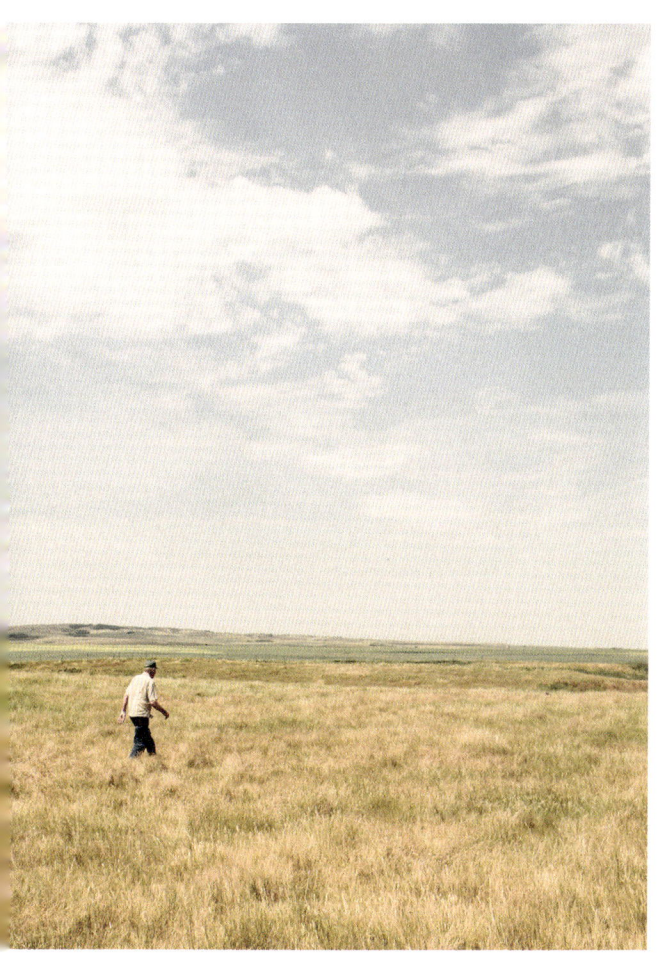

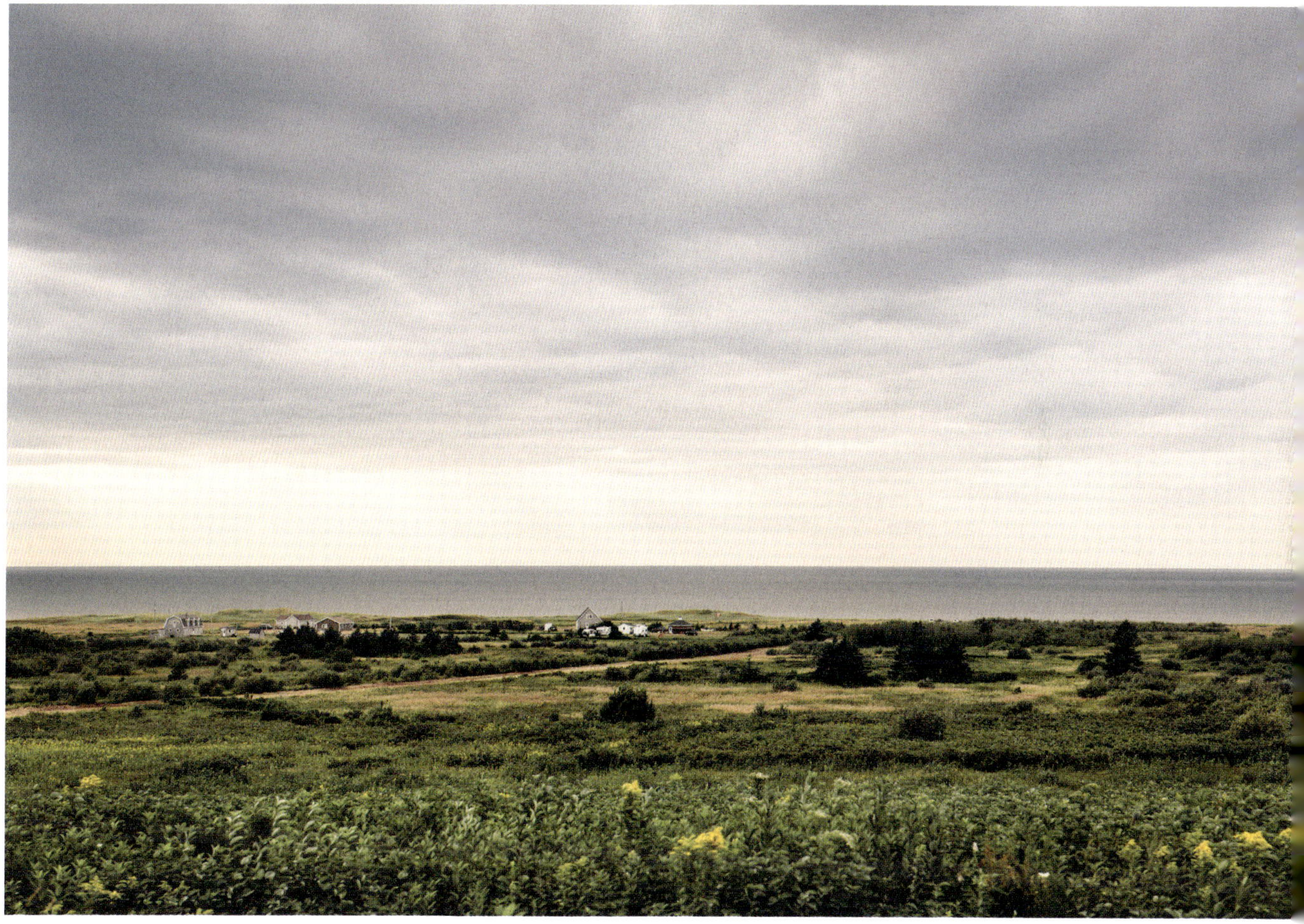

LEFT TO RIGHT THE PACIFIC OCEAN, NEAR TOFINO, BRITISH COLUMBIA, MAY 2016. MY GREAT-UNCLE ON THE HOMESTEAD WHERE HE AND HIS 18 SIBLINGS GREW UP AFTER EMIGRATING FROM AUSTRIA. NEAR MOOSE JAW, SASKATCHEWAN, JULY 2017. THE ATLANTIC OCEAN, NEAR TIGNISH, PRINCE EDWARD ISLAND, AUGUST 2017.

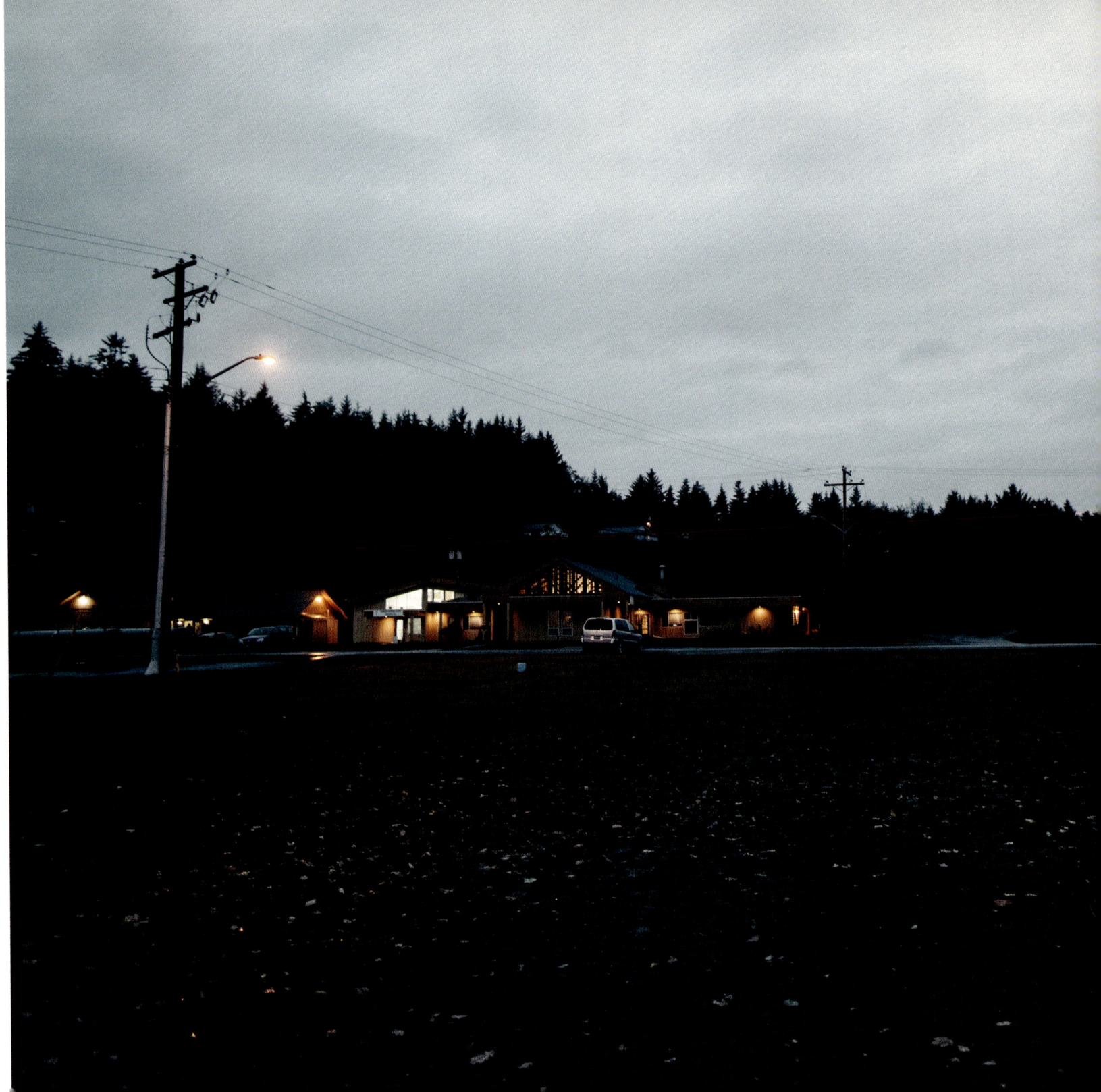

THE FORMER SITE OF ST. MICHAEL'S INDIAN RESIDENTIAL SCHOOL. IN FEBRUARY 2015, FIRST NATIONS, POLITICIANS AND FORMER STUDENTS ATTENDED A HEALING CEREMONY HOSTED BY THE 'NAMGIS FIRST NATION TO MARK THE DEMOLITION OF THE CLOSED SCHOOL'S BUILDING. ALERT BAY, BRITISH COLUMBIA, OCTOBER 2017.

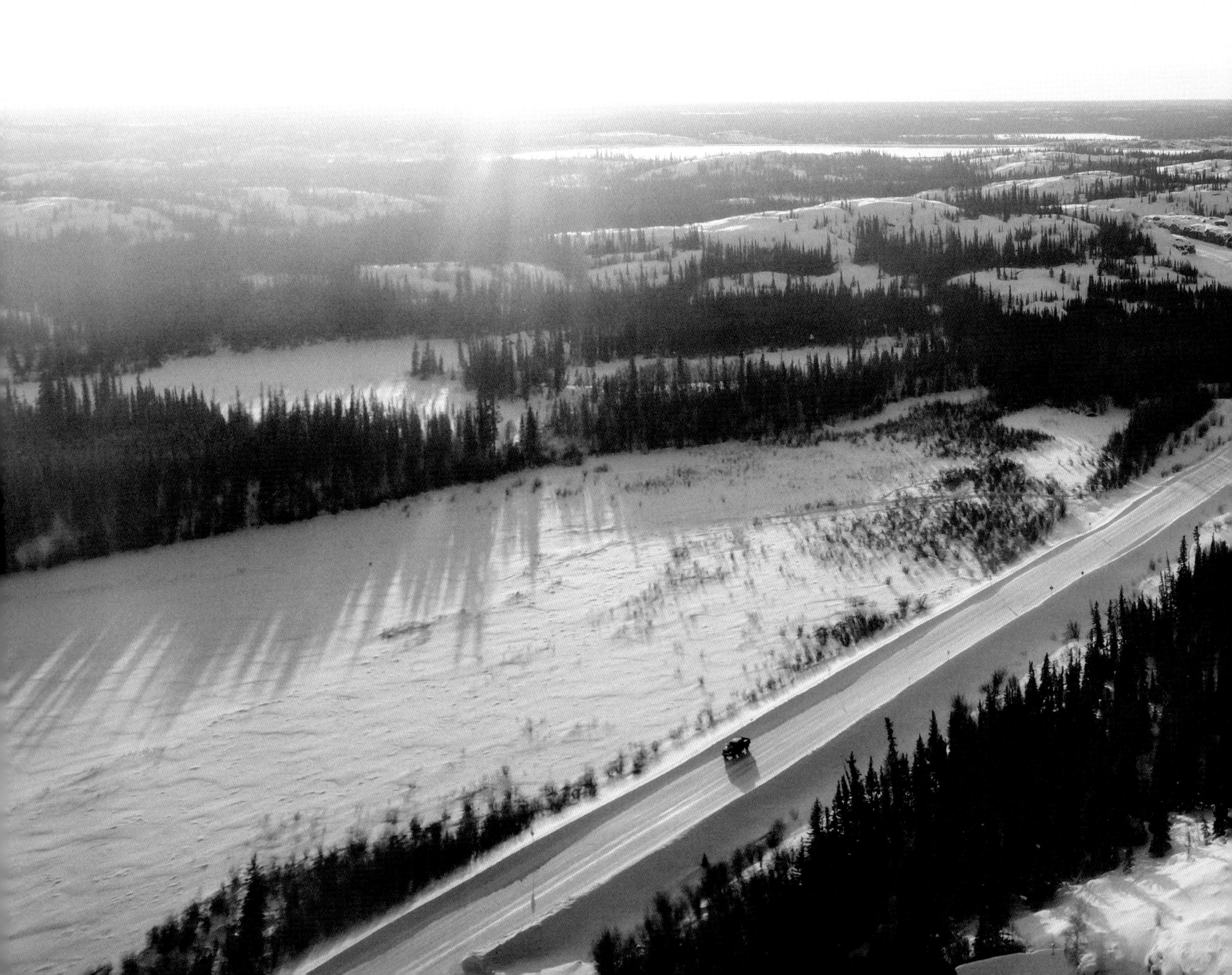

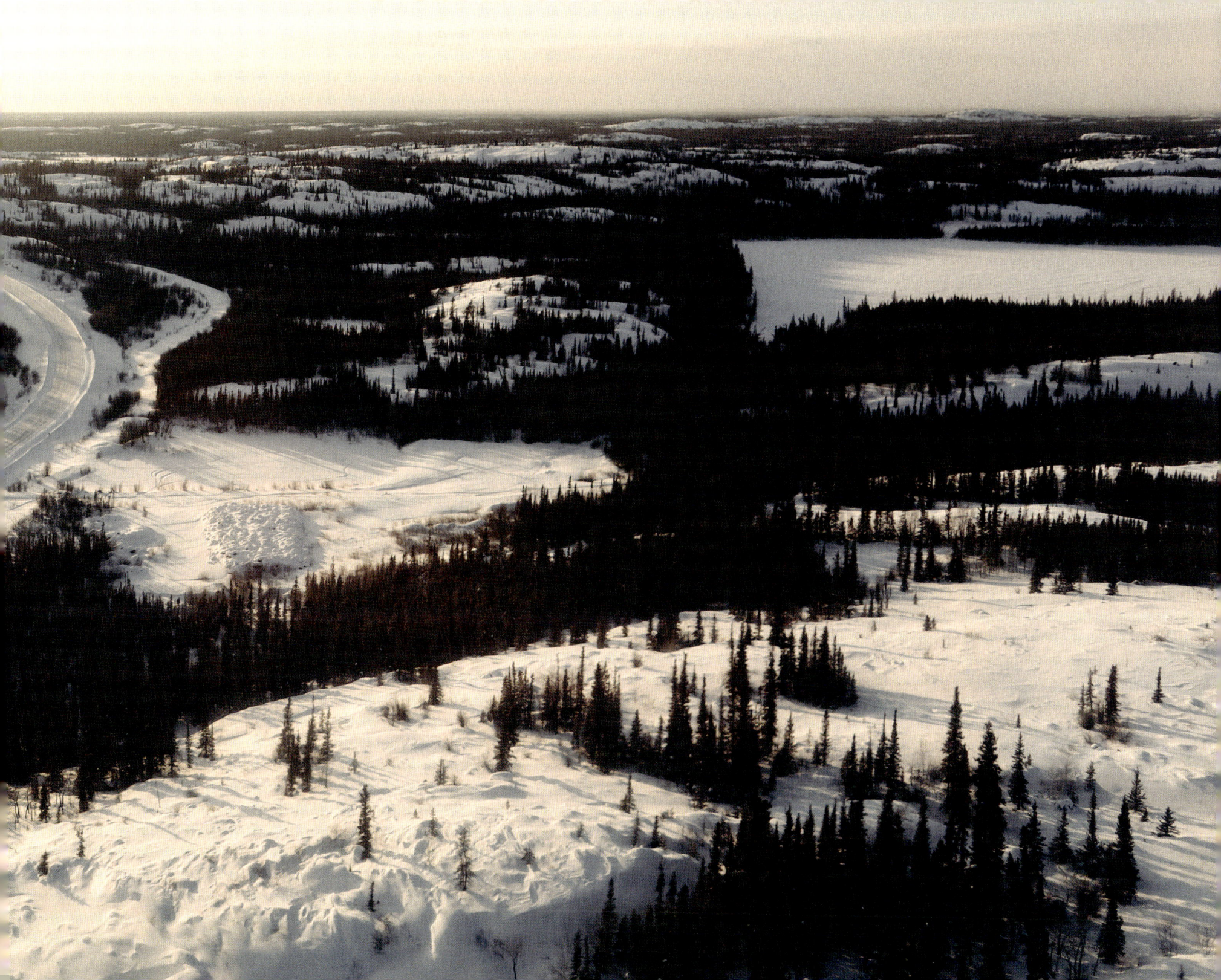

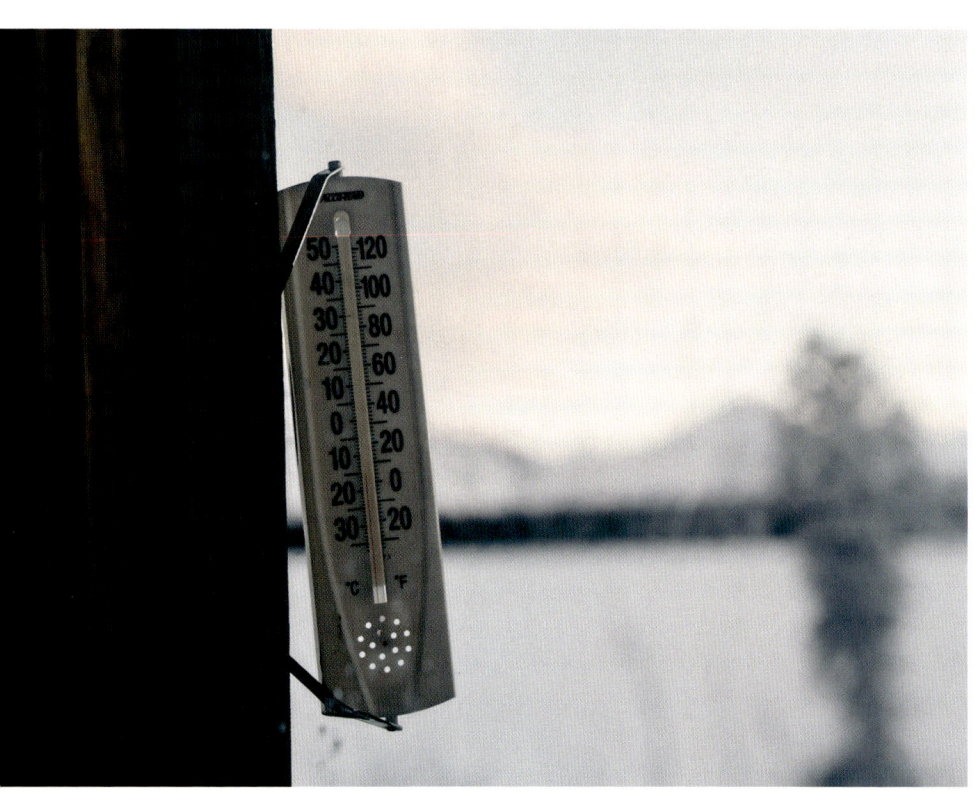

OVERLEAF ICE ROADS CROSS EIGHT ARCTIC COUNTRIES, AND CANADA ALONE HAS 5400 KM OF THEM. THEY ARE MOSTLY USED TO RESUPPLY SMALL COMMUNITIES AND MINING TOWNS IN THE FAR NORTH THAT WOULD OTHERWISE BE FLY-IN ACCESS ONLY. GLOBAL WARMING IS WREAKING HAVOC AND CREATING MAJOR SAFETY ISSUES FOR THIS VITAL INFRASTRUCTURE. YELLOWKNIFE, NORTHWEST TERRITORIES, MARCH 2017.

← MINUS 15°C, NEAR KLUANE NATIONAL PARK AND RESERVE, YUKON, MARCH 2017.

→ LEARNING TO SKATE IN HOPE, BRITISH COLUMBIA, DECEMBER 2015.

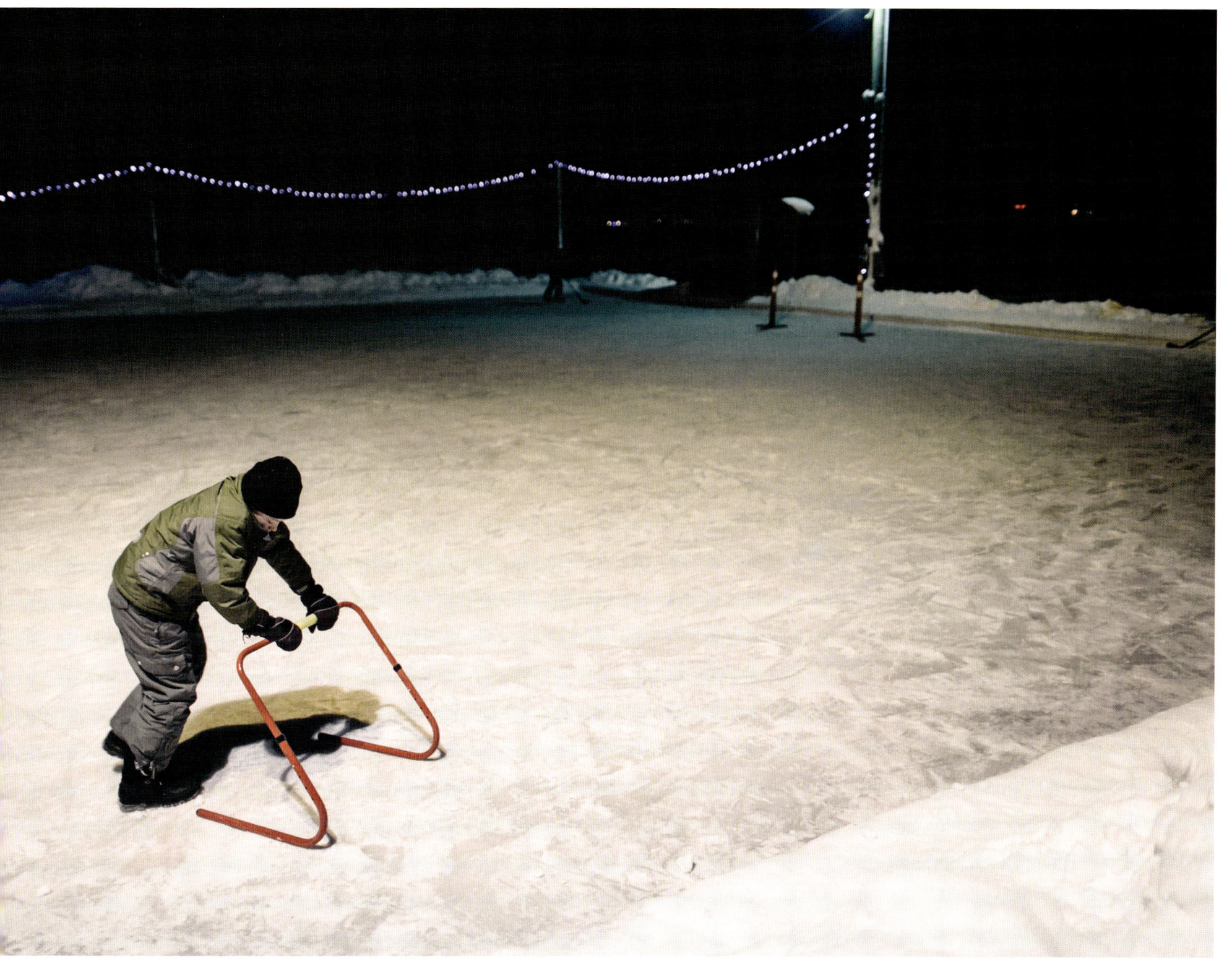

VANCOUVER HAS ONE OF THE MOST EFFICIENT RECYCLING AND WASTE MANAGEMENT SYSTEMS IN CANADA. ALLEYWAY AND BIN IN MOUNT PLEASANT, VANCOUVER, BRITISH COLUMBIA, APRIL 2016.

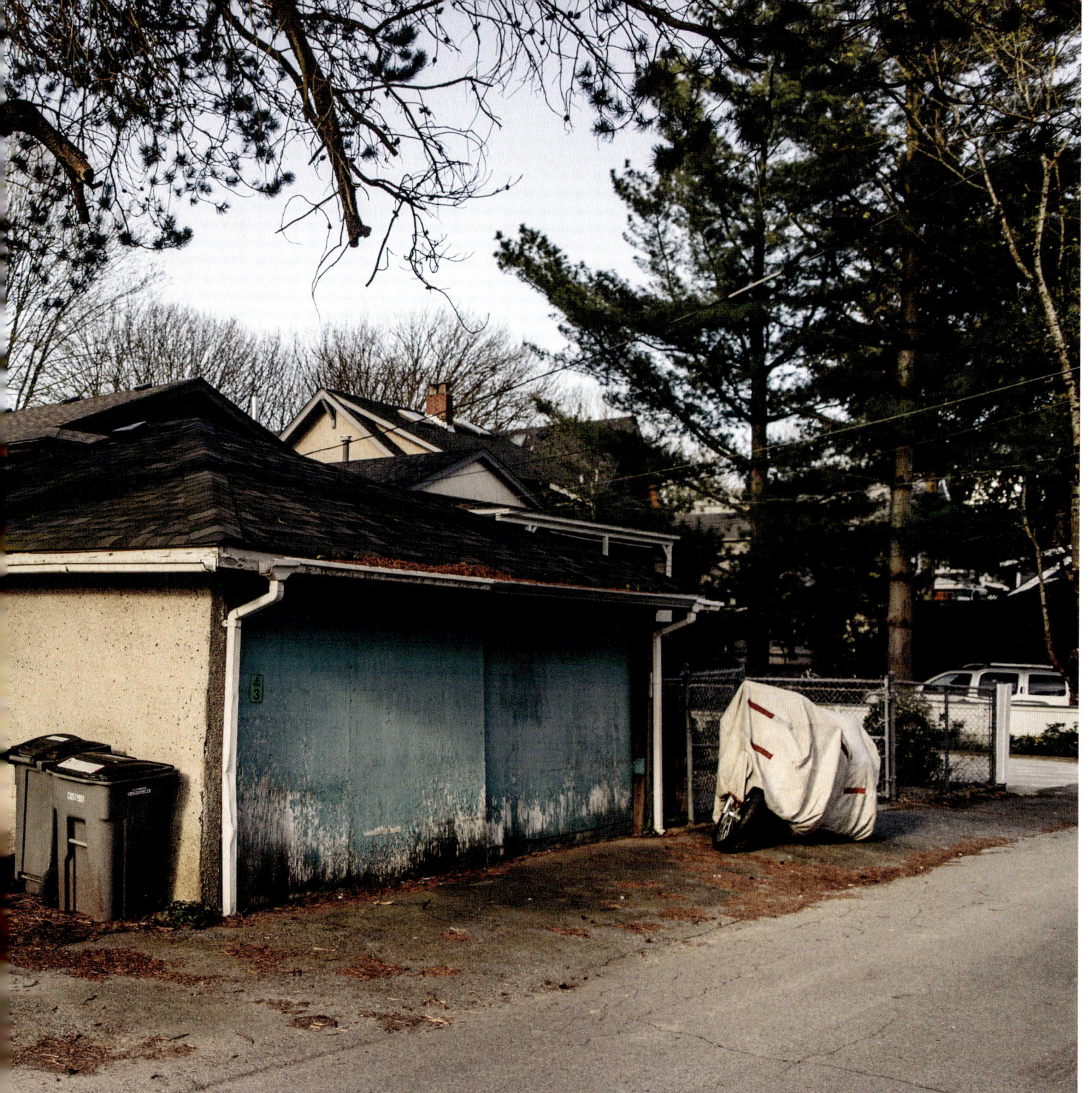

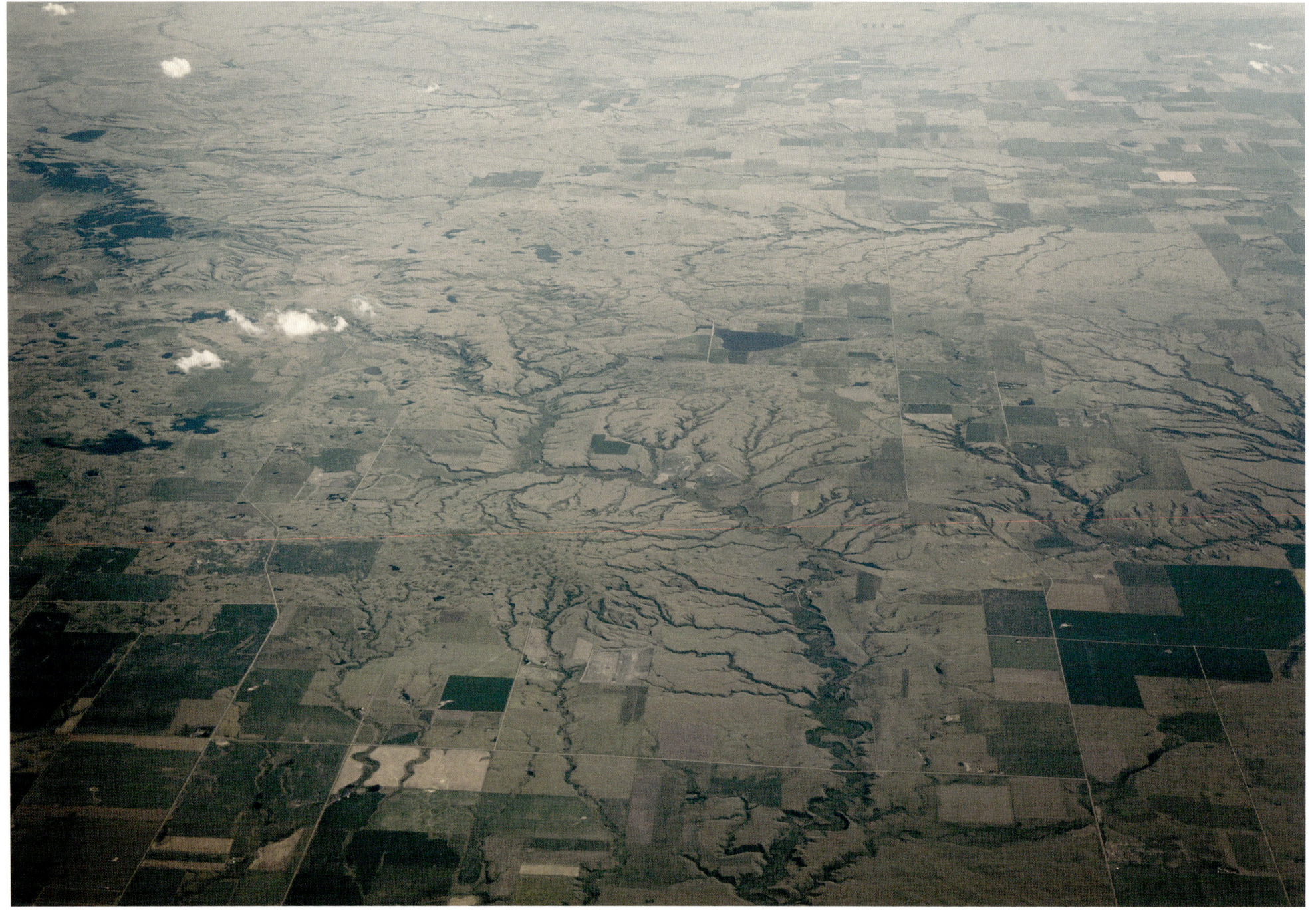

← ABOVE THE PRAIRIES, SOMEWHERE
BETWEEN SASKATCHEWAN AND
MANITOBA, JUNE 2017.

↓ TORONTO SKYLINE, TORONTO,
ONTARIO, JUNE 2022.

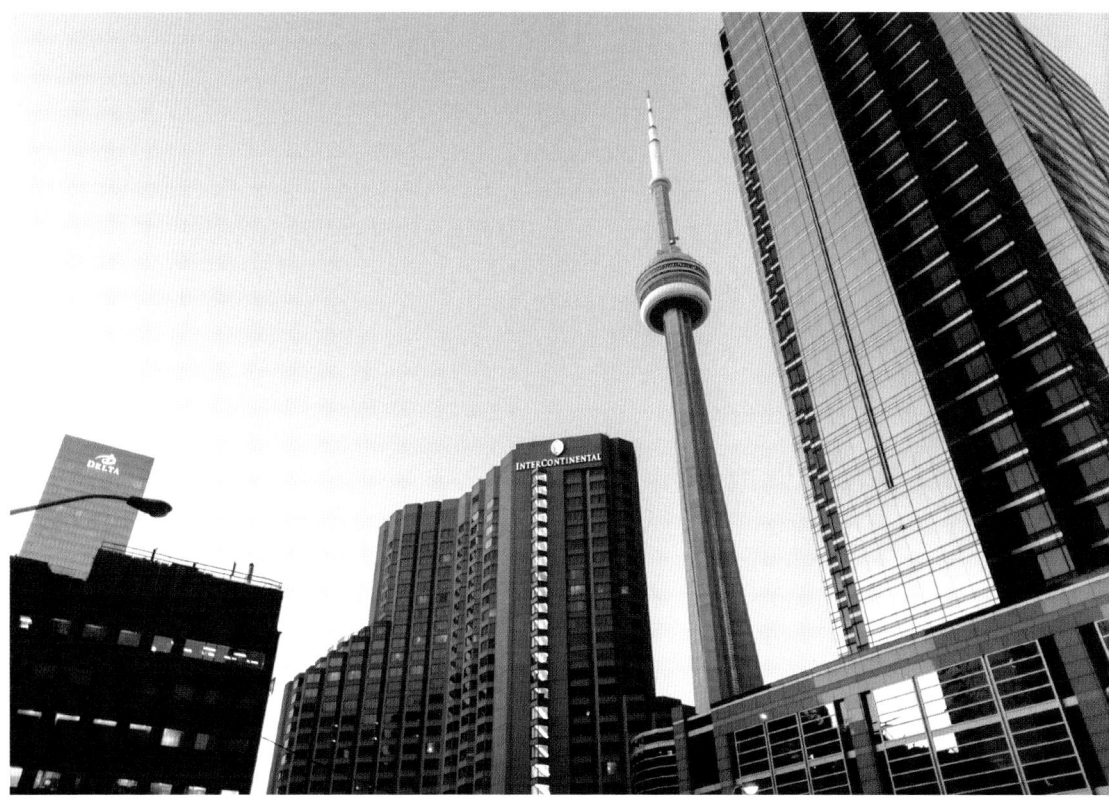

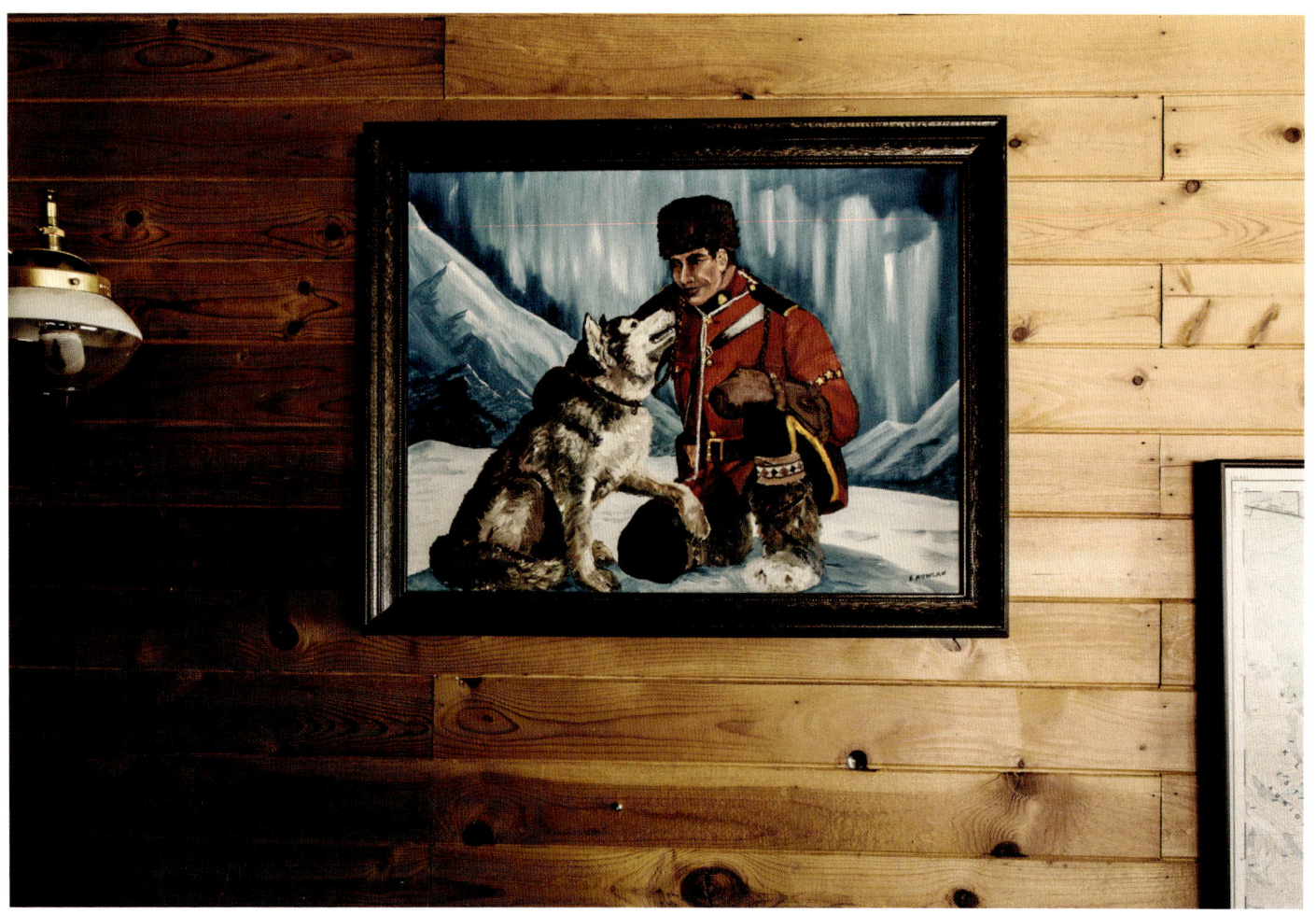

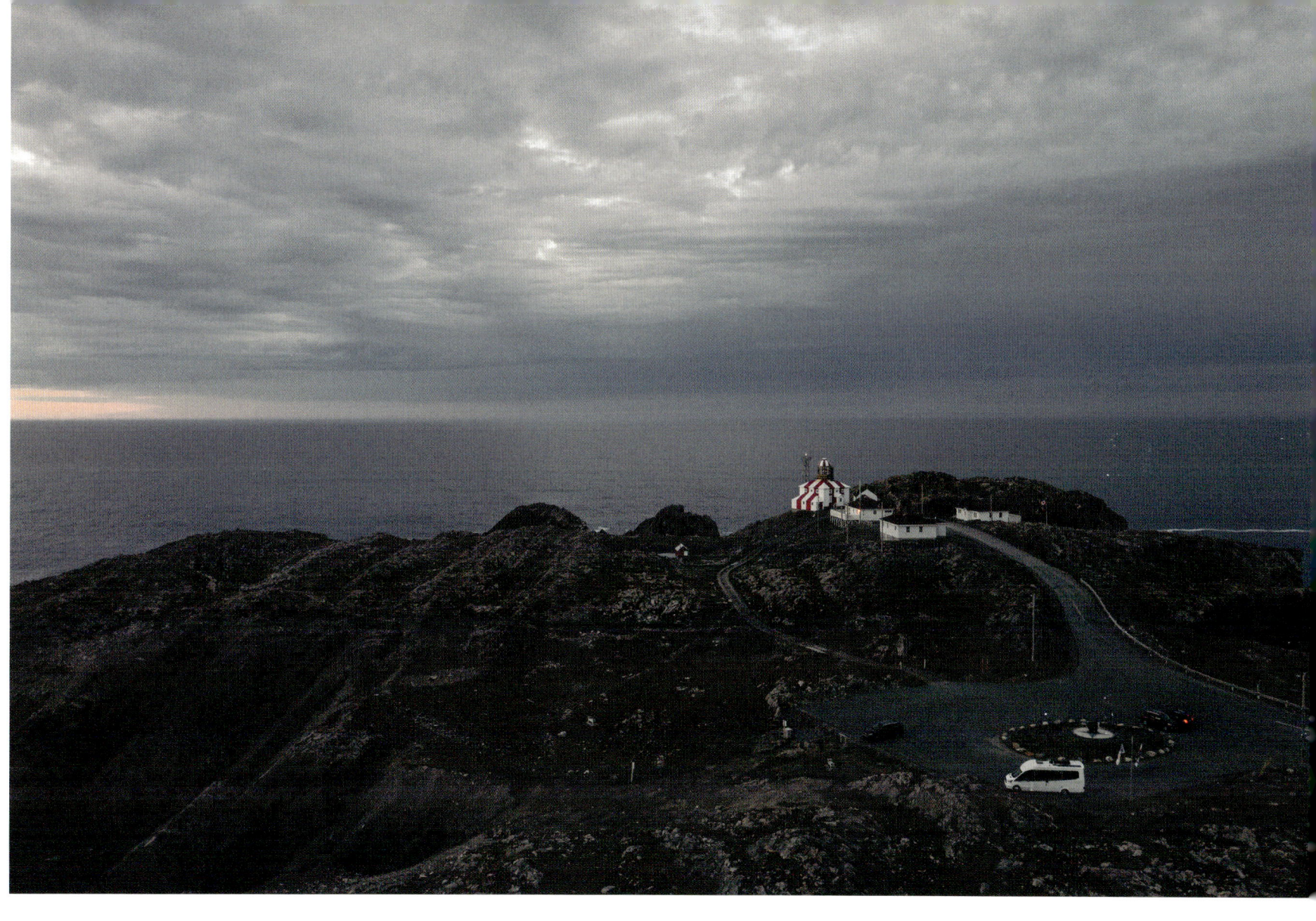

CAPE BONAVISTA LIGHTHOUSE STANDS IN THE LAST LIGHT
OF DAY. BONAVISTA, NEWFOUNDLAND, MAY 2022.

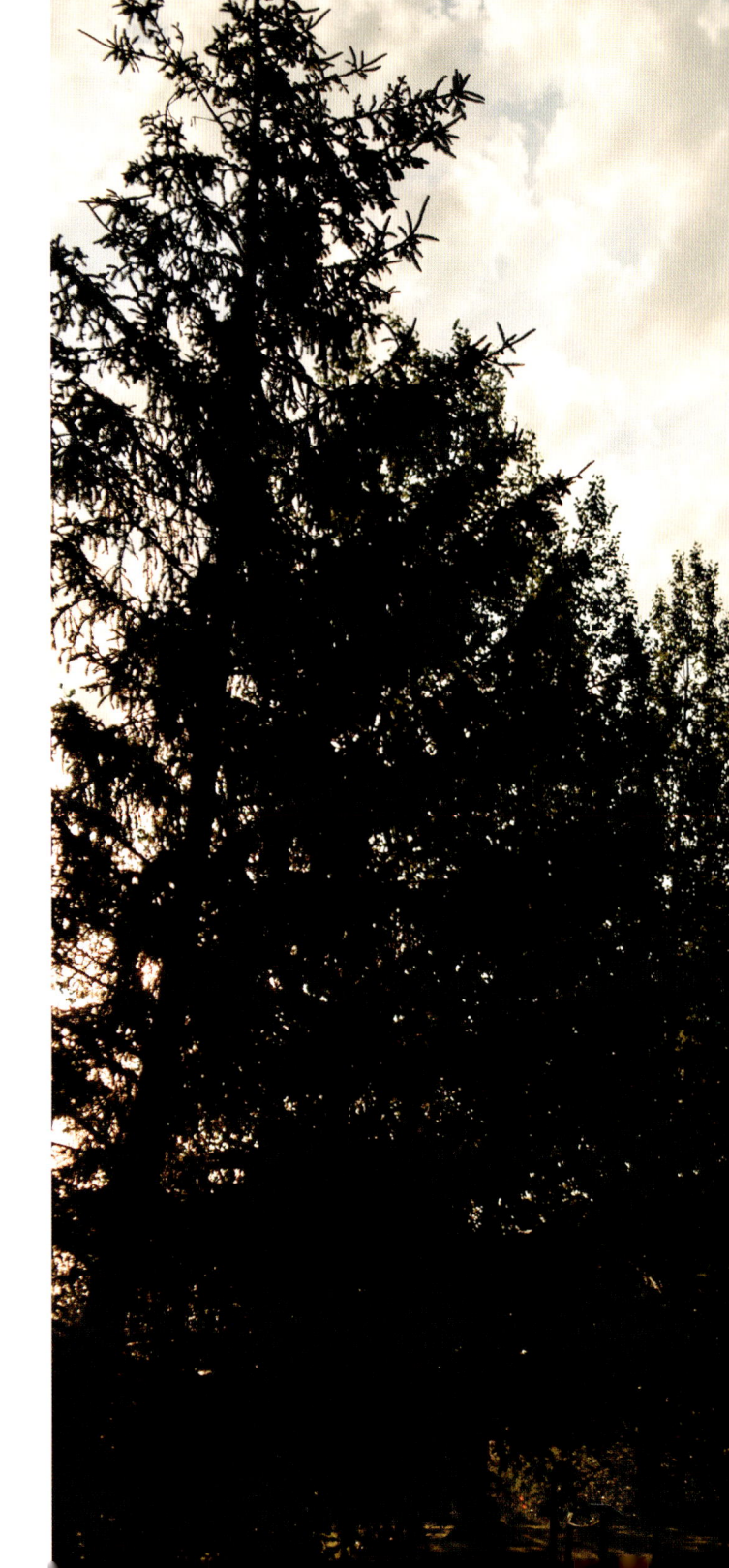

MOTEL IN MOOSE JAW, SASKATCHEWAN, JULY 2017.

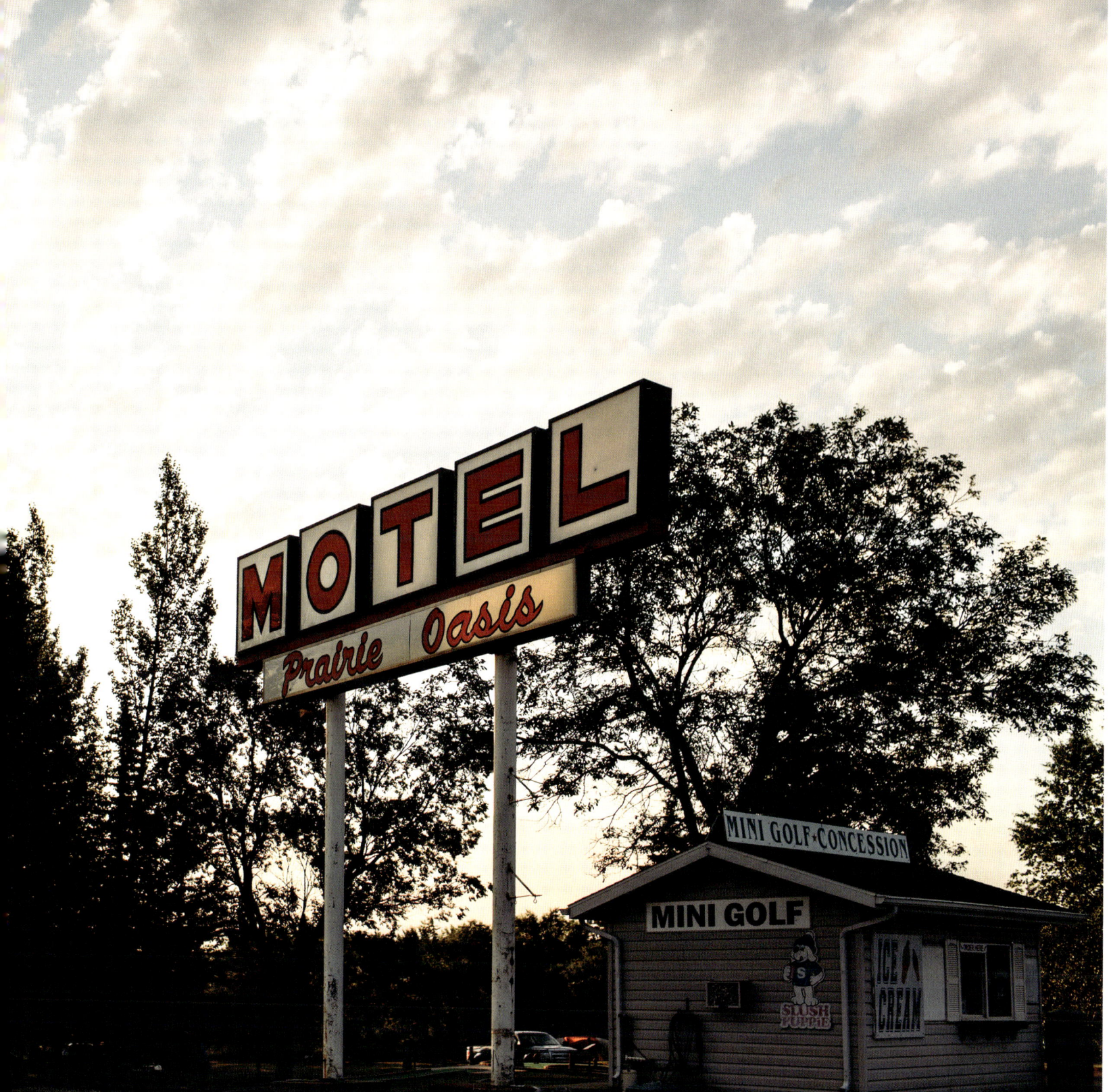

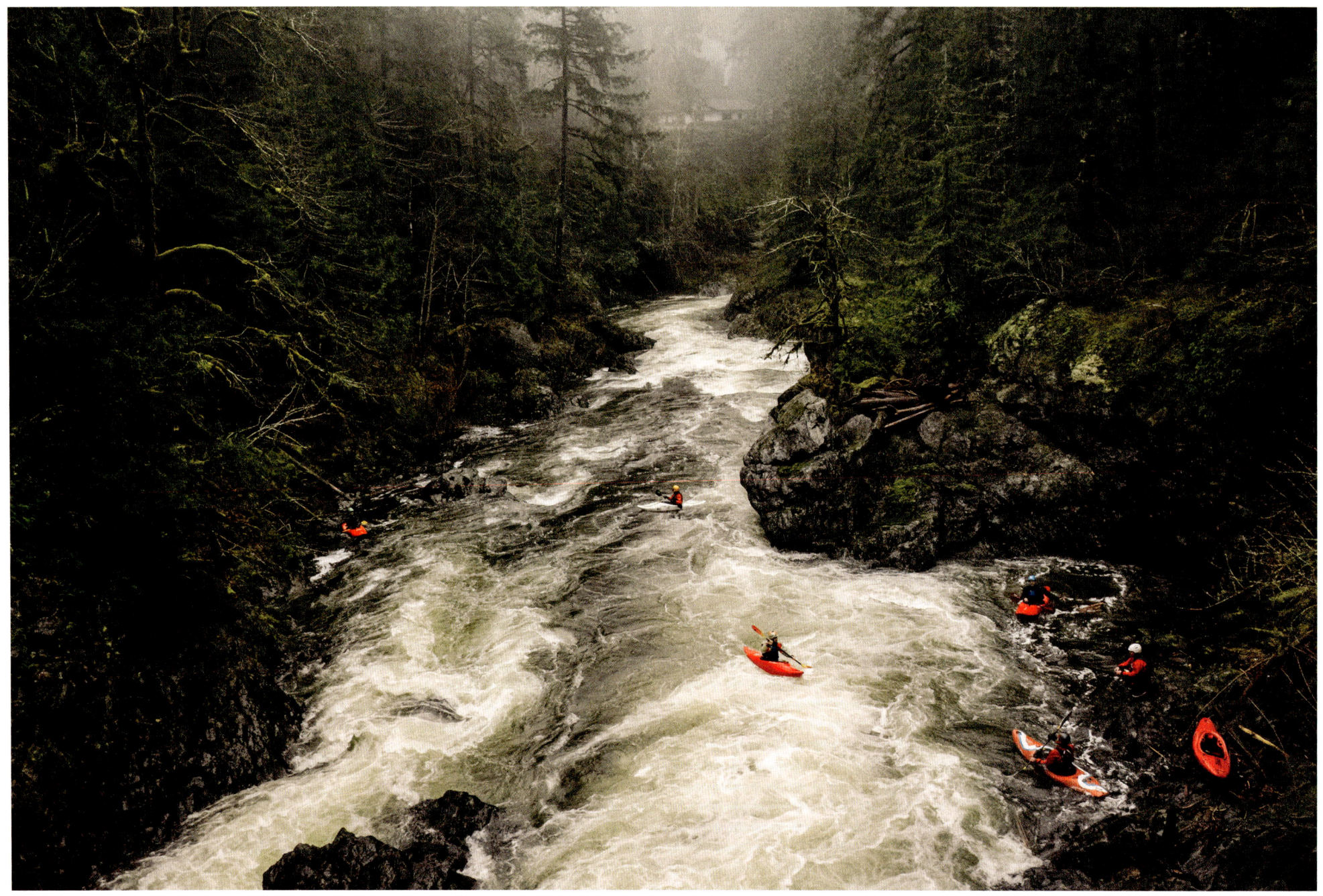

KOKSILAH RIVER, COWICHAN VALLEY, BRITISH COLUMBIA, DECEMBER 2020.

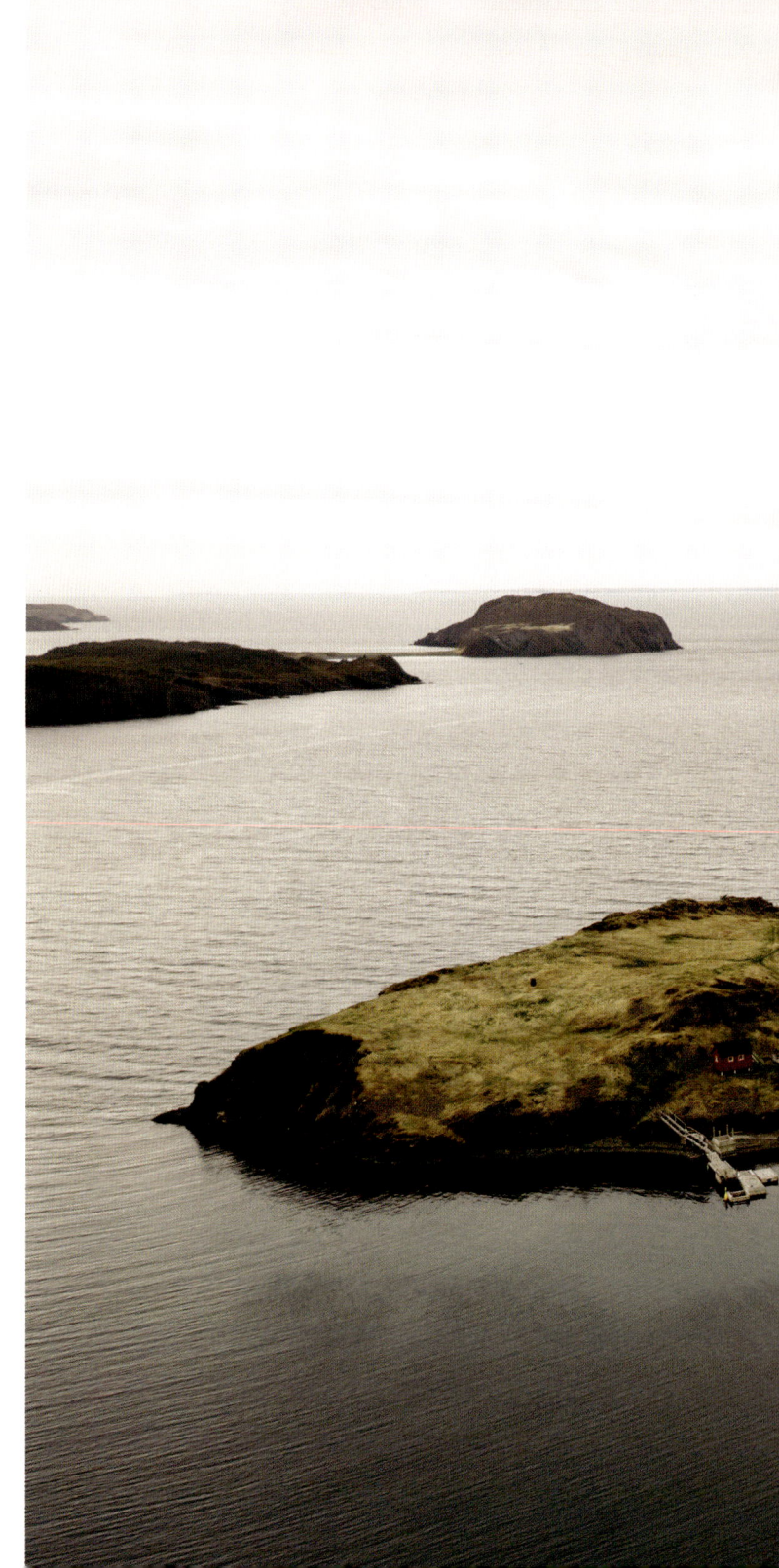

THE COMMUNITY OF PORT REXTON, NEWFOUNDLAND, MAY 2022.

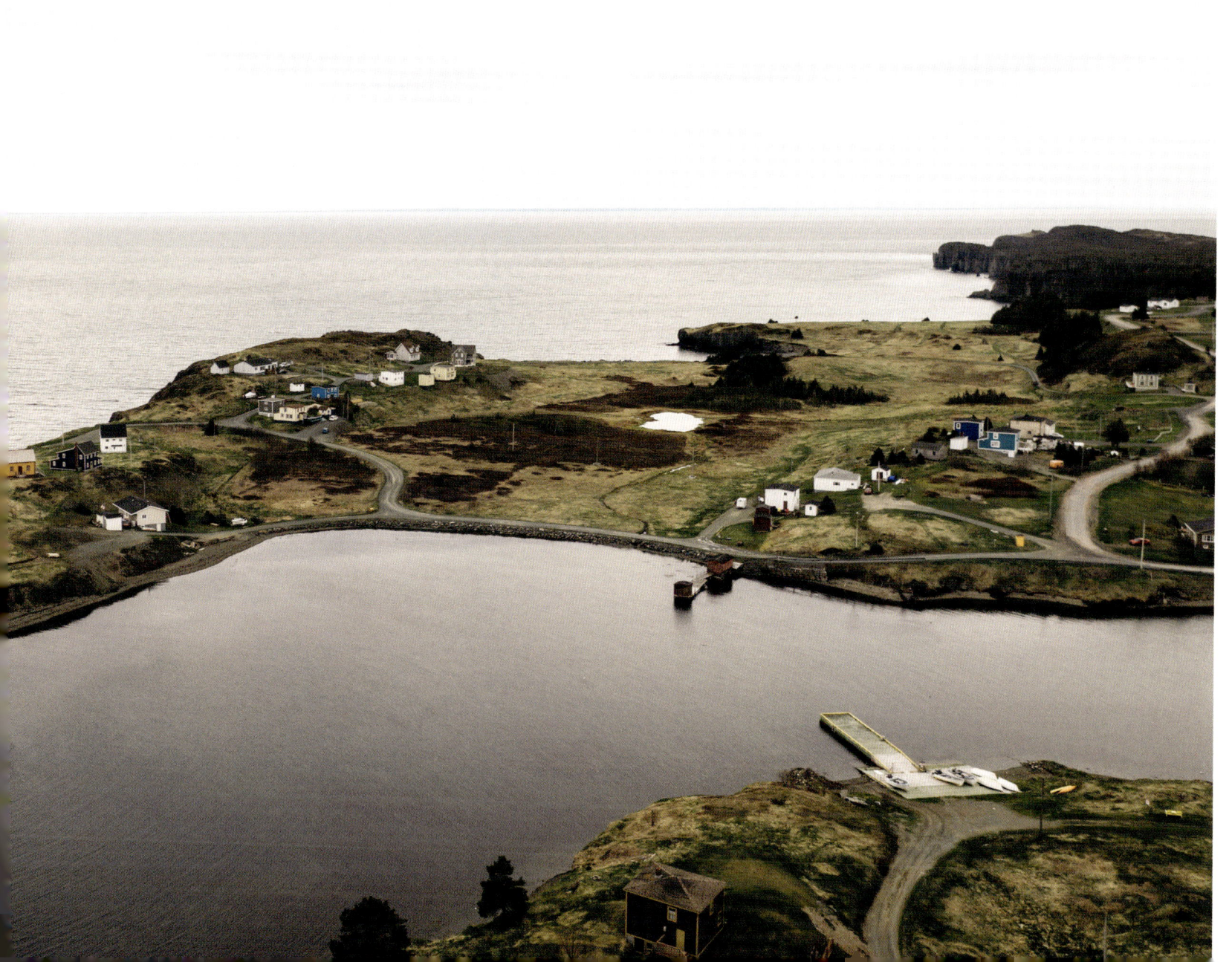

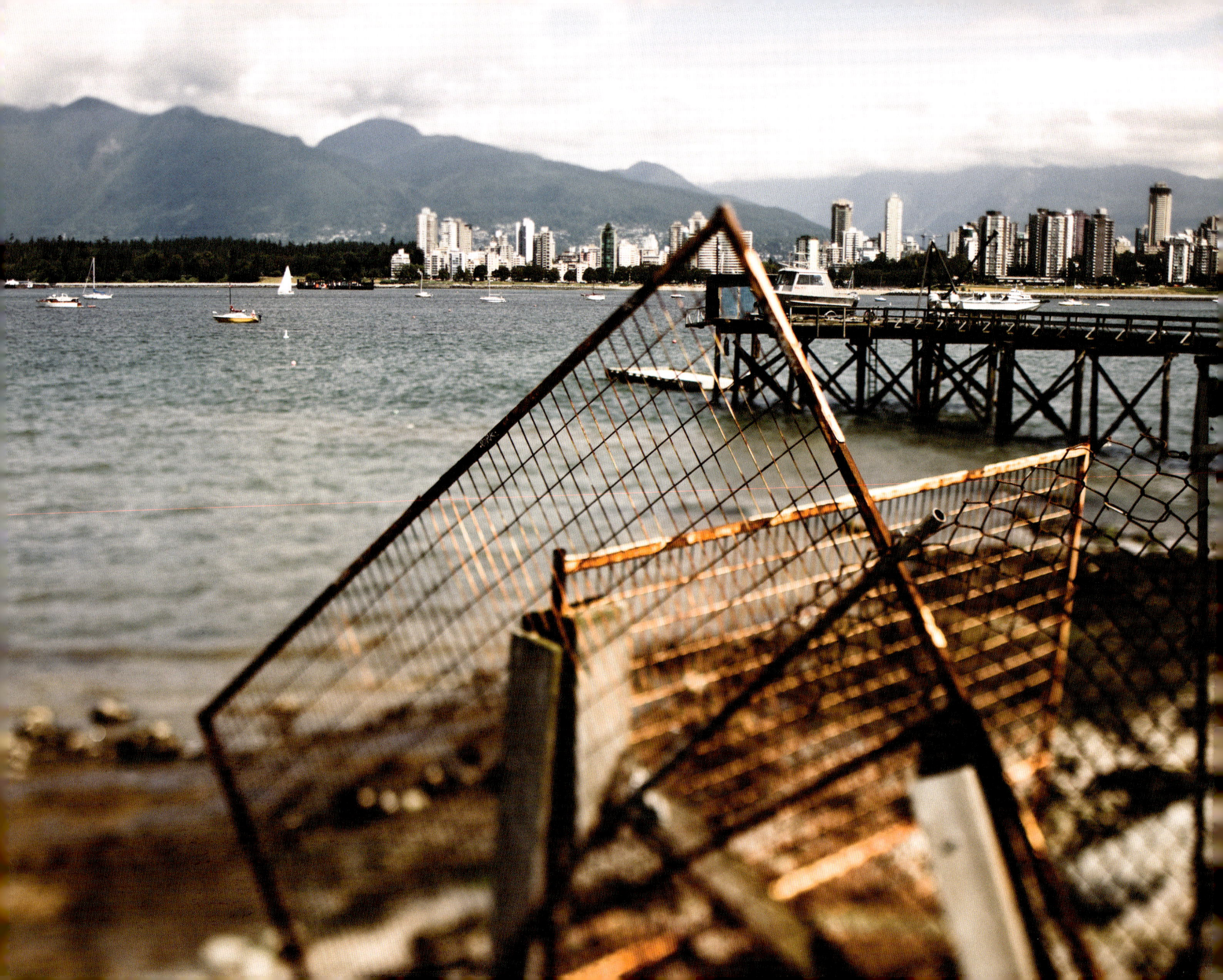

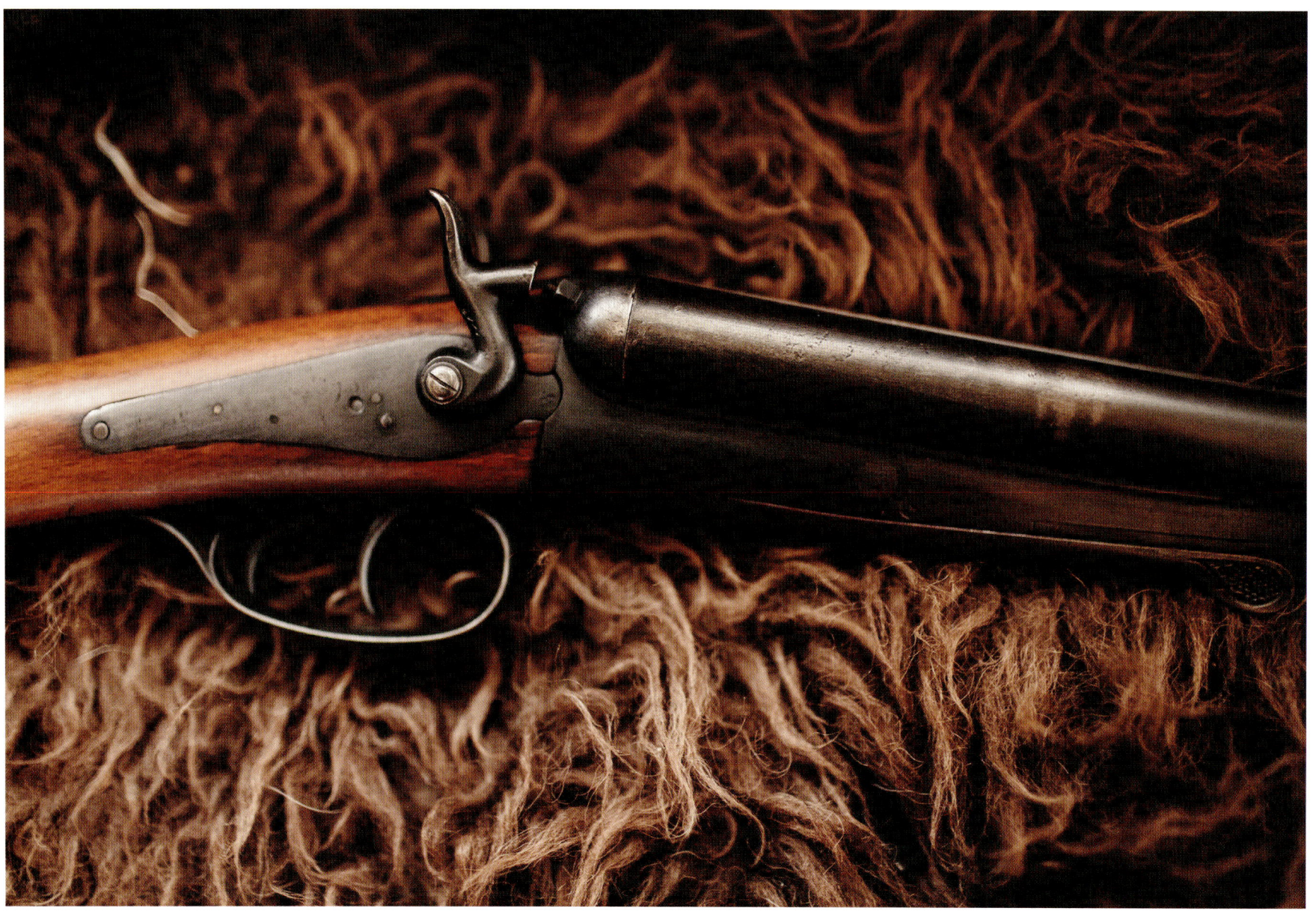

← HUNTING RIFLE ON A PILE OF FURS IN CLEARWATER COUNTY, ALBERTA, JANUARY 2019.

→ "EATON'S AUGUST FUR SALE MINK AND MUCH MORE!" MACTIER, ONTARIO, SEPTEMBER 2013.

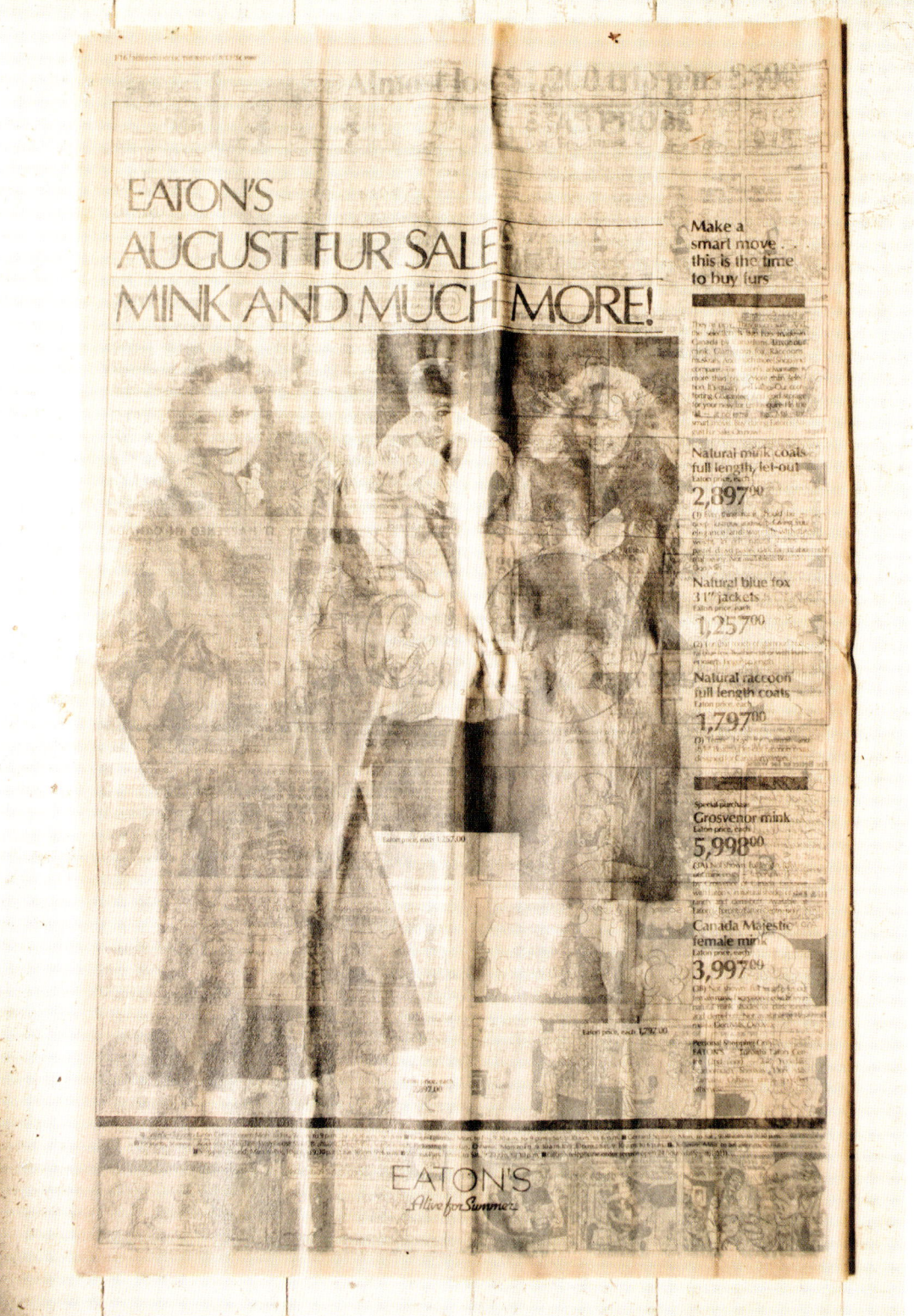

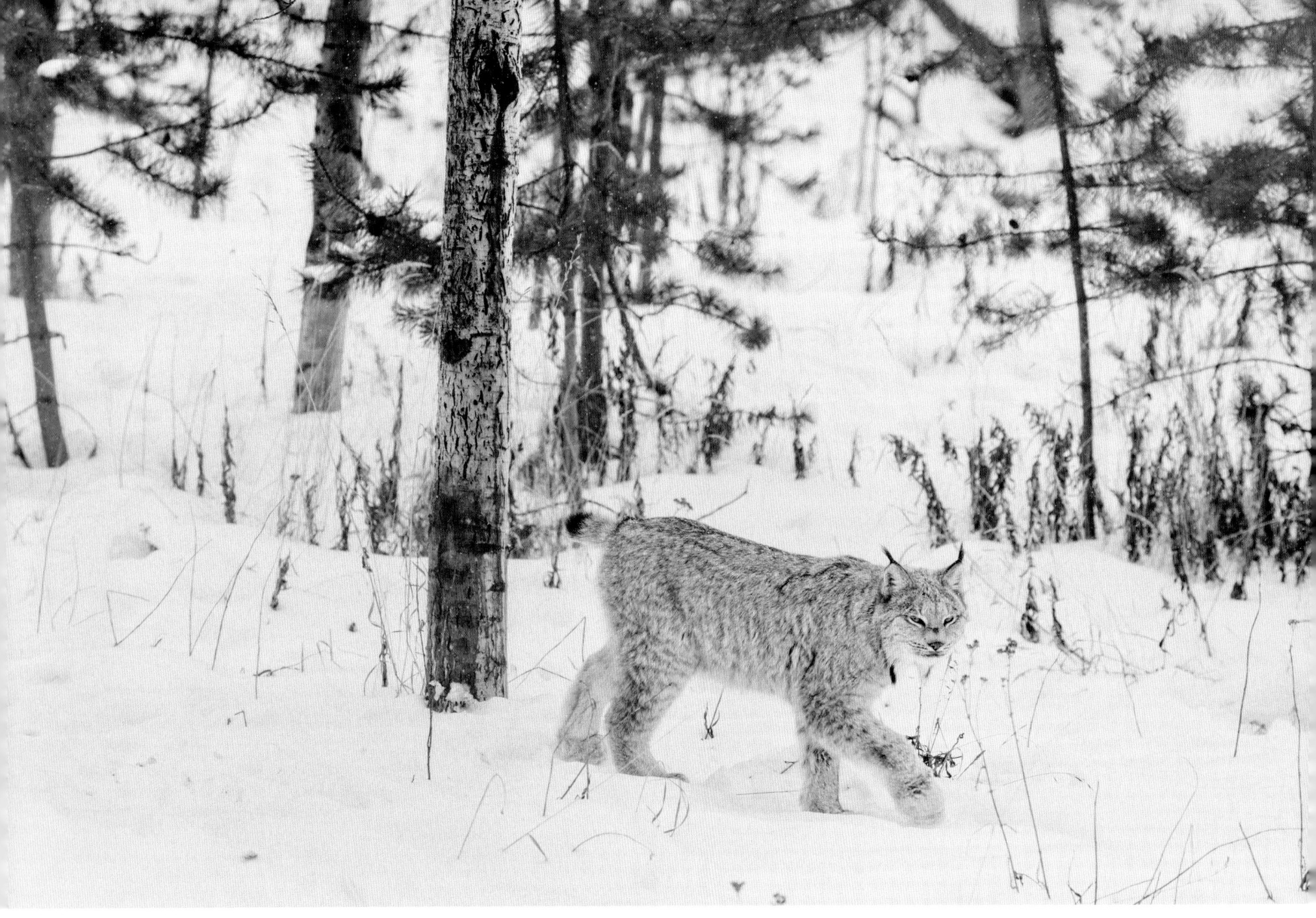

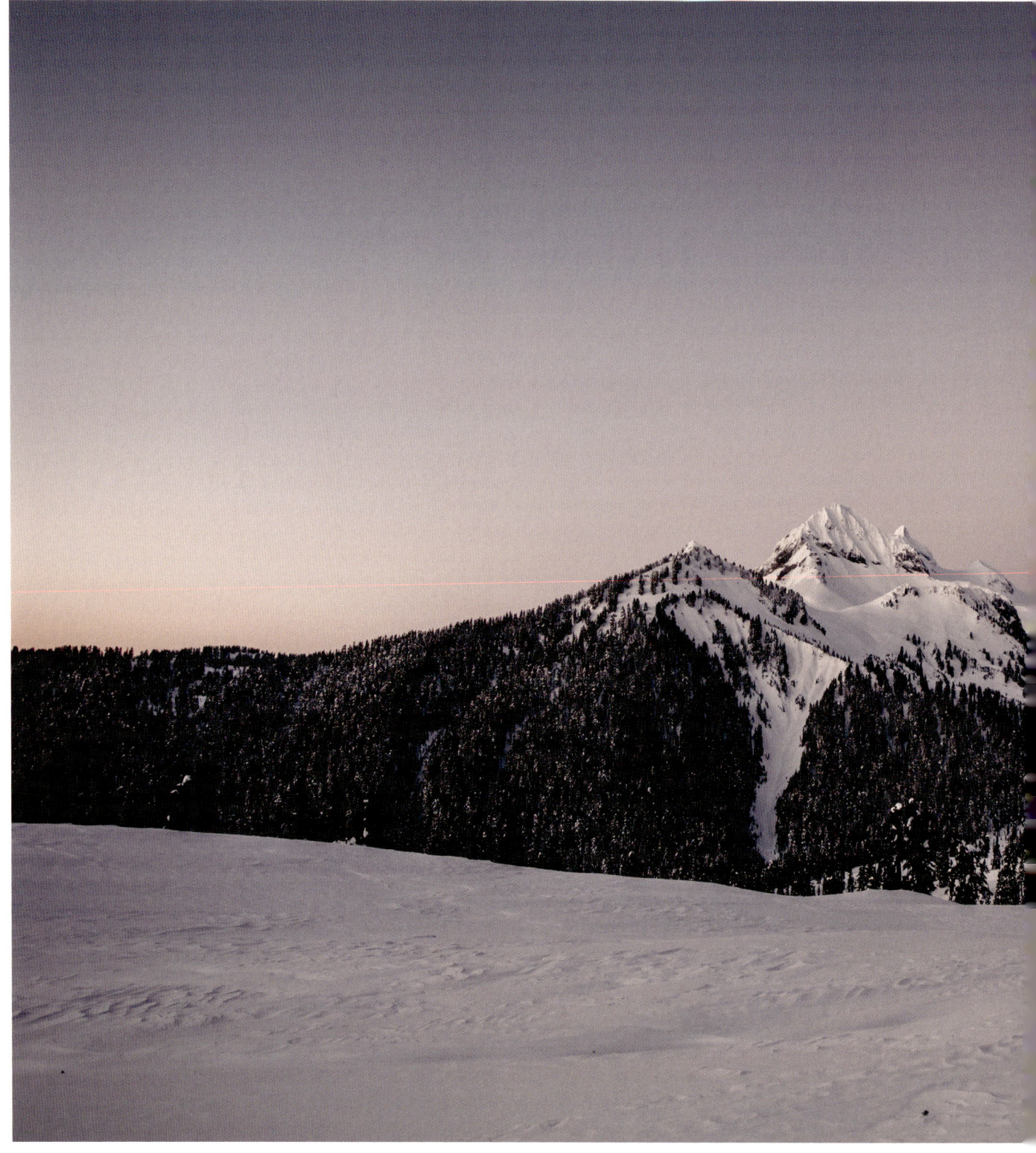

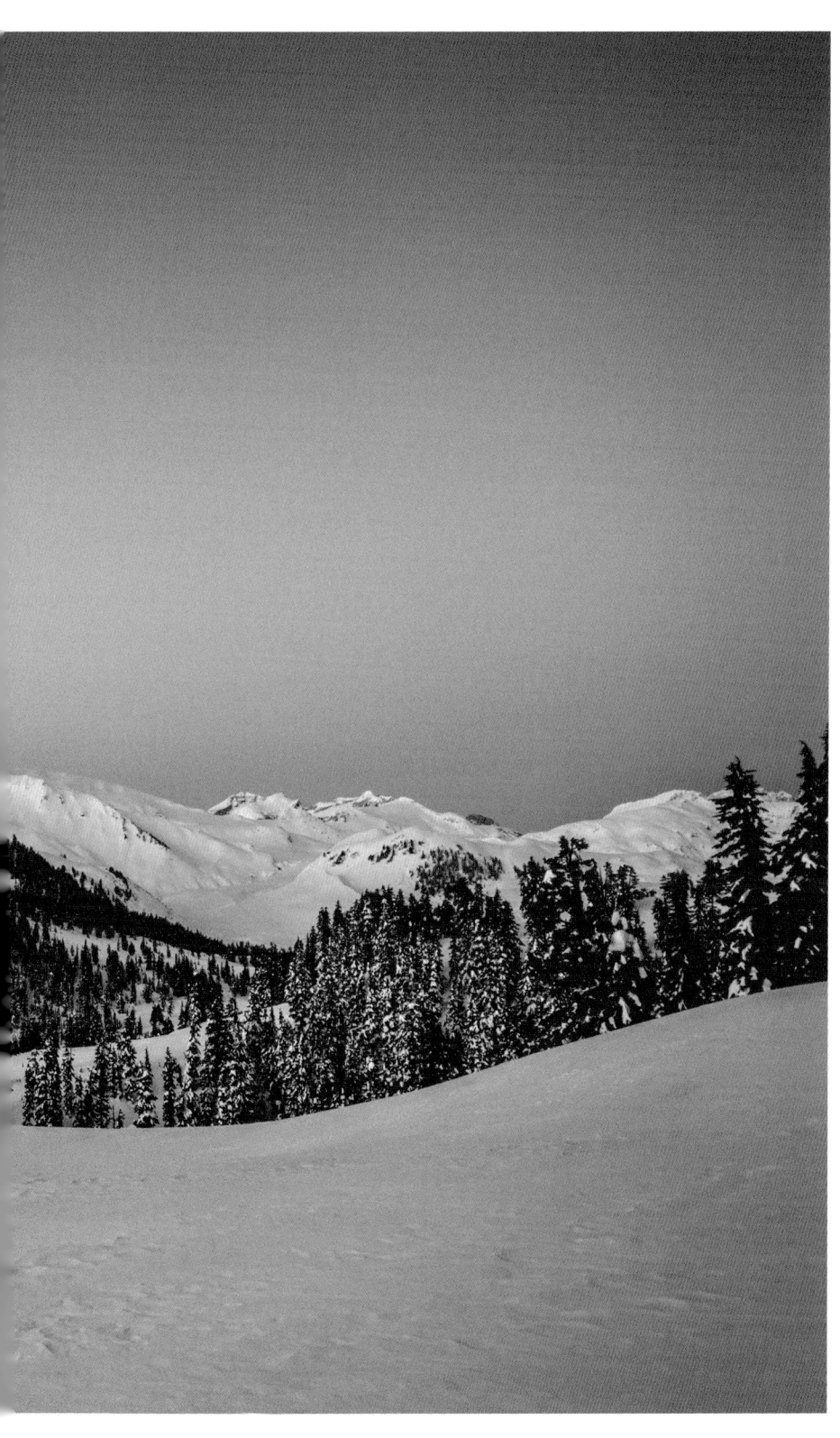

TWILIGHT IN SQUAMISH, BRITISH COLUMBIA, JANUARY 2017.

POLAR BEAR IN THE SNOW, DENE FIRST NATION,
YELLOWKNIFE, NORTHWEST TERRITORIES, MARCH 2017.

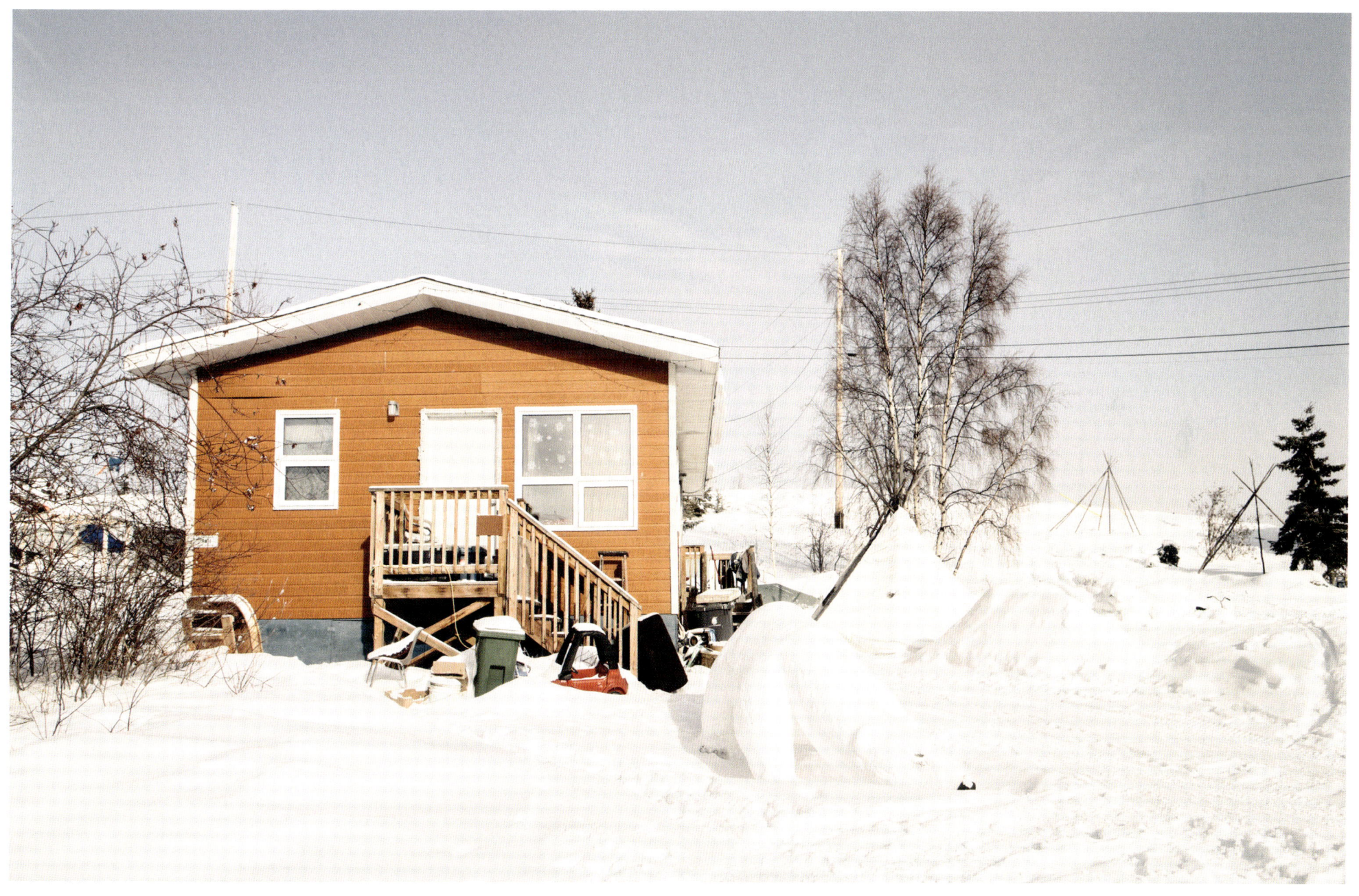

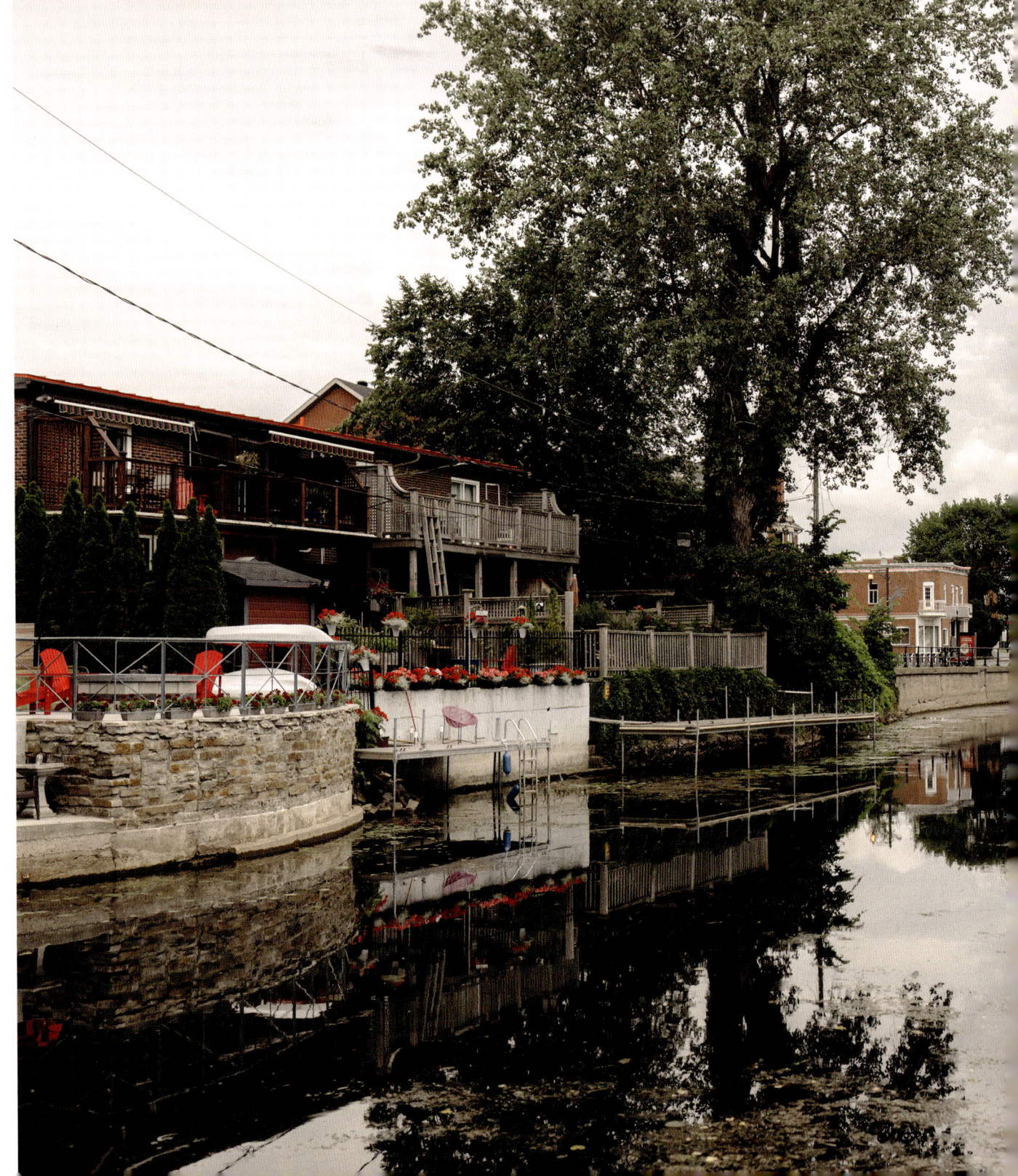

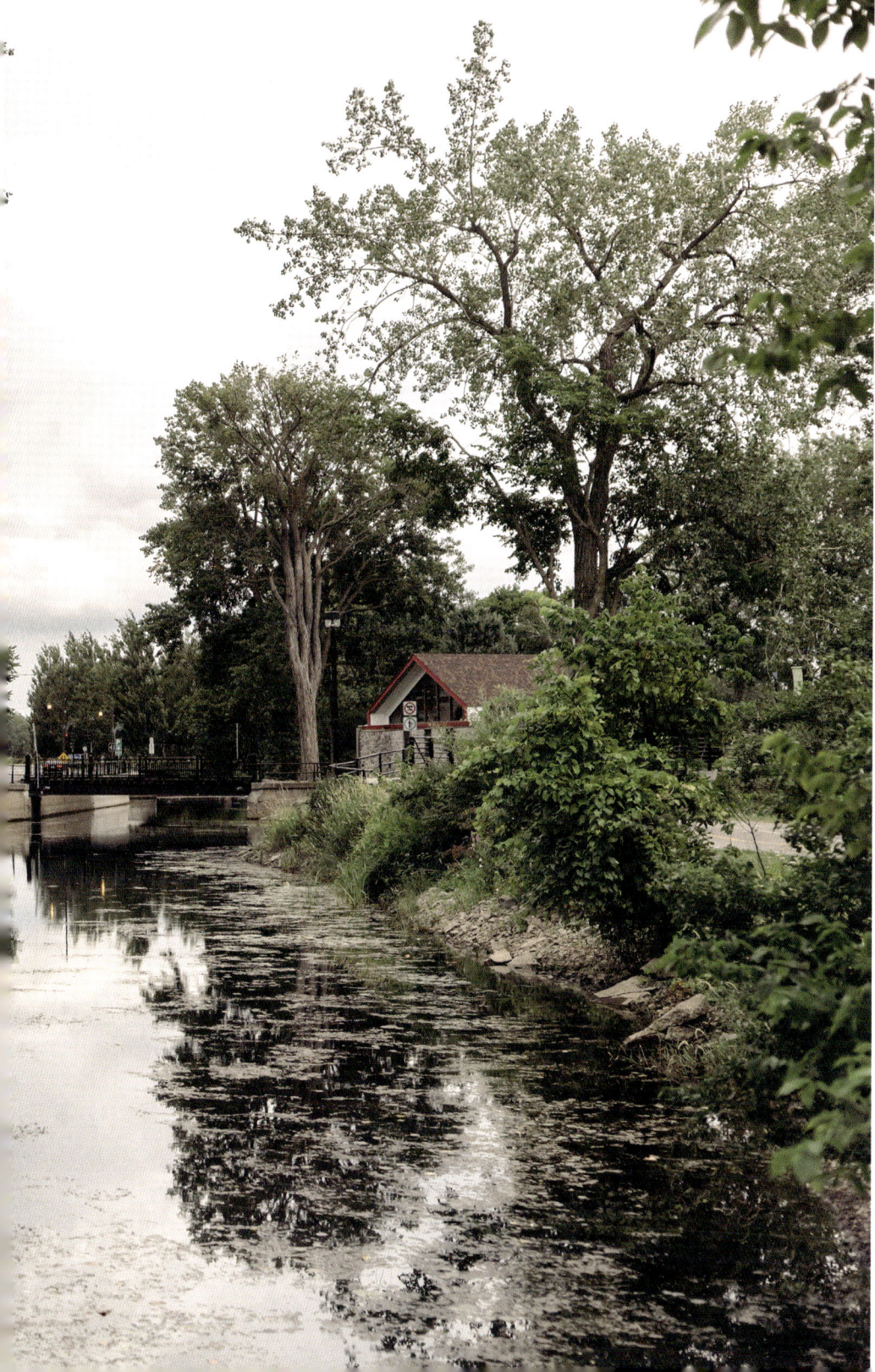

LACHINE, MONTREAL, QUEBEC, JULY 2022.

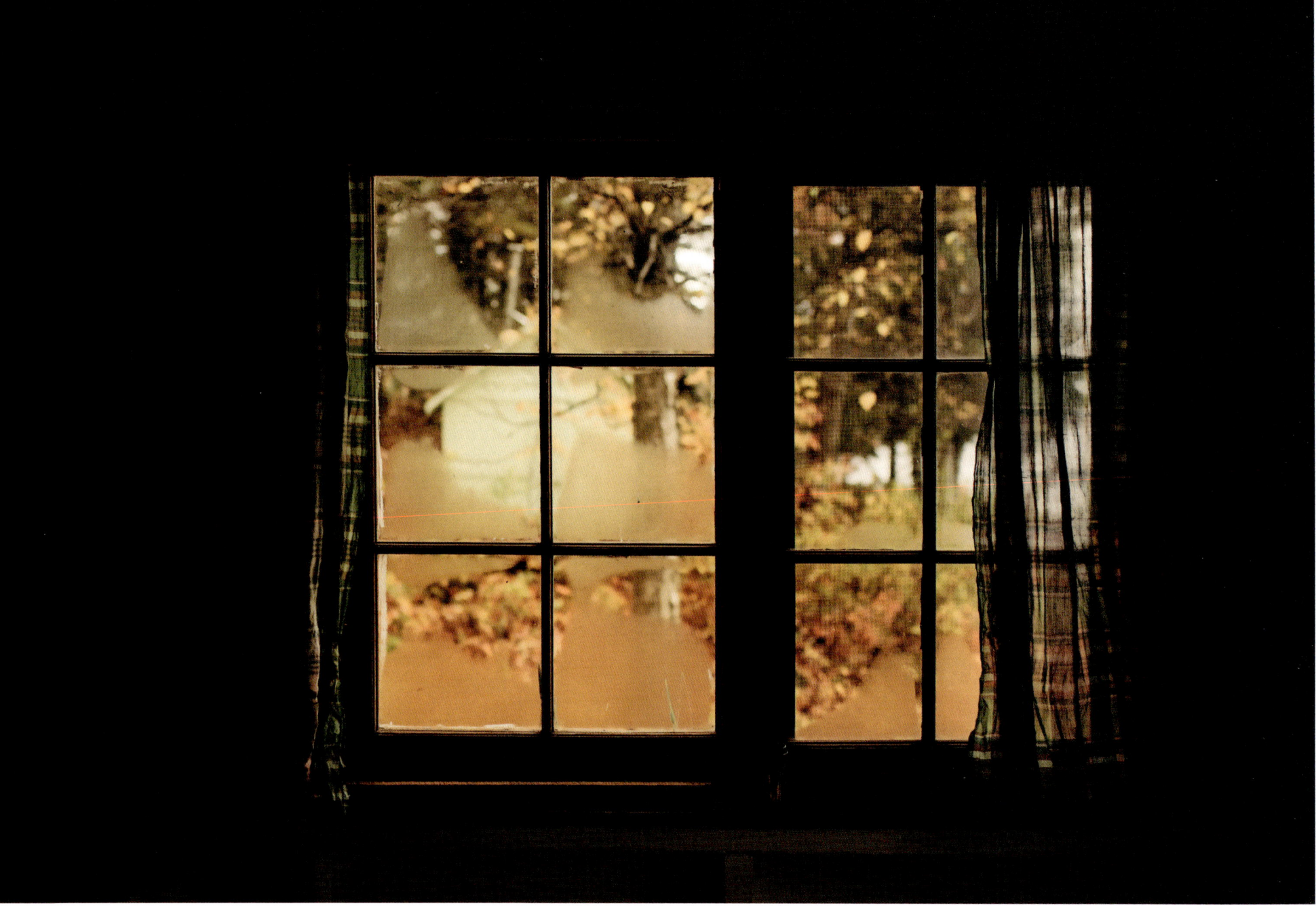

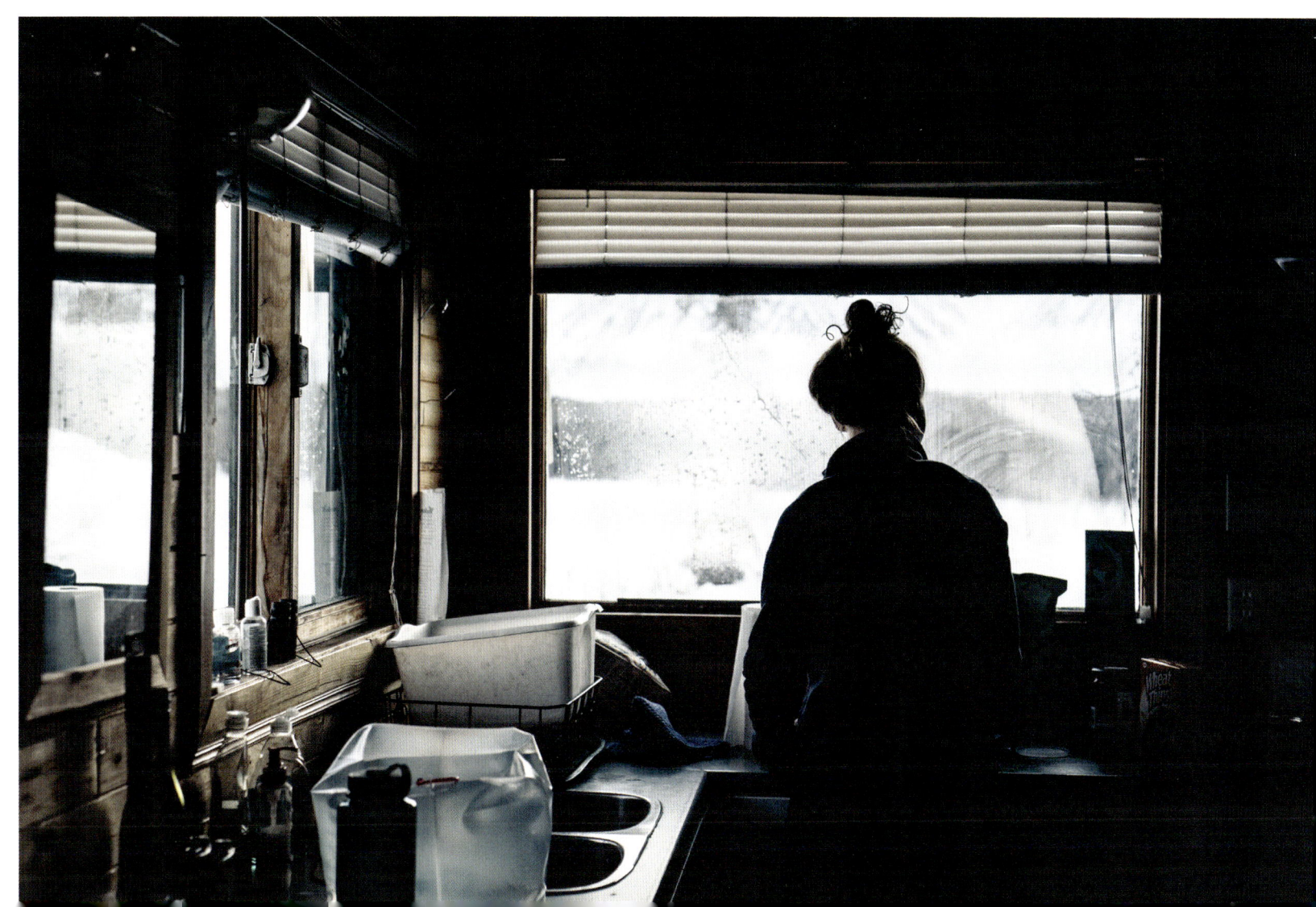

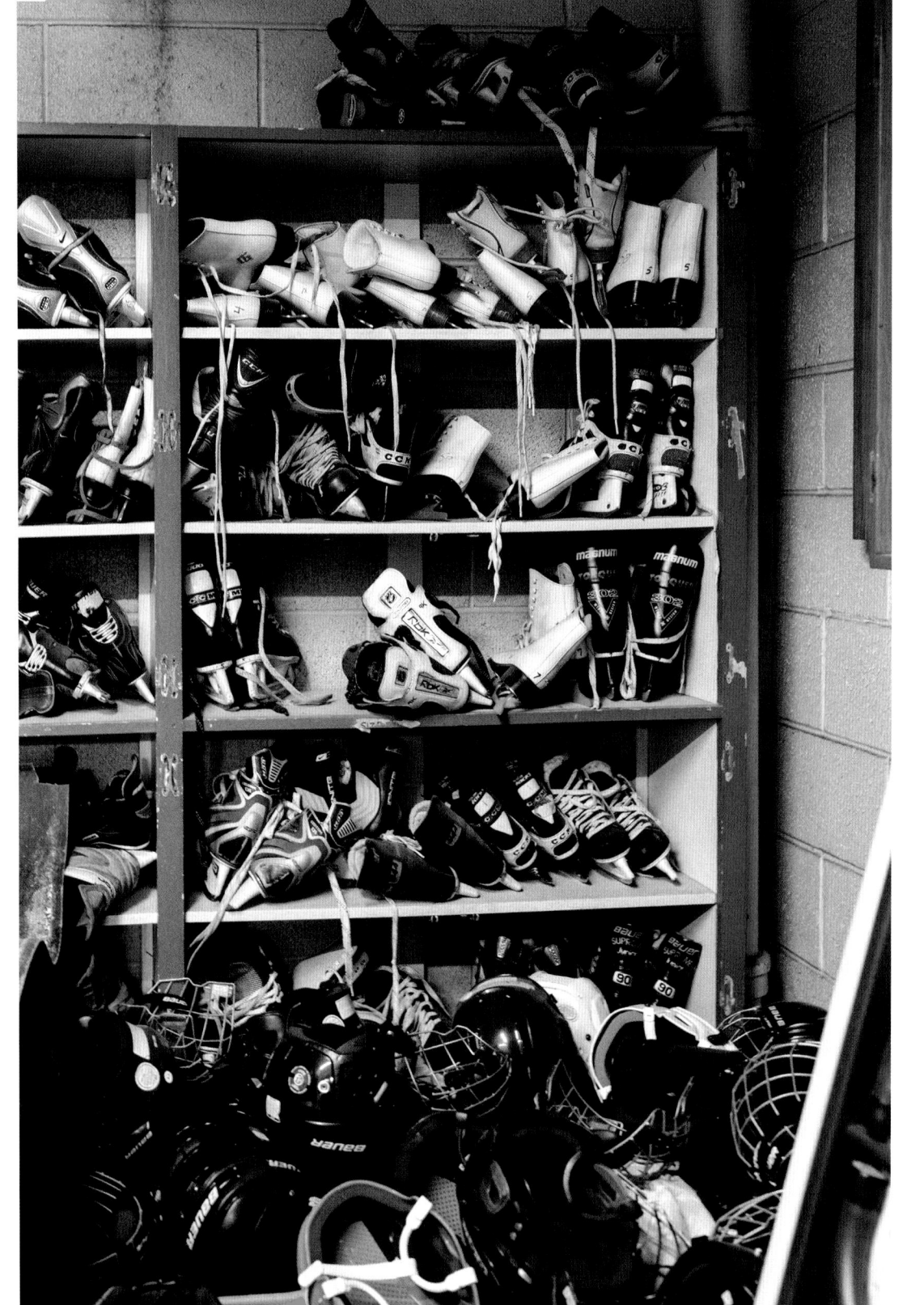

← SKATE STOREROOM IN A PUBLIC ELEMENTARY SCHOOL, TORONTO, ONTARIO, DECEMBER 2021.

→ AN EMPTY CHANGE ROOM AWAITS SUMMER SWIMMERS IN THE SPRING RAIN. FOGO ISLAND, NEWFOUNDLAND, MAY 2022.

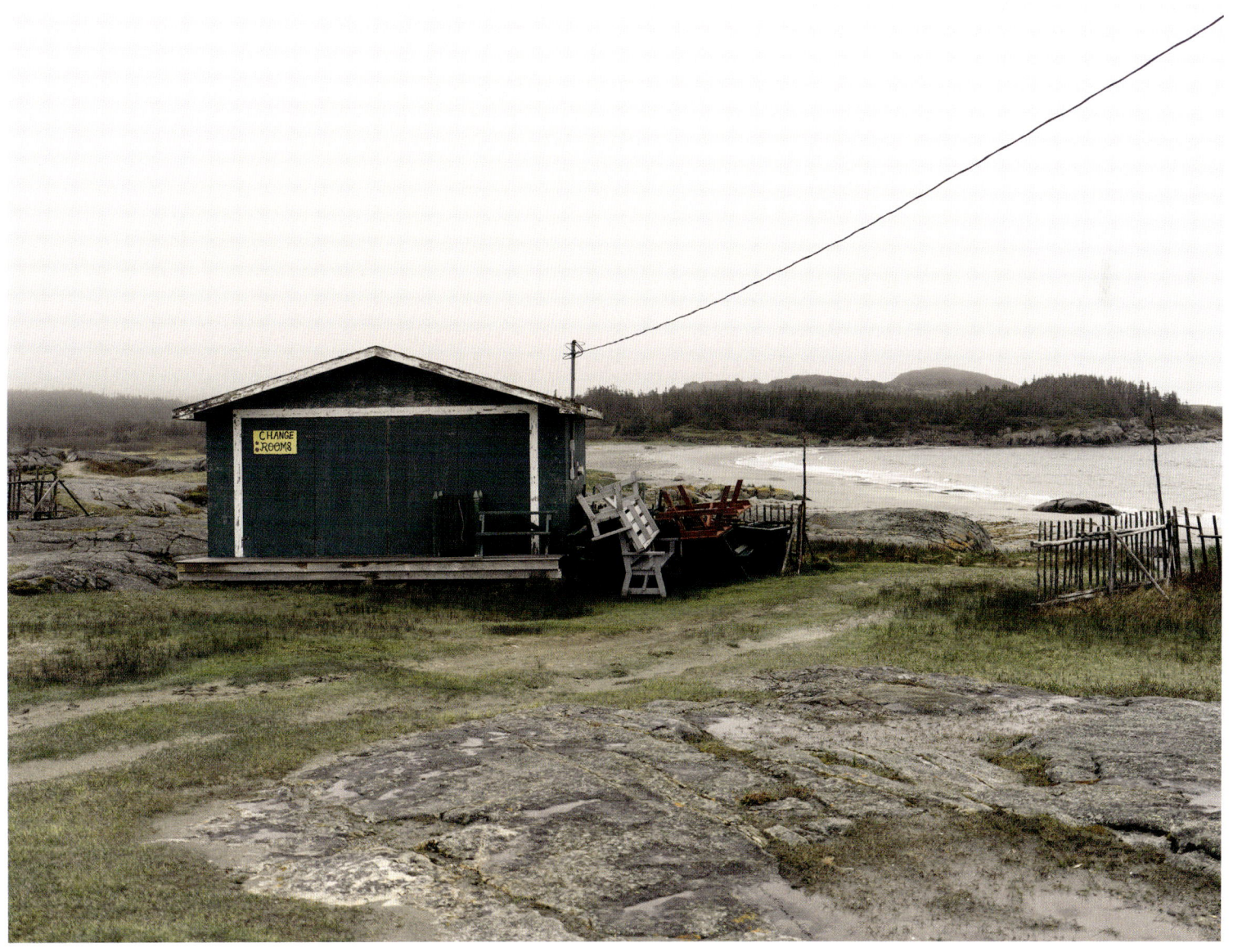

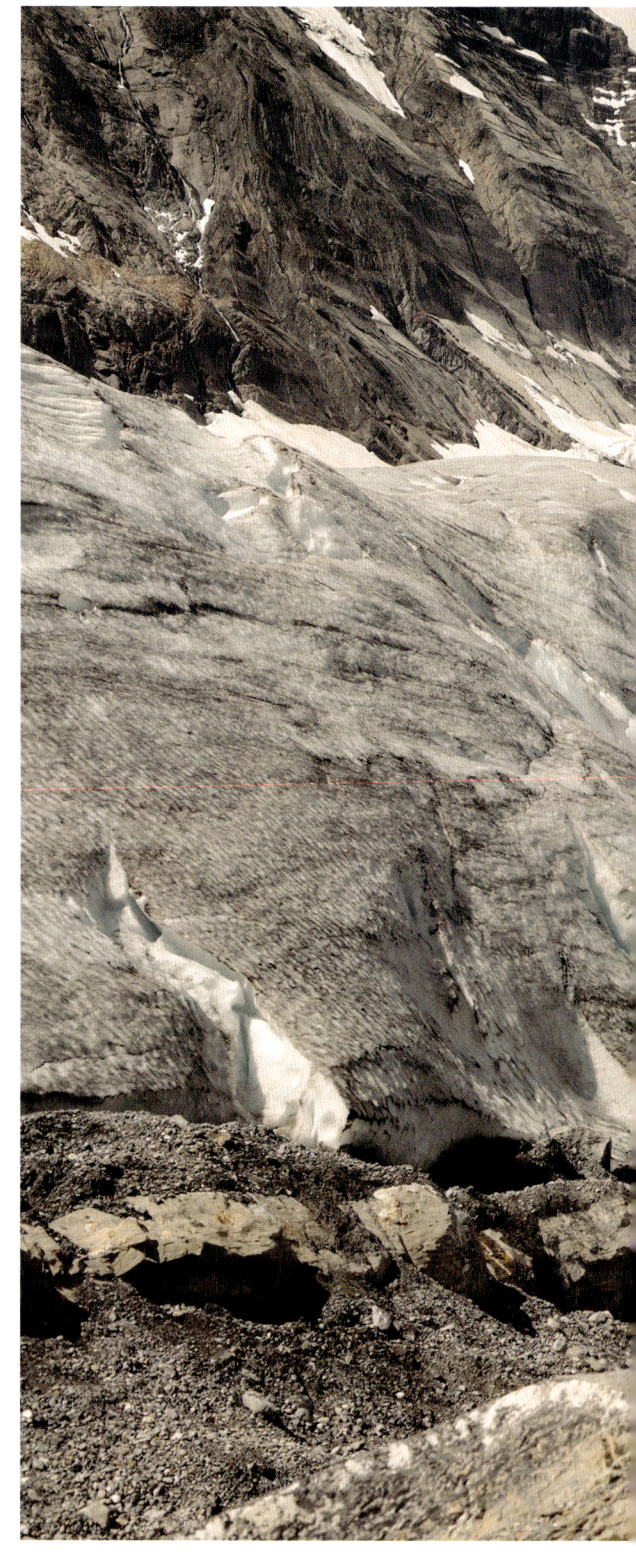

MUMMERY GLACIER, GOLDEN, BRITISH COLUMBIA, AUGUST 2022.

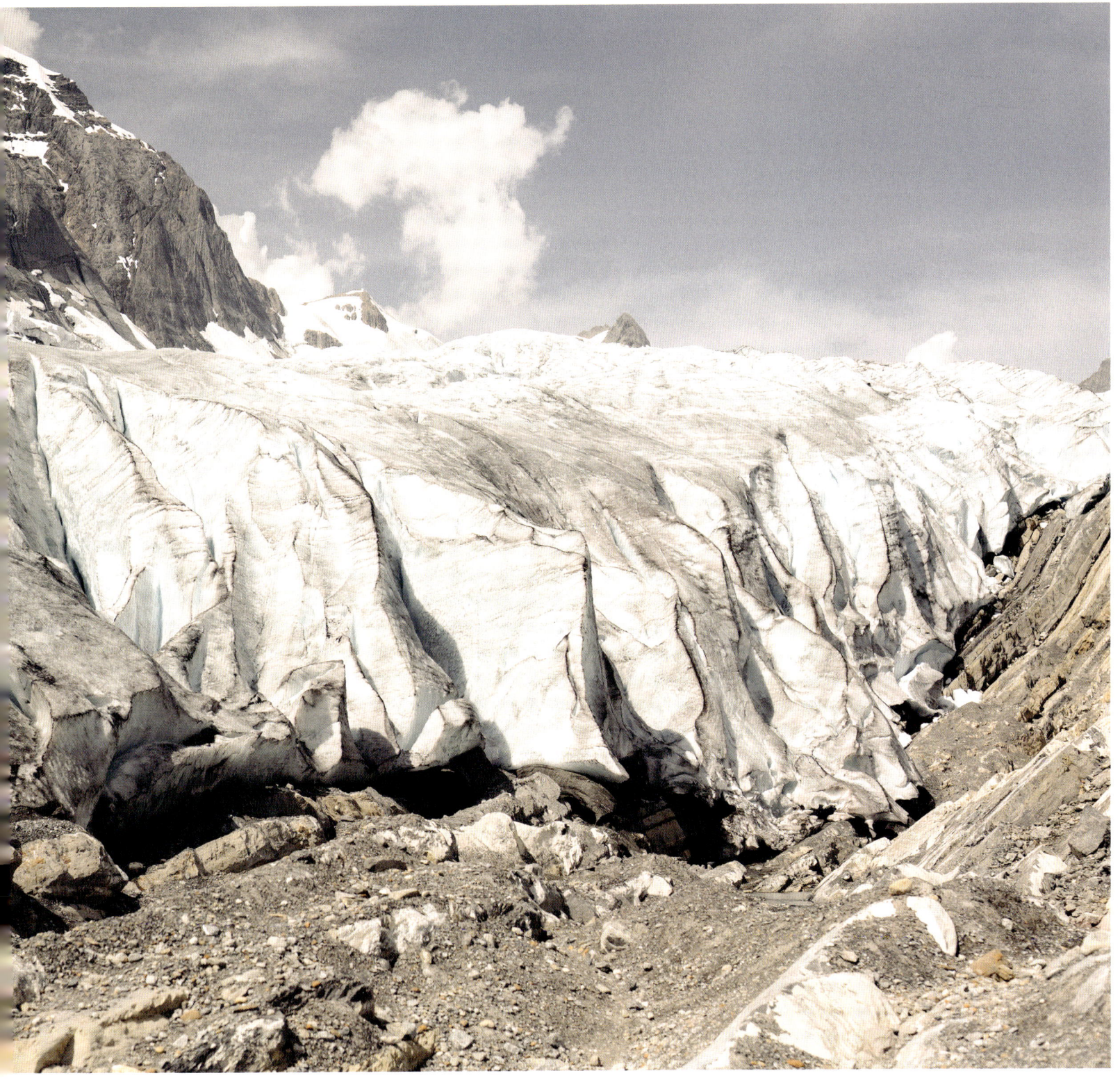

STOP SIGN IN BOTH ENGLISH AND KWAKWALA ON THE
TRADITIONAL TERRITORY OF THE 'NAMGIS FIRST NATION.
ALERT BAY, BRITISH COLUMBIA, OCTOBER 2017.

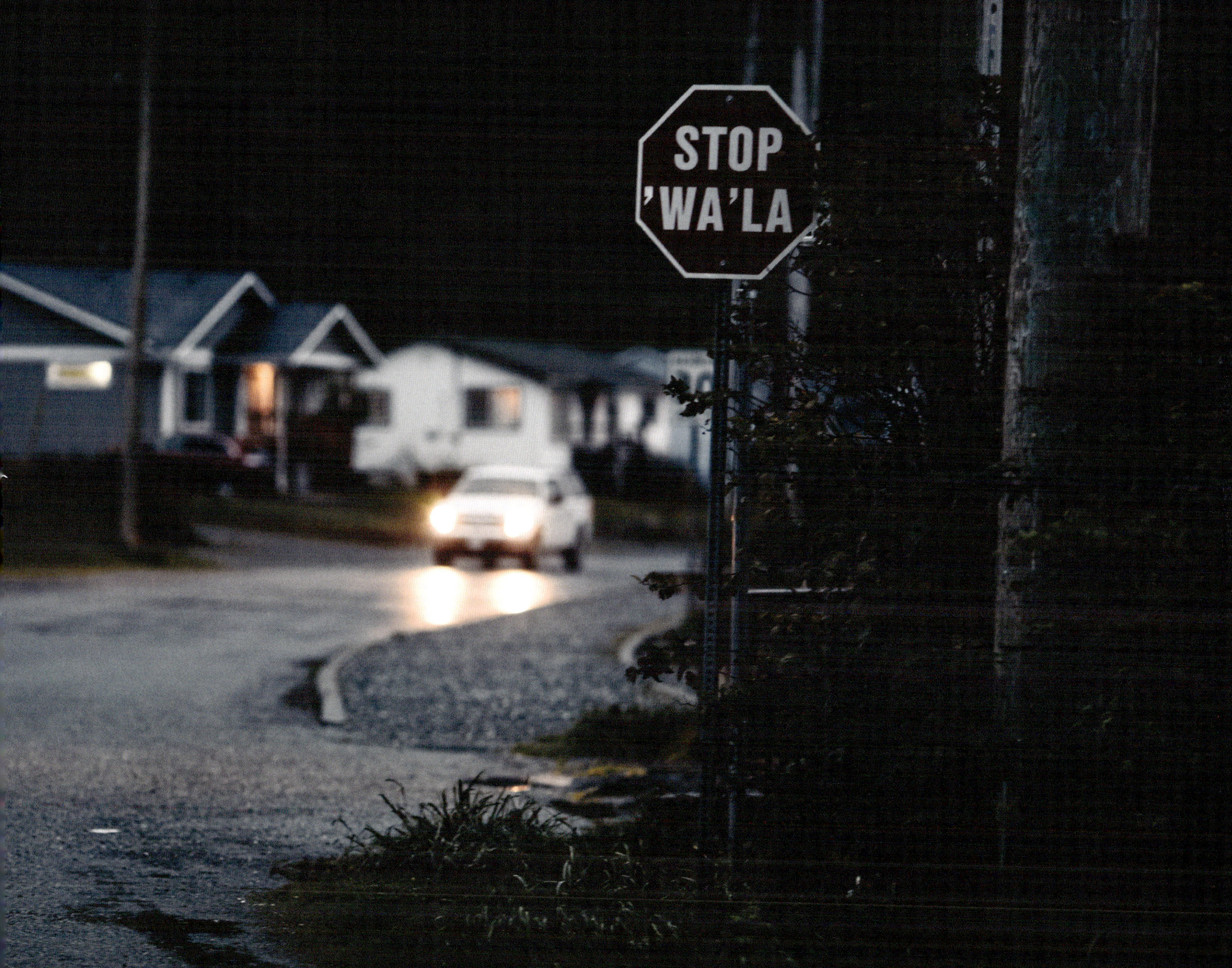

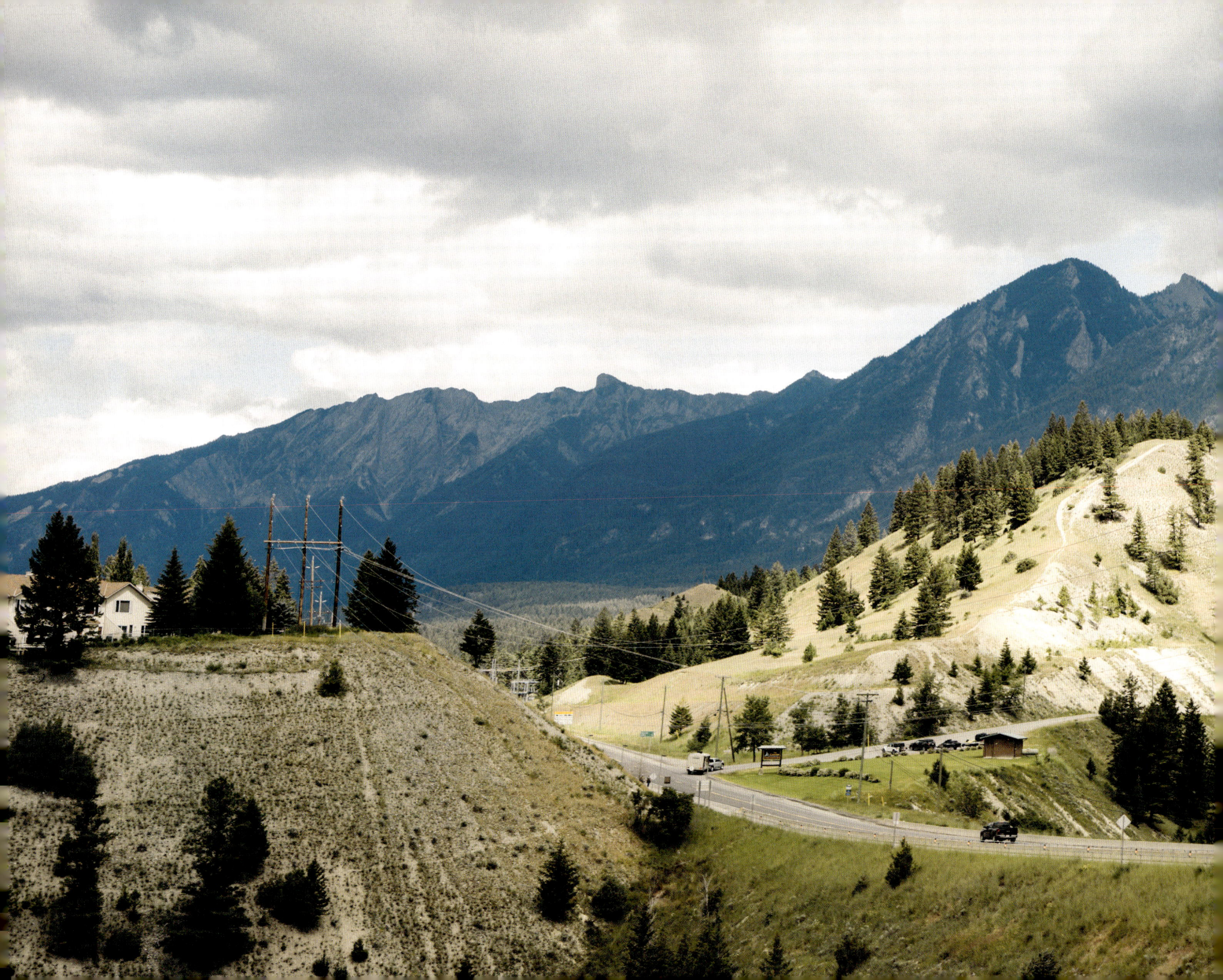

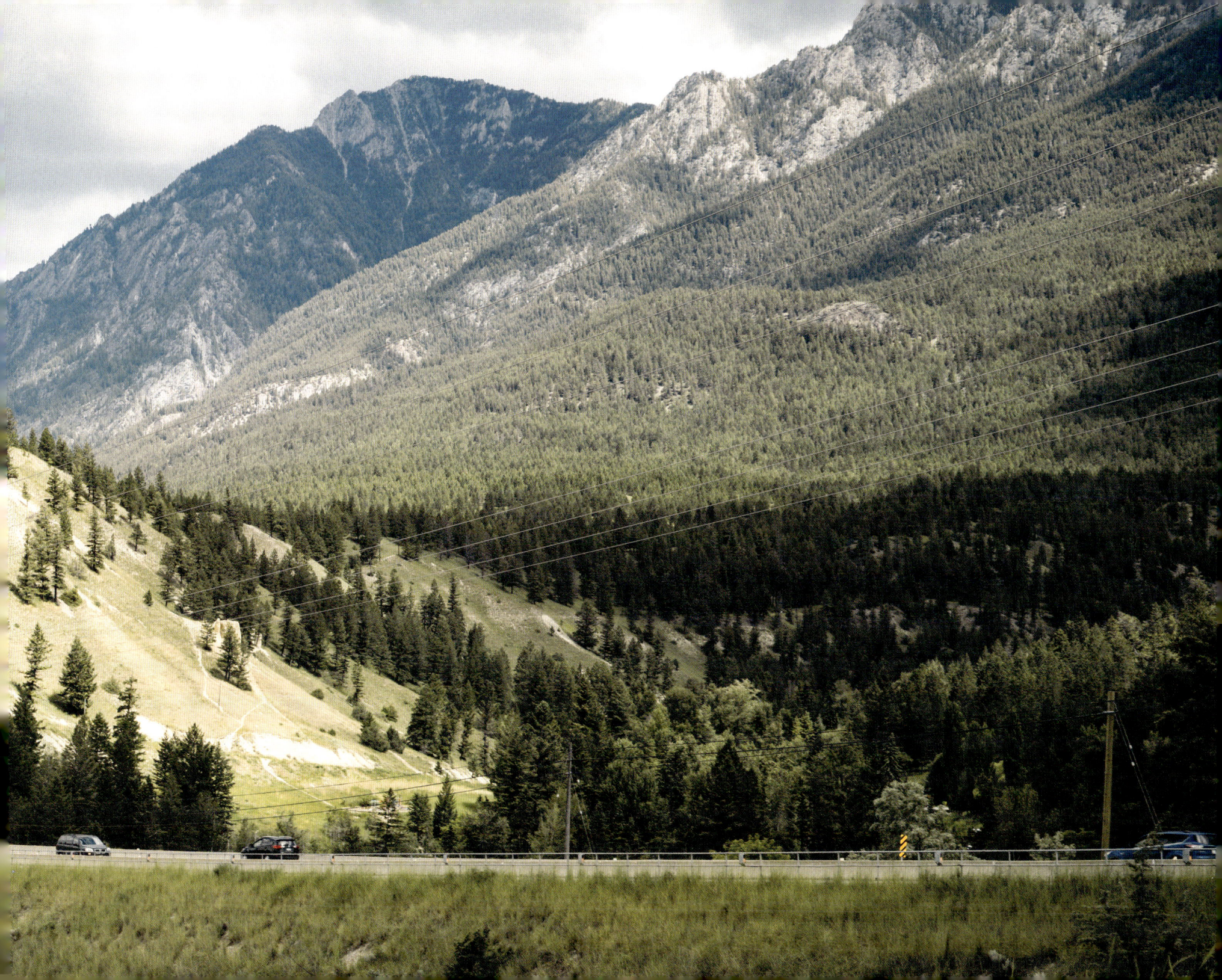

THE CONFLUENCE OF THE SILTY
KECHIKA RIVER FLOWING INTO THE
CRYSTALLINE LIARD RIVER, NEAR
THE NORTHERN BOUNDARY OF THE
PROPOSED KASKA INDIGENOUS
PROTECTED AND CONSERVED AREA.
KASKA DENA TRADITIONAL TERRITORY,
BRITISH COLUMBIA, AUGUST 2019.

OVERLEAF RADIUM HOT SPRINGS,
BRITISH COLUMBIA, JULY 2020.

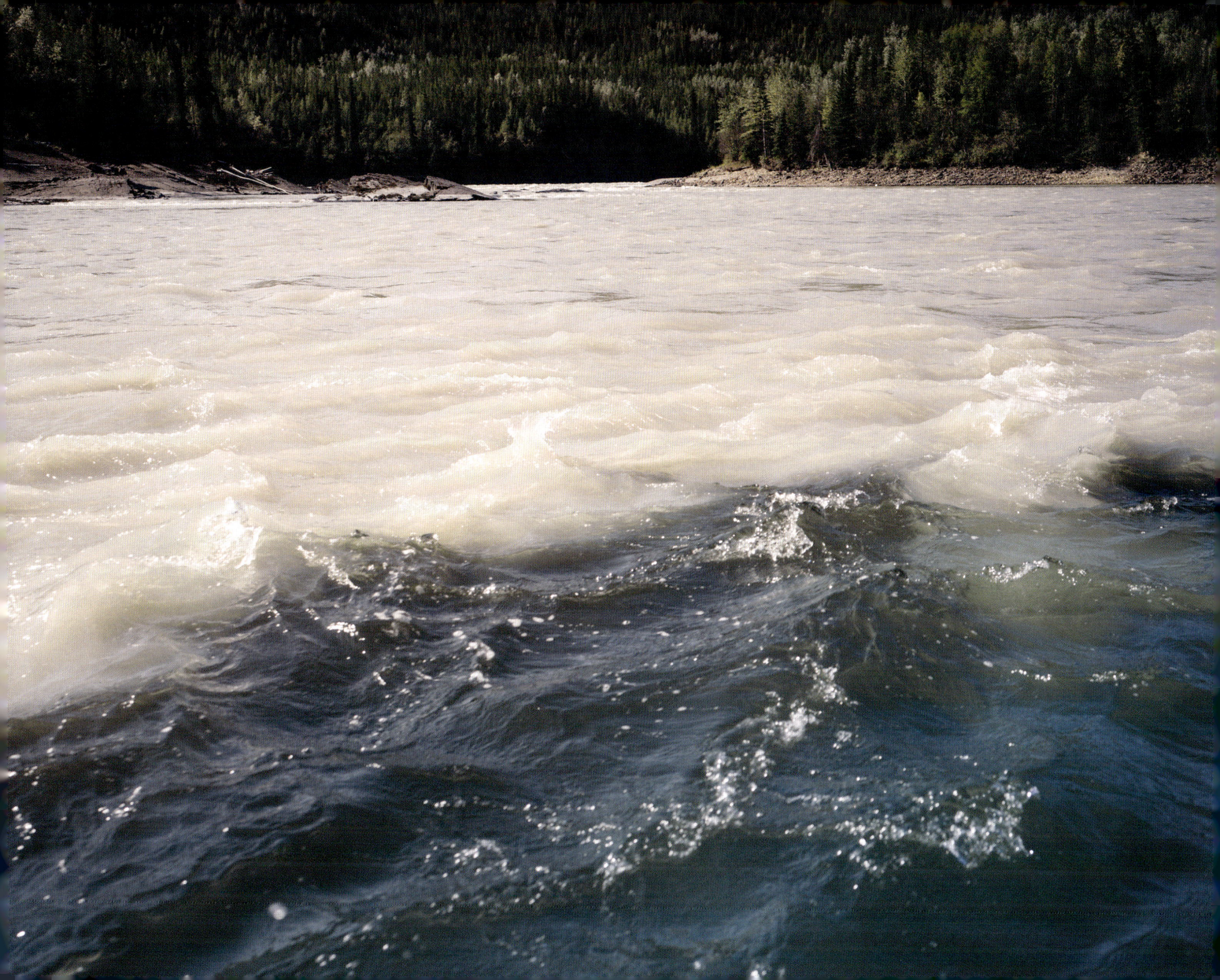

TELEGRAPH COVE, VANCOUVER ISLAND,
BRITISH COLUMBIA, JULY 2015.

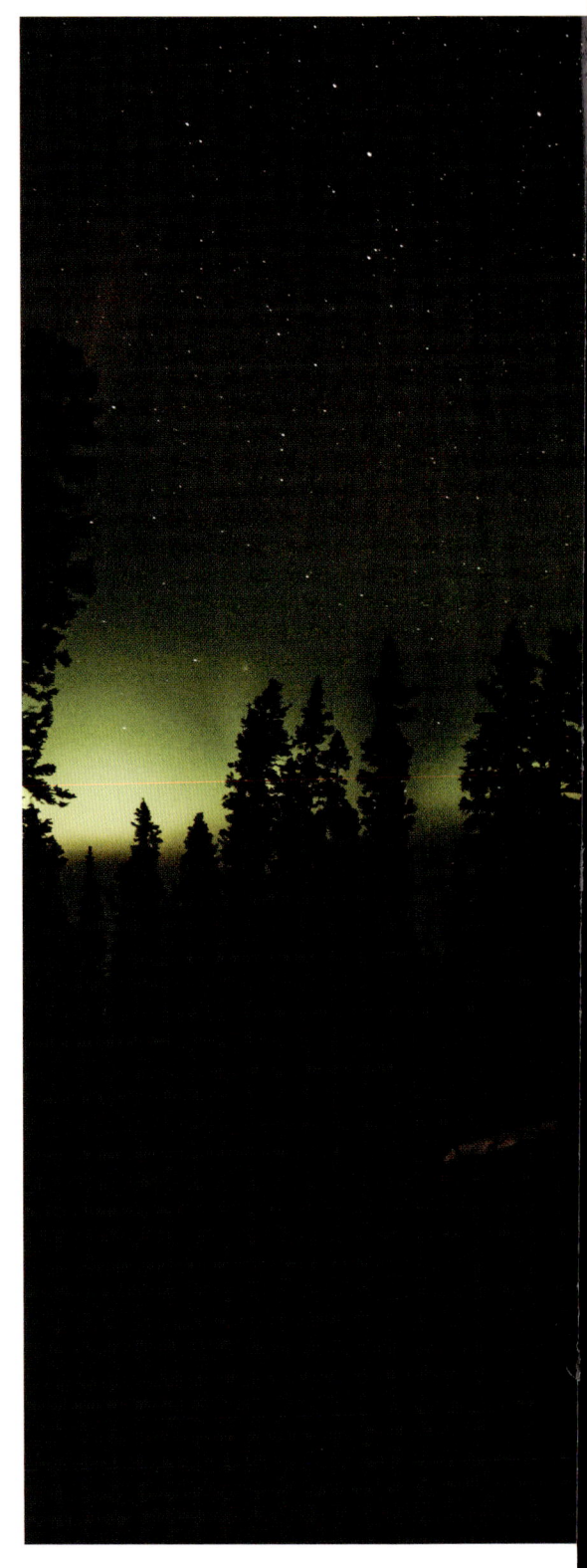

AURORA BOREALIS, YUKON, MARCH 2017.

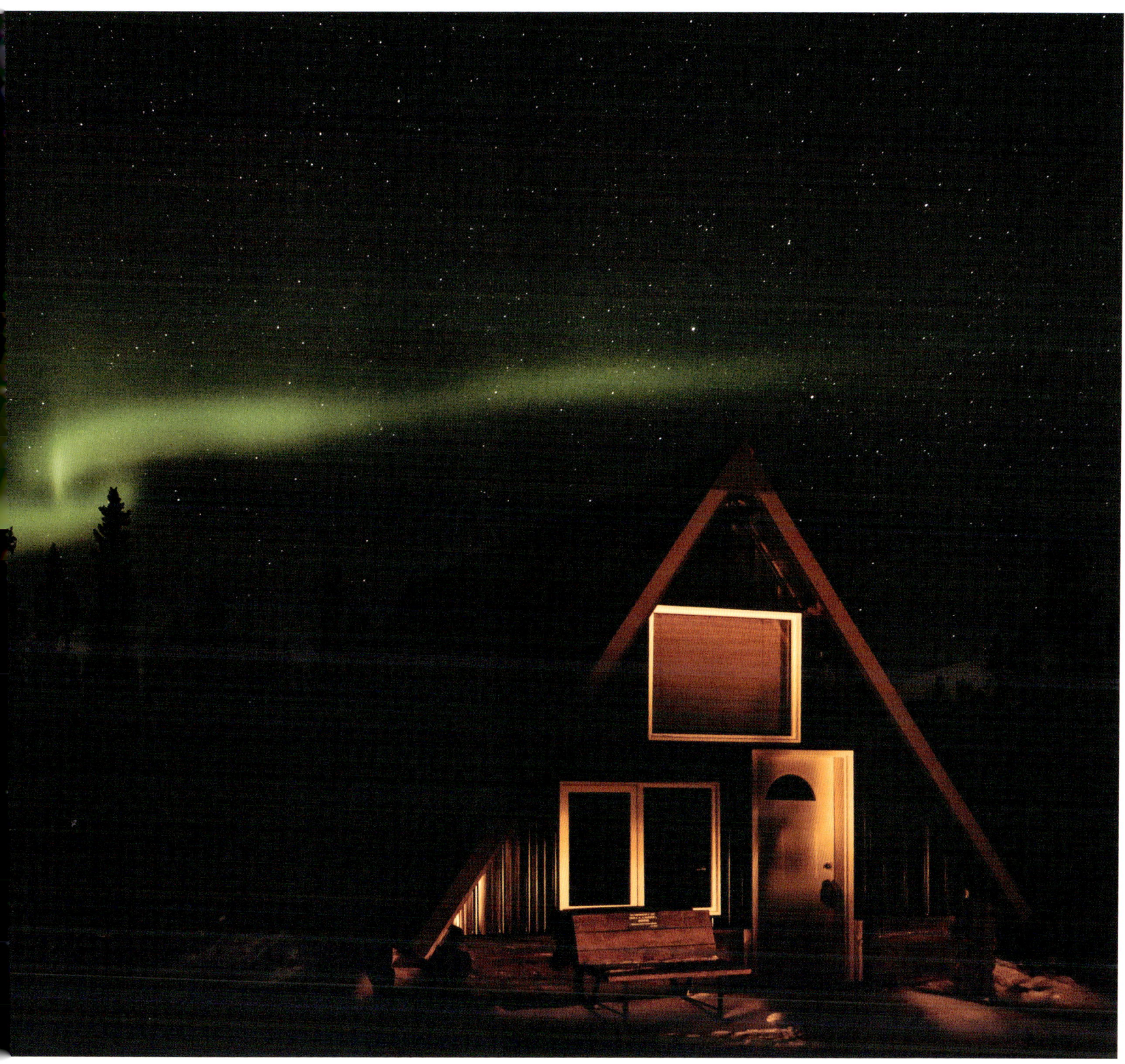

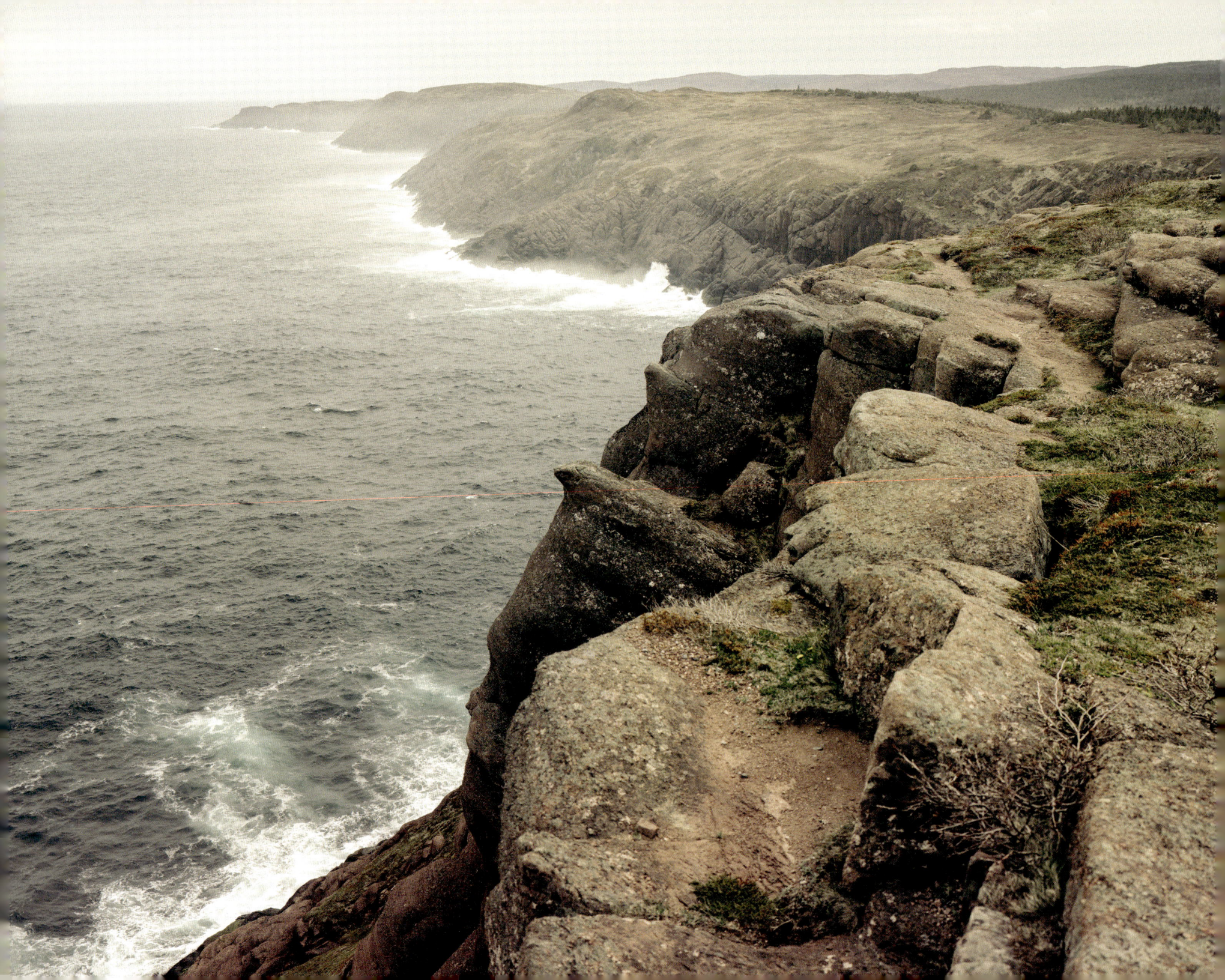

← CAPE SPEAR IS NOT JUST CANADA'S
BUT THE ENTIRE CONTINENT'S
EASTERNMOST POINT OF LAND.
CAPE SPEAR, NEWFOUNDLAND,
MAY 2022.

→ THE MARMOT IS A PARTICULARLY
STUNNING RODENT. A SPECIES
OF SQUIRREL, IT HAS SPURRED A
PLETHORA OF OUTDOOR ADVENTURE
BRANDING, FROM MARMOT CLOTHING
TO MARMOT MOUNTAIN IN ALBERTA,
TO THE WHISTLER MOUNTAIN RESORT
IN BC. THE LATTER IS NAMED NOT FOR
THE WIND THAT WHISTLES BETWEEN THE
HIGH-ALTITUDE PEAKS, AS SOME MAY
SUSPECT, BUT FOR, YOU GUESSED IT,
THE HIGH-PITCHED, EXCITED SQUEAL
OF THE MARMOT. GOLDEN, BRITISH
COLUMBIA, AUGUST 2022.

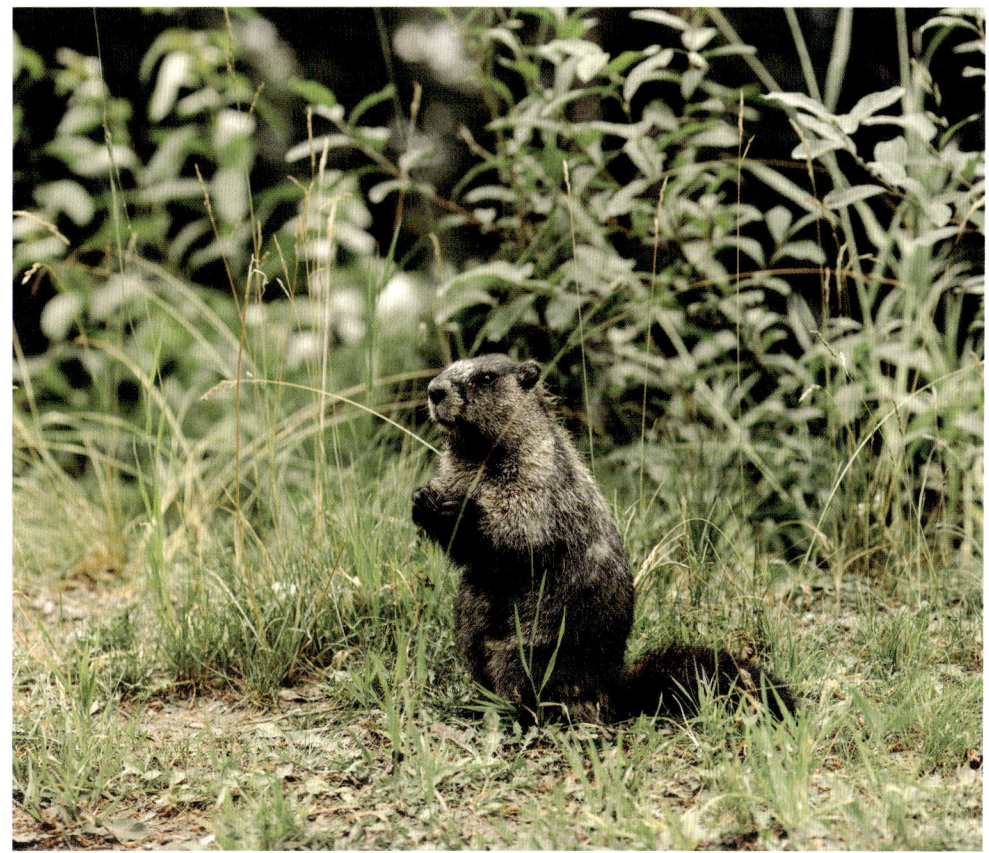

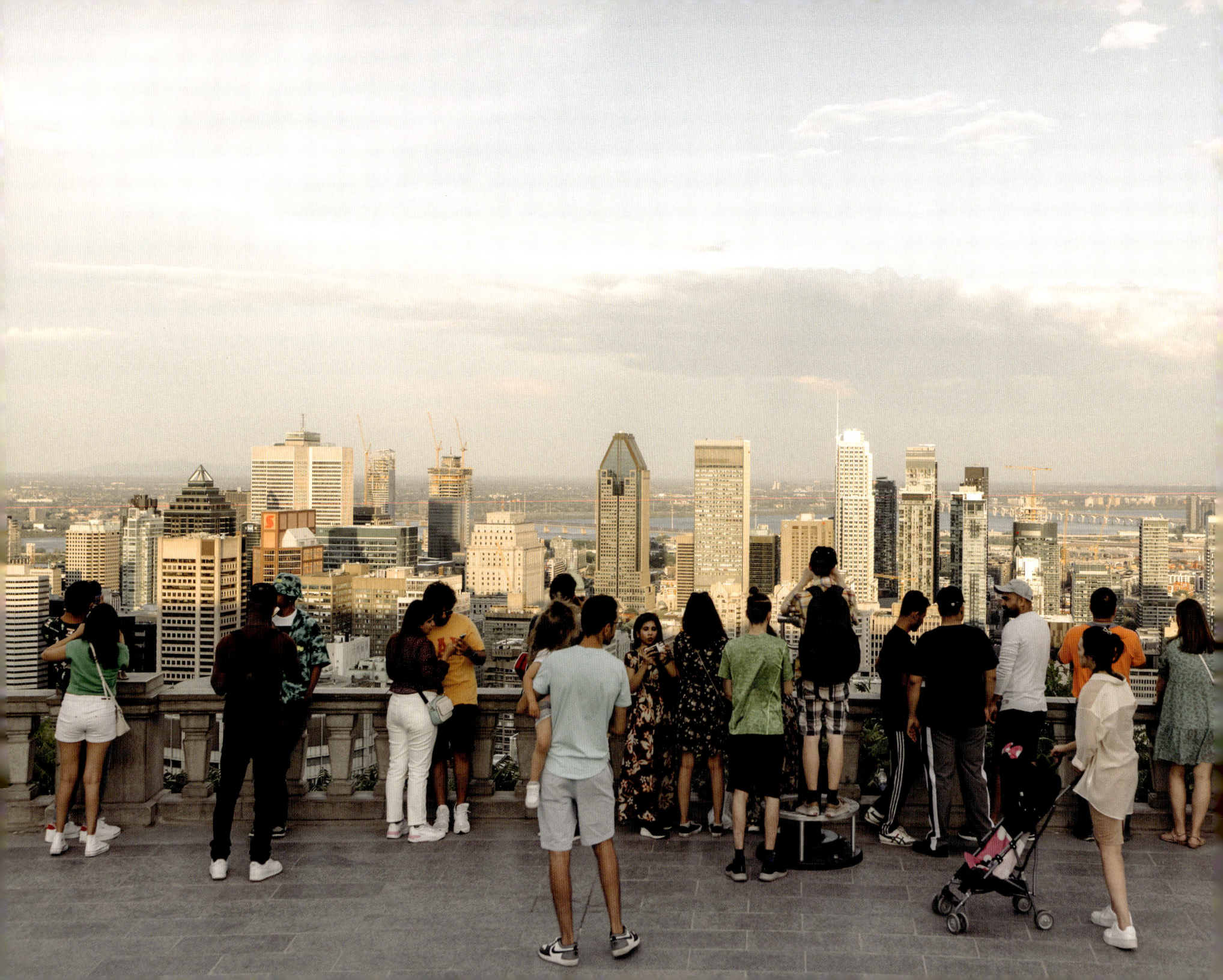

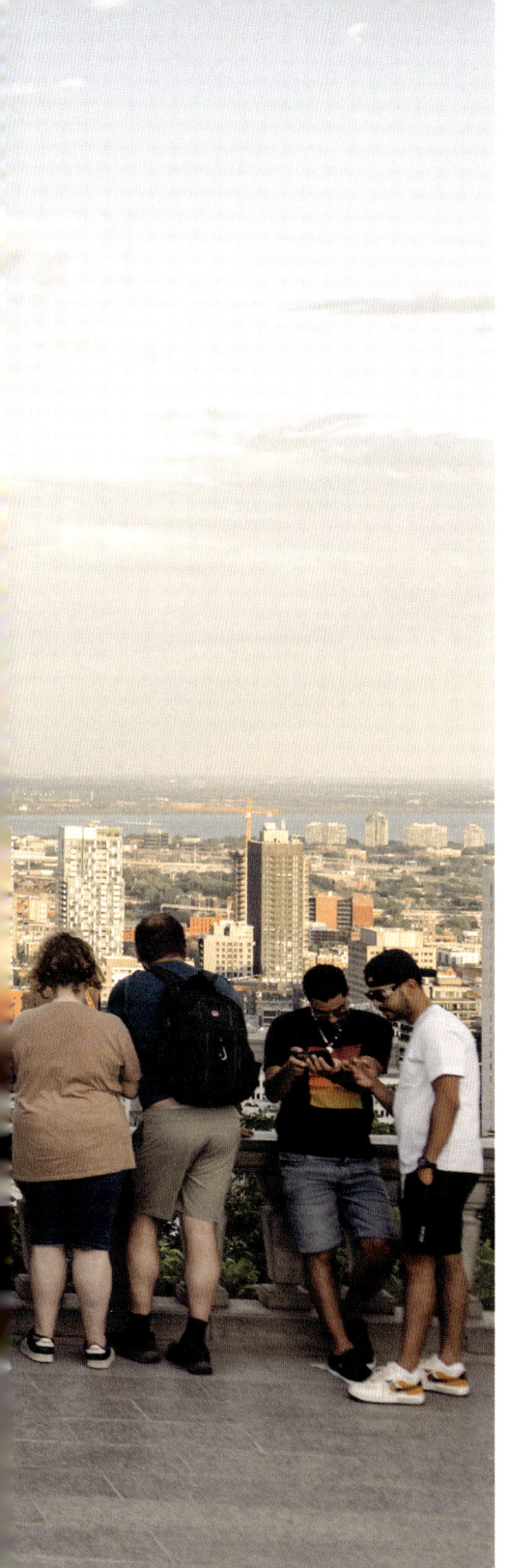

MONTREAL SKYLINE FROM MONT ROYAL. MONTREAL IS A CONTRACTION OF *MONT* AND *RÉAL*, WHICH IN 16TH-CENTURY FRENCH WAS USED INTERCHANGEABLY WITH THE WORD "ROYAL." MONTREAL, QUEBEC, JULY 2022.

STORM CLOUDS ALONG THE HIGHWAY ON THE WAY TO SLAVE LAKE, ALBERTA, JULY 2012.

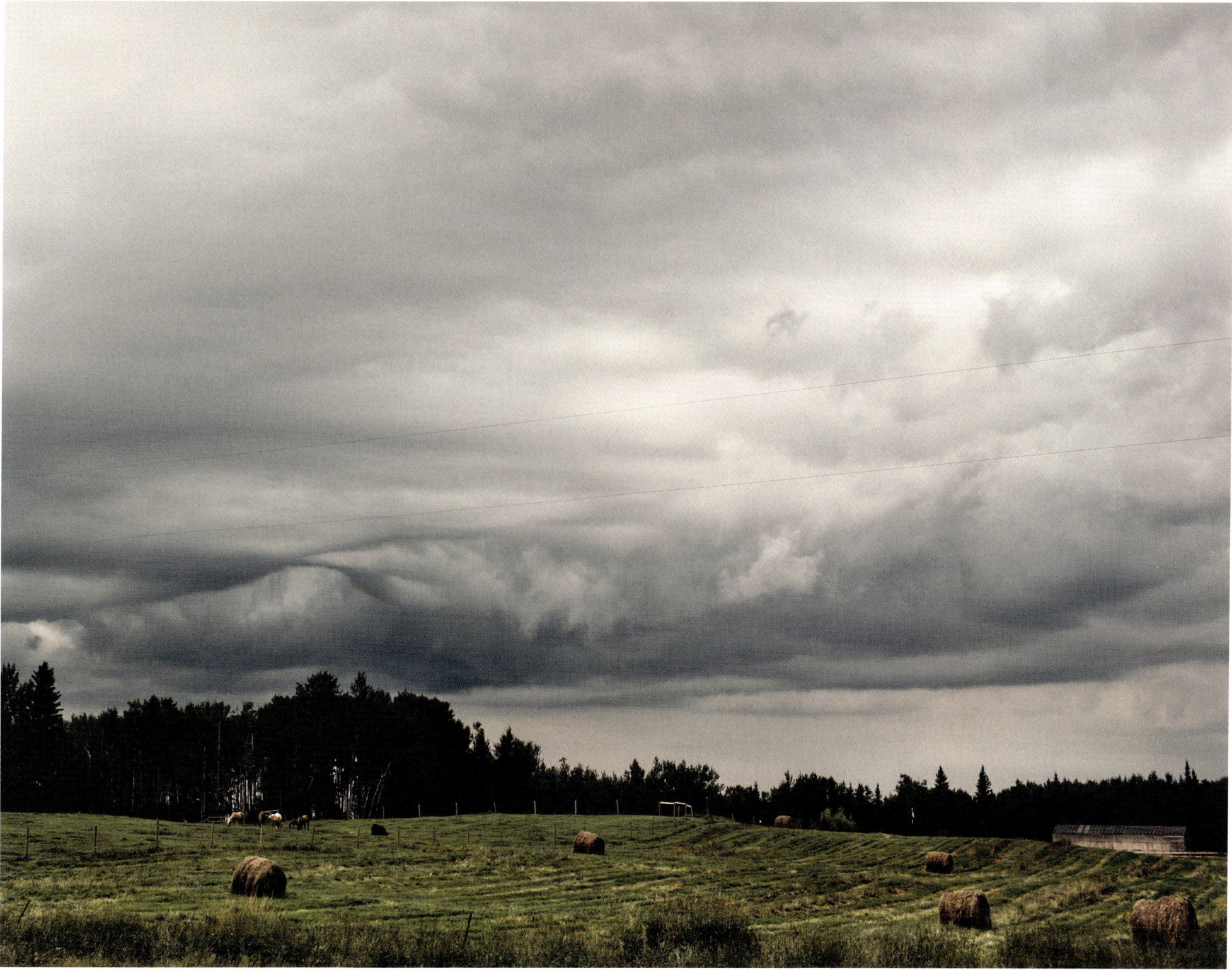

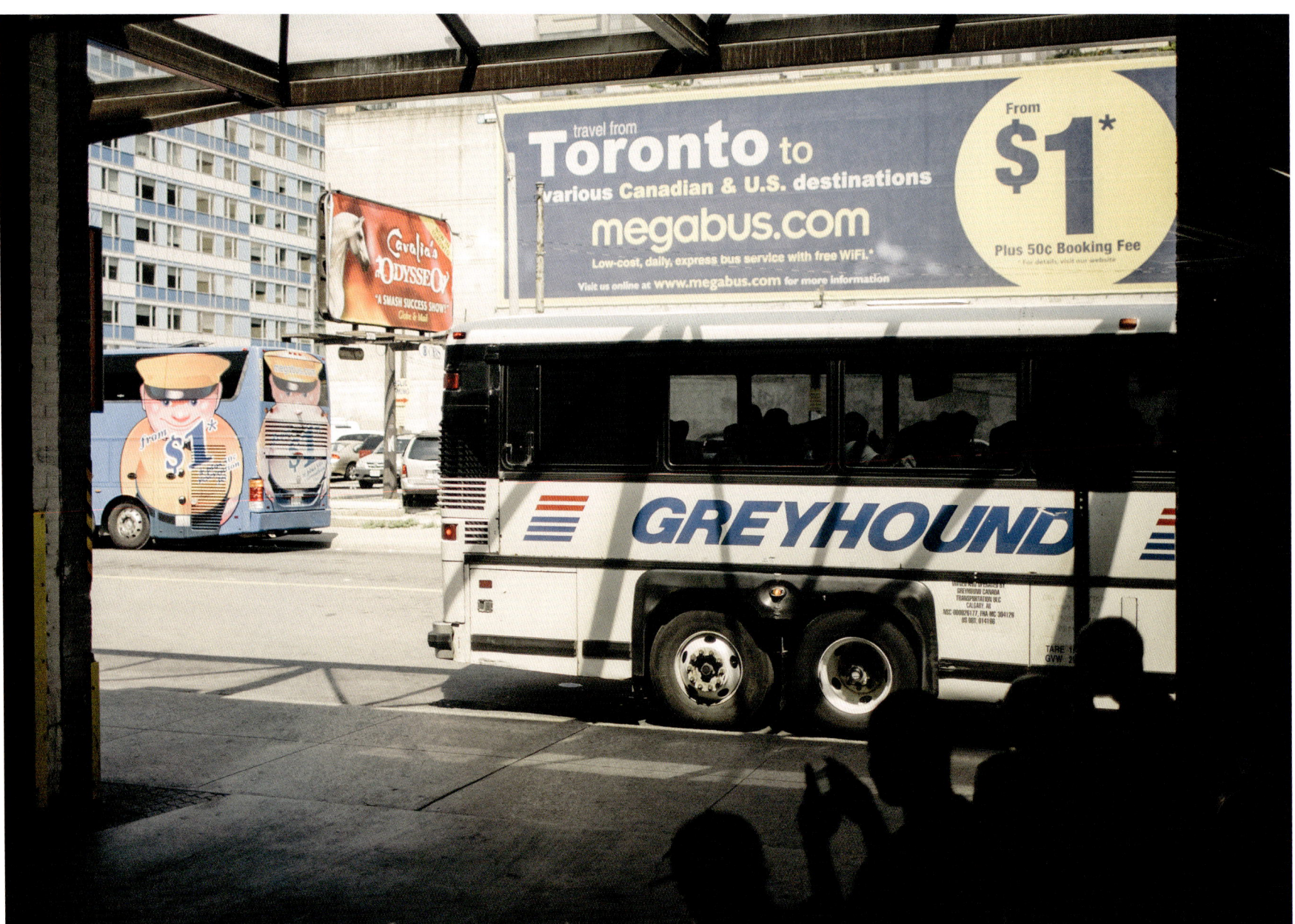

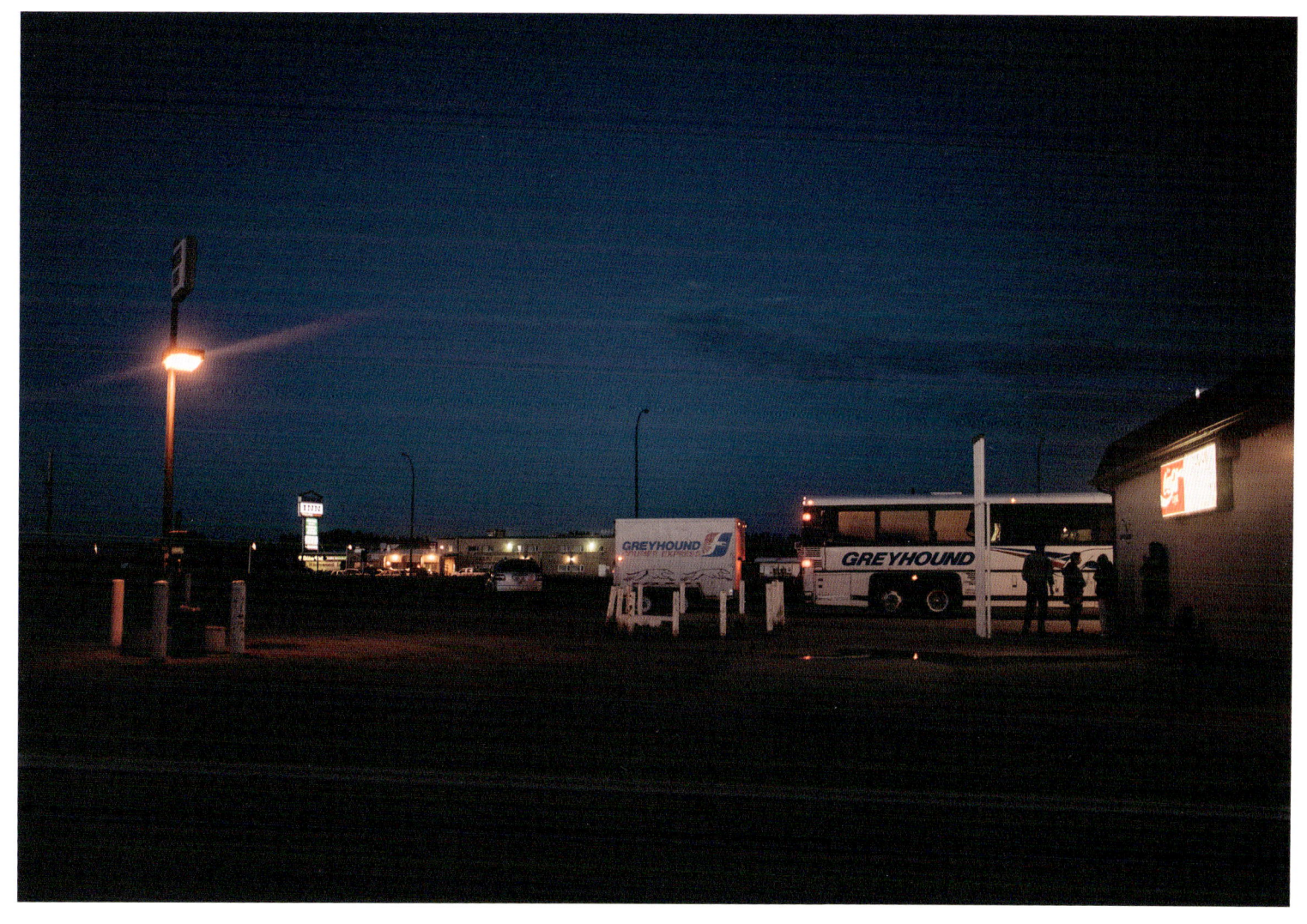

LEFT TO RIGHT GREYHOUND STATIONS IN TORONTO,
ONTARIO, AND A VERY EARLY MORNING SOMEWHERE
IN ALBERTA, JULY 2012.

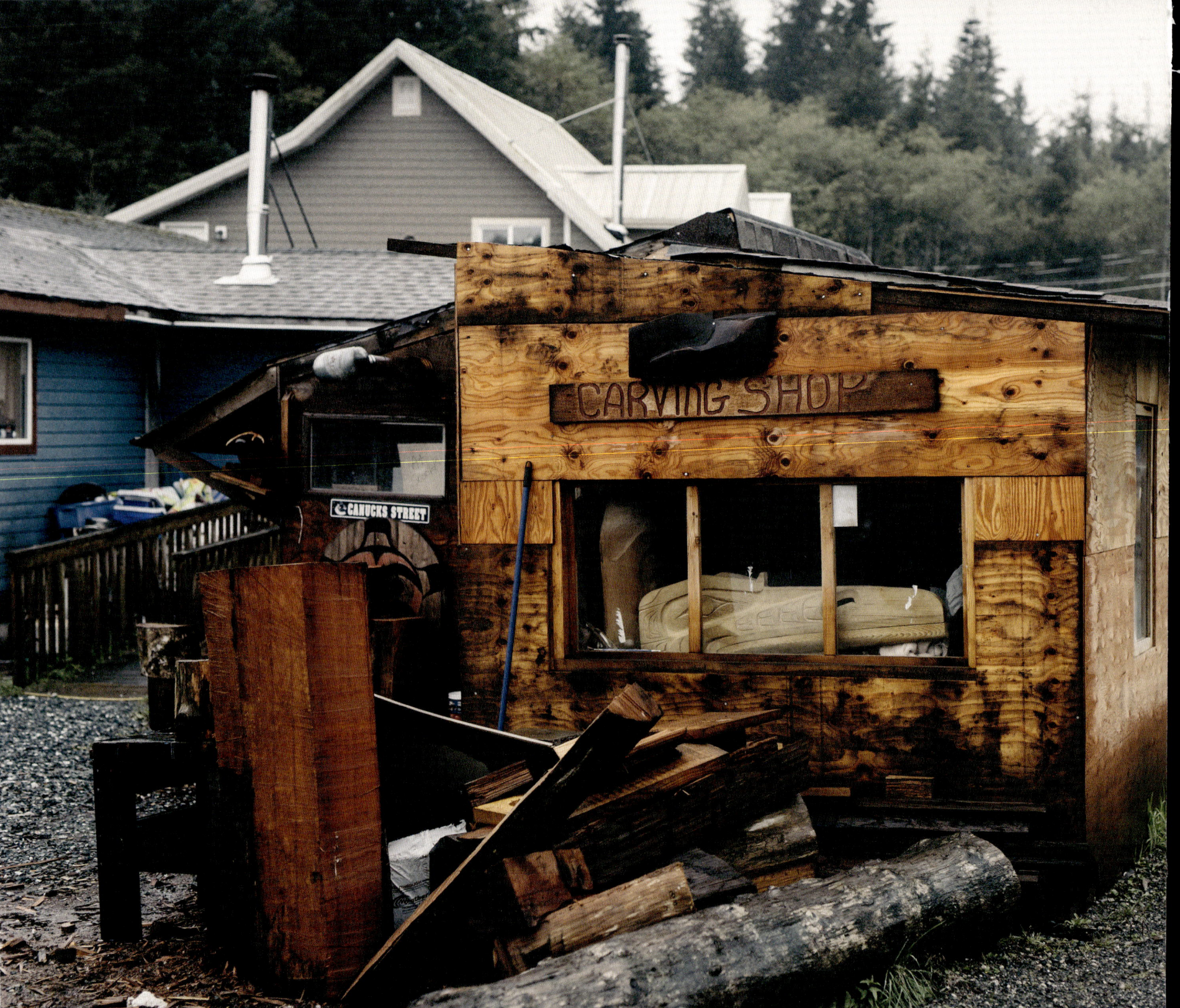

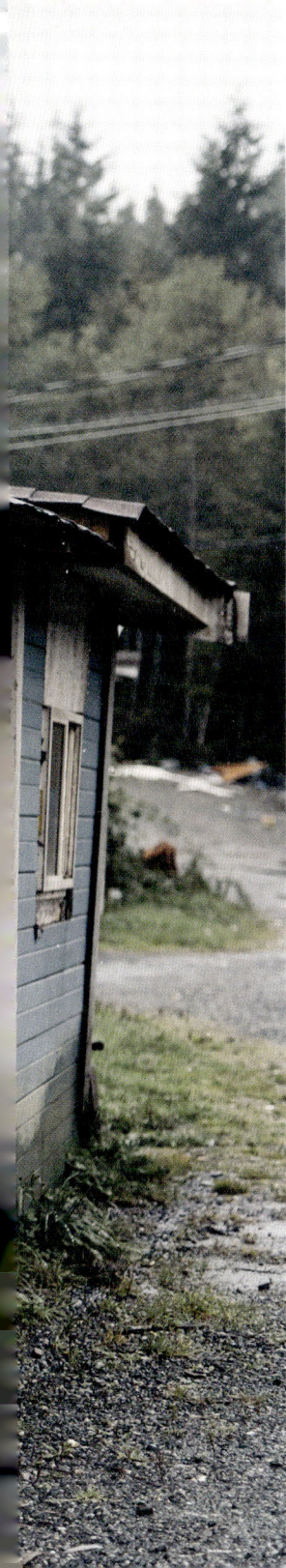

EAGLE HEAD IN A CARVING SHOP ON TSULQUATE RESERVE,
THE CURRENT BUT NOT TRADITIONAL HOMELAND OF MEMBERS
FROM GWA'SALA-'NAKWAXDA'XW NATIONS. PORT HARDY,
VANCOUVER ISLAND, BRITISH COLUMBIA, OCTOBER 2017.

EAGLE AFTER IT PICKS UP A FISH IN SKIDEGATE, HOME TO THE
HAIDA NATION. HAIDA GWAII, BRITISH COLUMBIA, AUGUST 2019.

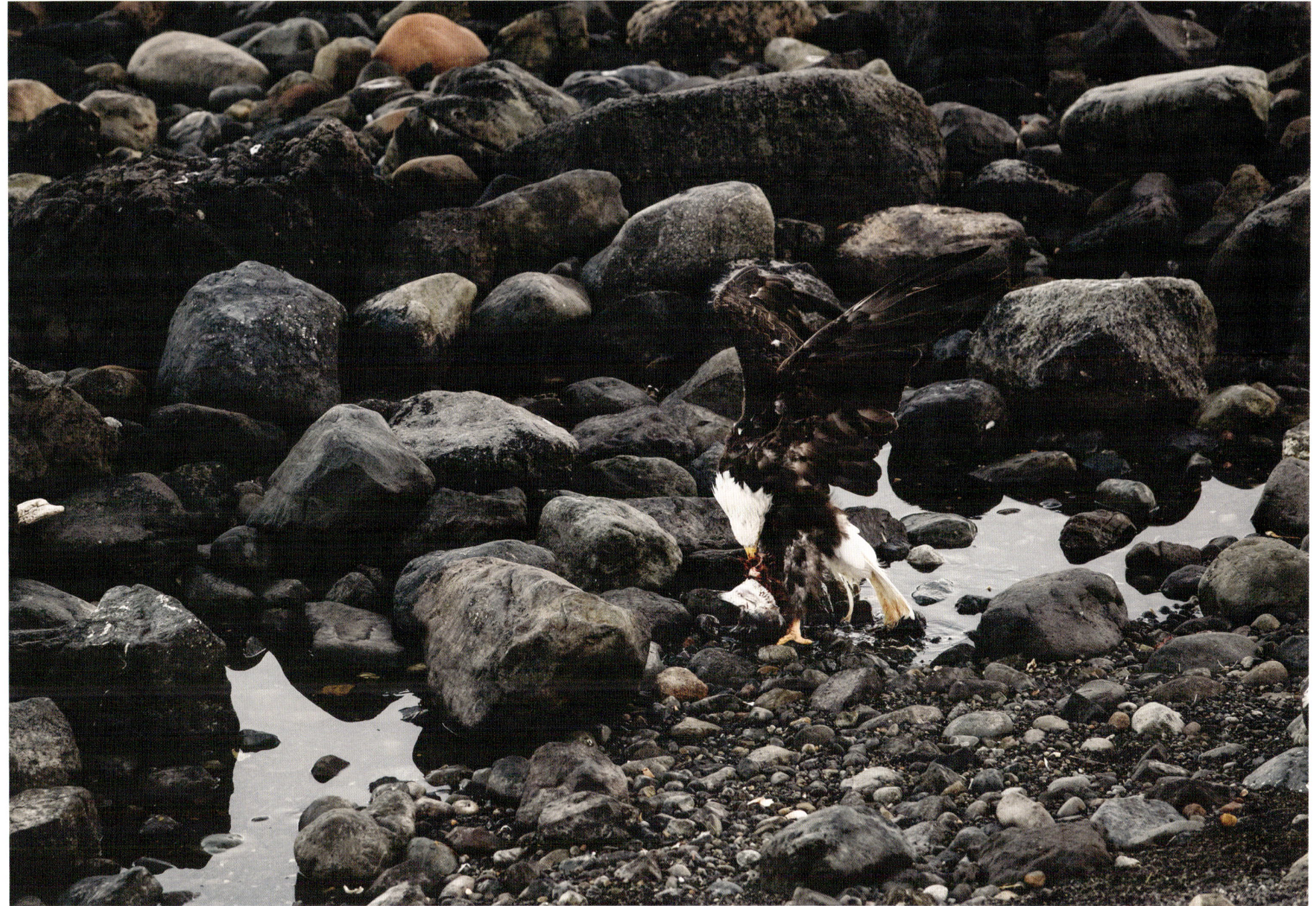

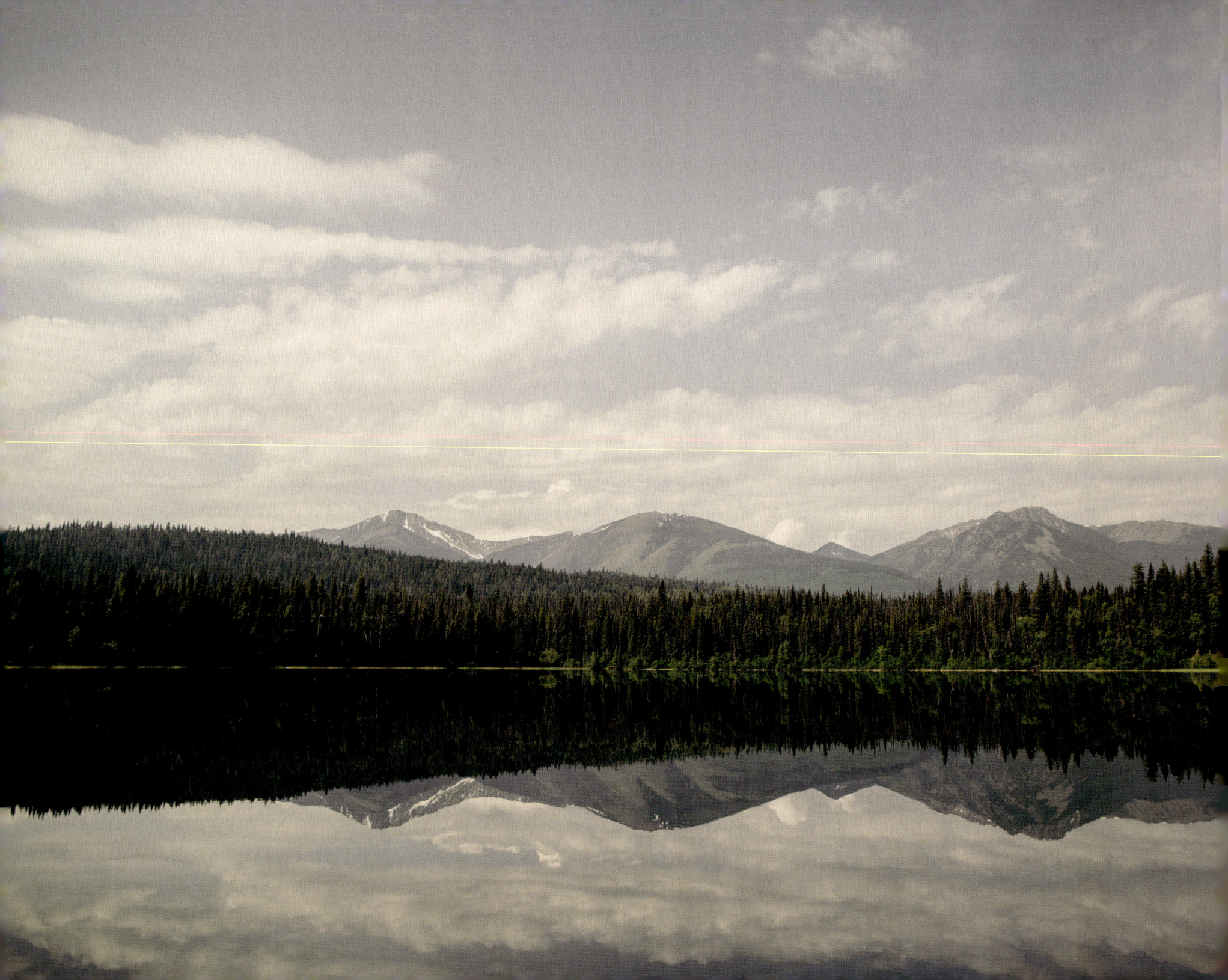

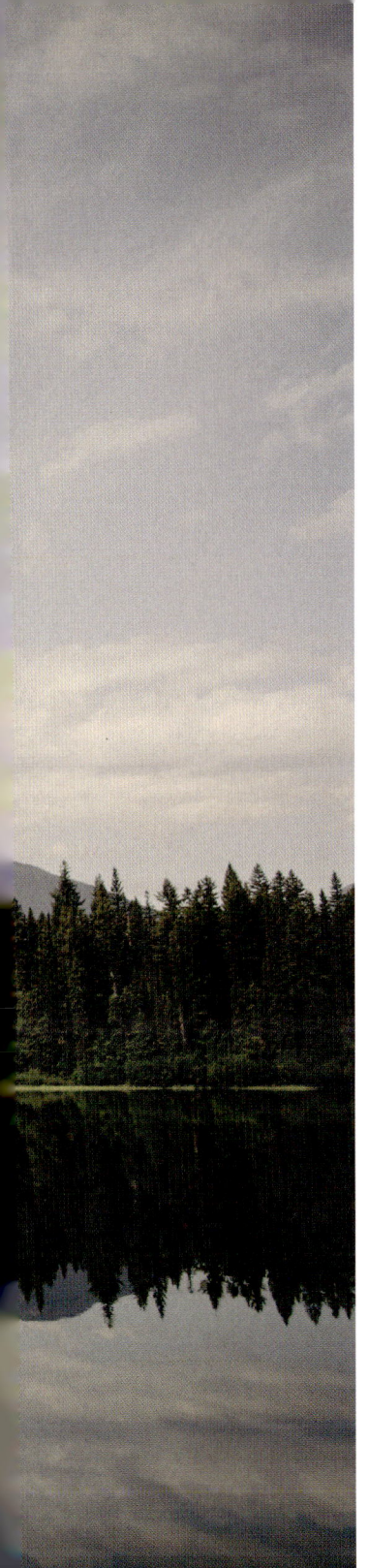

BLUE LAKE, BOWRON LAKE CANOE CIRCUIT, BRITISH COLUMBIA, JULY 2018.

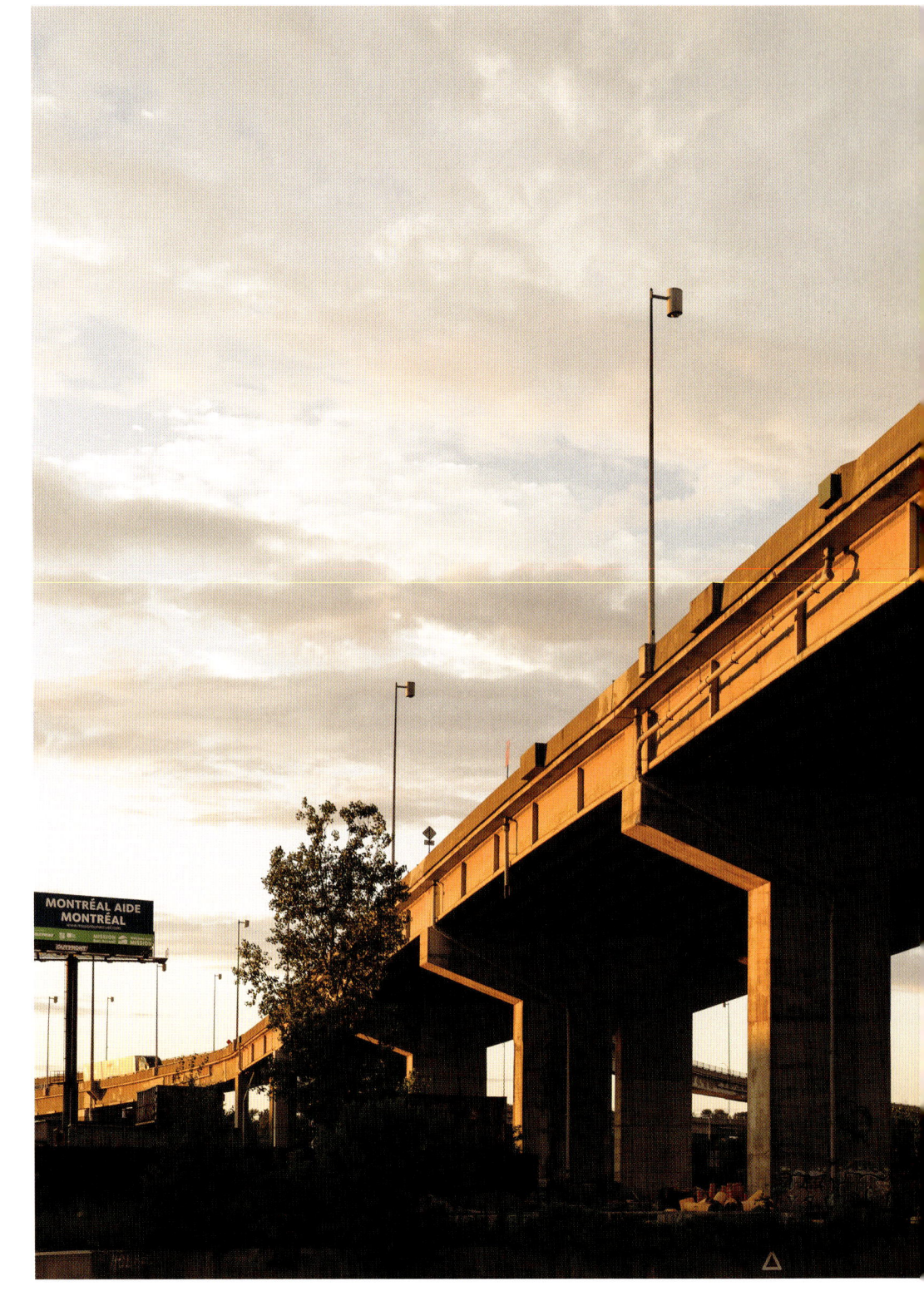

HIGHWAY BRIDGE OVER THE LACHINE
CANAL, MONTREAL, QUEBEC, JULY 2022.

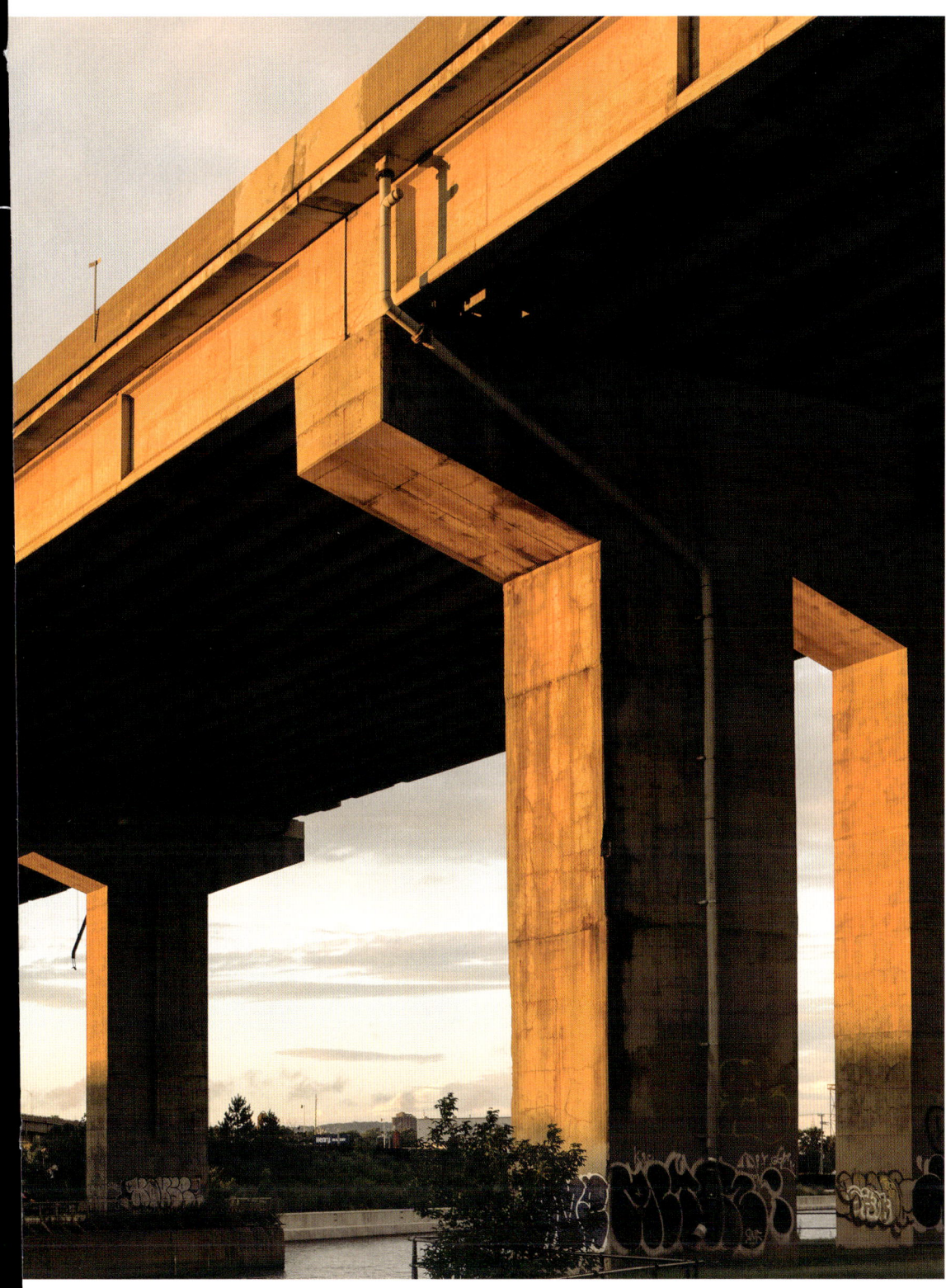

RODERICK LAKE, MACTIER, ONTARIO, SEPTEMBER 2013.

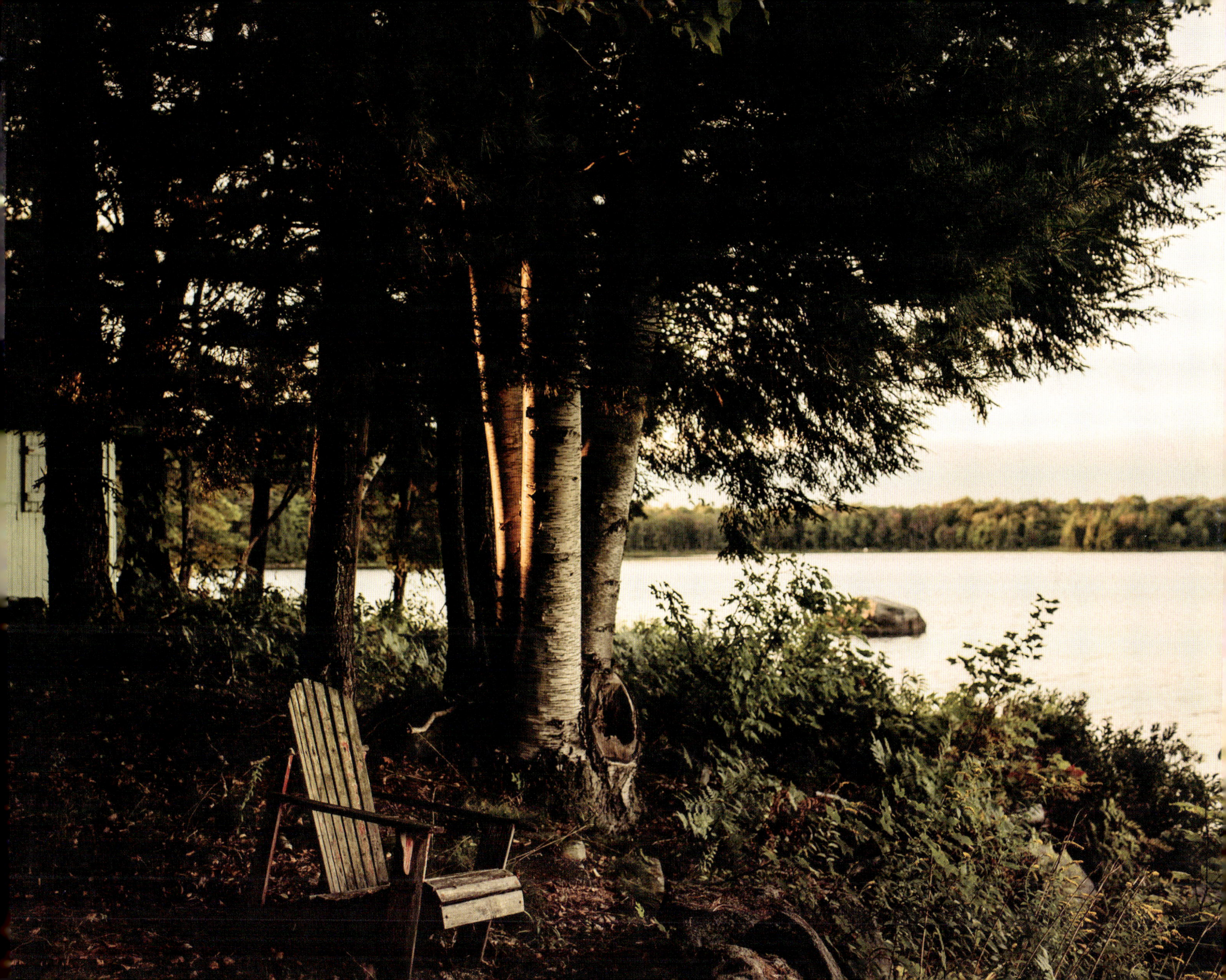

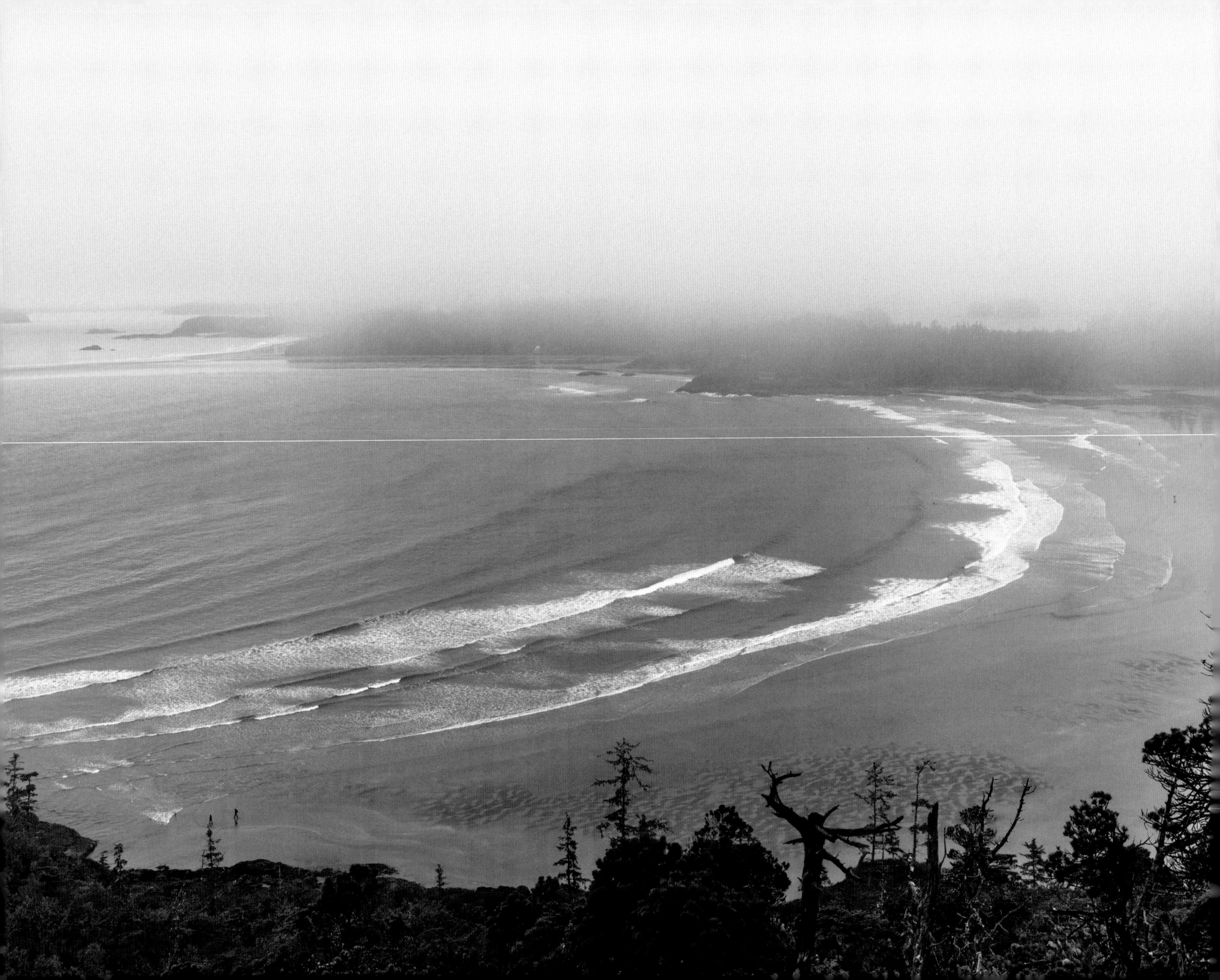

Acknowledgements

This book wouldn't have been possible without the countless sofas, guest beds and air mattresses I was able to lay my head on. Thank you to every friend, distant aunt, uncle and cousin, and sometimes kind-stranger-turned-into-friend who has given me a place to put my head for the night. Specifically, Jordan Jackson, my baby sister, whose couch I've occupied the most. Jessica Stadnick and Nicole Brissard for hosting me in the North, Lana and Rod Ludwar for a last-minute tour of the Prairies, Aunt Mary and Aunt Hilda, Brittany Staddon and Sam Le in Alberta. Brenda and Dan King in Prince Edward Island, Samantha Morton, and Amy Collier-Holmes in Newfoundland, and Brian Van Wyk, Rachel and Zaac Pick, Tomasz Wagner and Amy Tran, Sarah and Graeme Nickerson, Shannon and Natalie Lovelle, Elora Braden, Blaire Mackenzie, Thanushi Eagalle, Alexa Mazzarello, Chelsea Kanstrup and Bryan Smith, for sharing your British Columbia with me. Maddy and Deb MacDonald, and Paul Harding, Lauren Phillips and Leslie Campbell for our Ontario.

Thank you to Jacqueline Salomé. The foreword to this book couldn't have been more perfect. I couldn't have asked for a better adventure buddy, from our days and nights in Vancouver, and every stop from our grade school days in Nobleton to Waterloo, and all the places in between.

To my mom, dad, Braydon, Jordan, my baba and didi, my grandma and grandpa and extended family: Thank you for being a safe place to land, and for every early morning airport pickup, warm dinner and curious ear. It is my grandpa's Canadian coin collection on the bookends, and I'm very proud to have them on display.

To my island girls and extended family – Katie Brissard, Breanna and Sydele Merrigan, Kimberley Mackenzie, Jessica Knowler and Mary Mcneill-Knowles – exploring remote British Columbia with you all has made this province feel like home.

Uriel Conod, thank you for looking at every single iteration of this project, waking up before dawn to assist me on shoots and tagging along when I say I have a project a ten-hour drive away. Life wouldn't be nearly as wonderful without you.

And last but not least: Jo Dwhytie and Liz Greenway – the women behind Camp Tapawingo –

and my teacher Bill Schoenhardt, who inspired a lifelong love of nature. Emma Gilchrist and Carol Linnitt of *The Narwhal*, for every single photography assignment you've given me – it has been a chance to explore and learn, and an honour to photograph stories for you, which is all I ever wanted when I began to shoot. To Peter Wall and the *Canada C3*, who took me on the trip of a lifetime down the remote coast of British Columbia on an icebreaker ship. To Destination Canada, for hiring me to explore, camera in hand. To the Canada Council for the Arts, which believed in this project first – thank you for the digital originals grant and the motivation to finally make it happen. And, of course, to Don at Rocky Mountain Books – to hold this book is a dream.

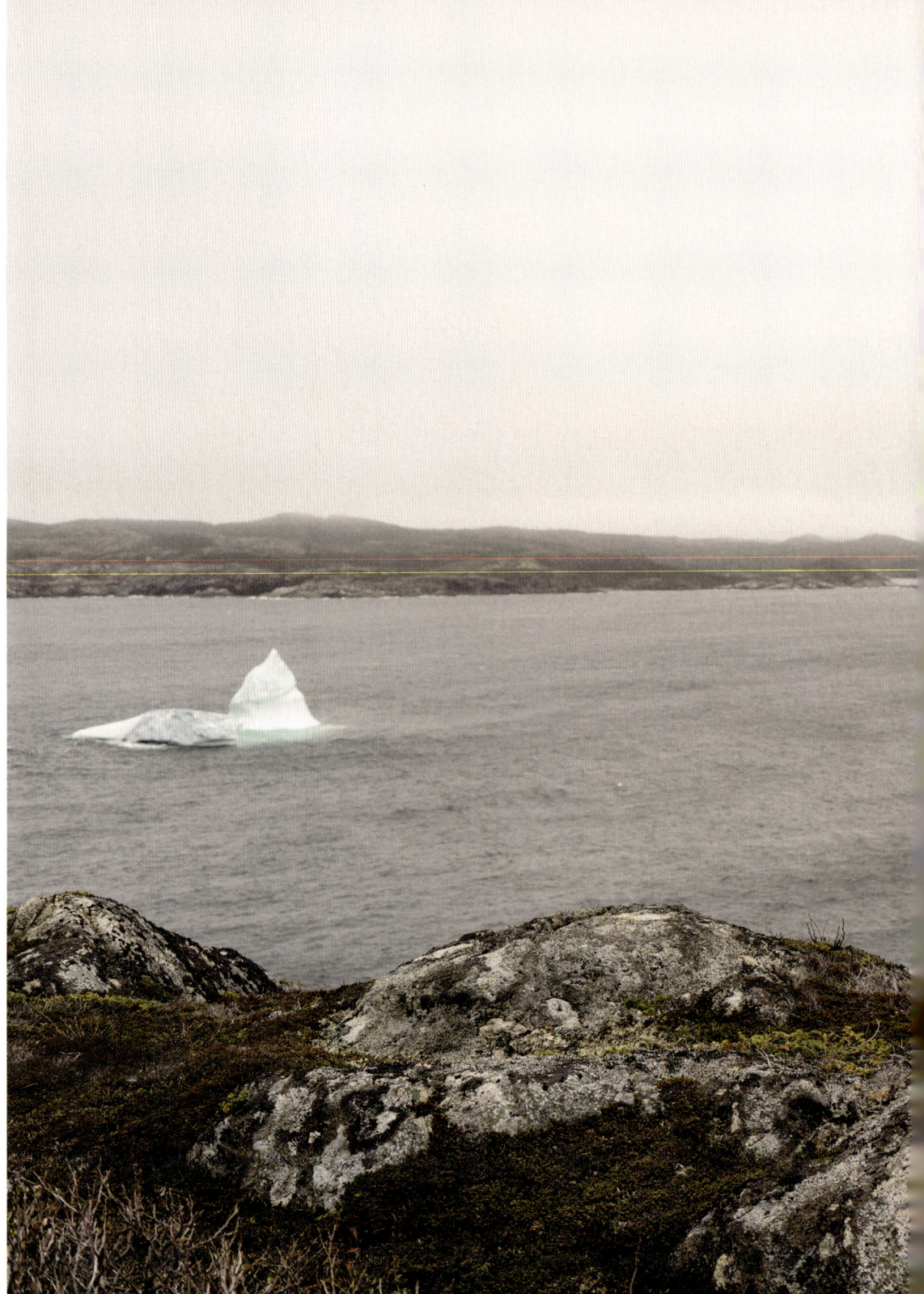

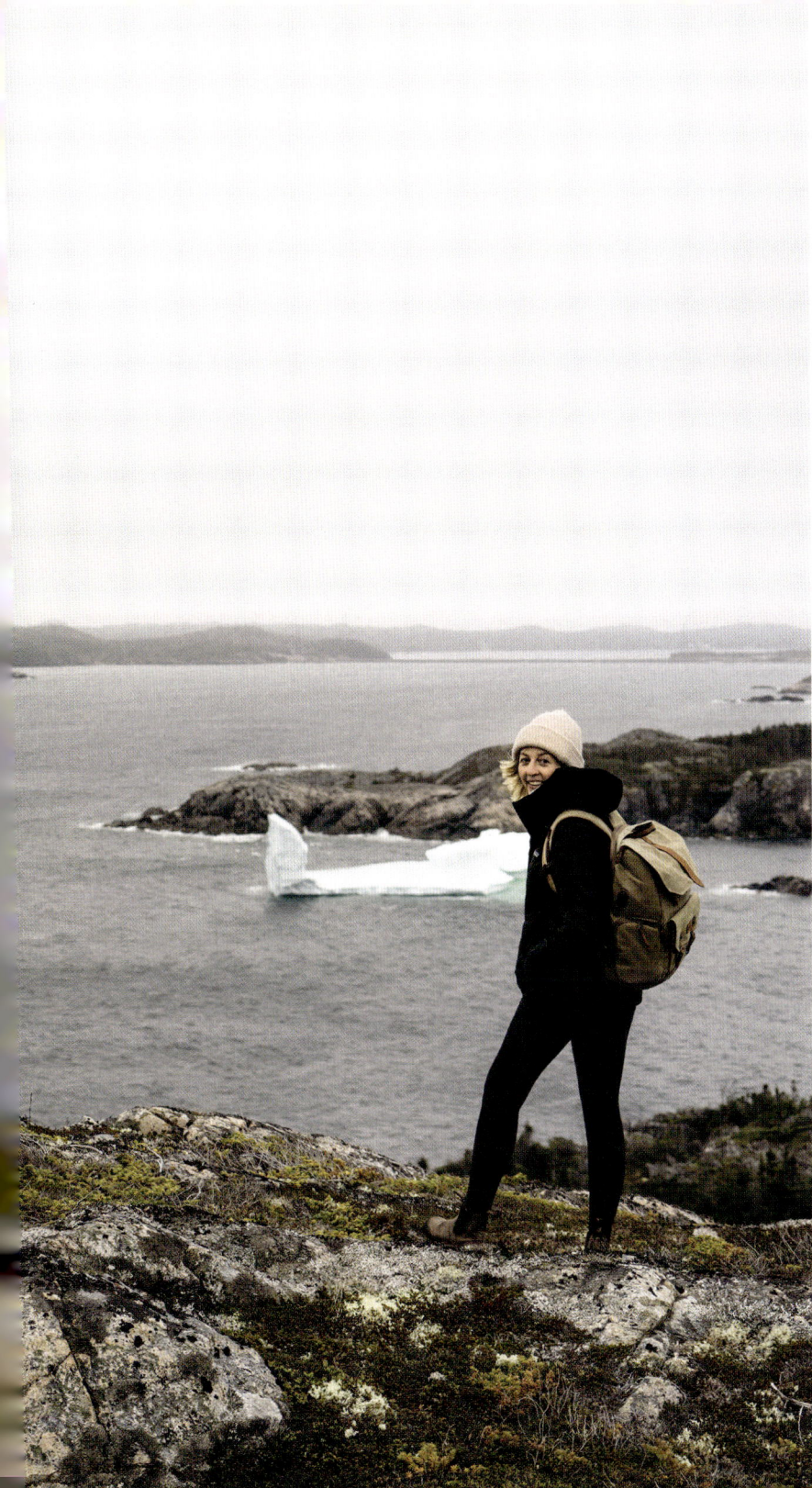

About the Author

Taylor Roades was born in Etobicoke and raised in Nobleton, Ontario. She has been a freelance photographer since the age of 20, working in both the advertising and editorial worlds. Her love of travel, curiosity in the realm of science, and compassion for issues related to climate change have led to a variety of assignments near and far. She was a part of the Canada C3 – a 150-day voyage around the three coasts of Canada on a retired Coast Guard icebreaker ship, and is a regular contributor to the *Globe and Mail* and *The Narwhal*. Taylor opened a photography studio in 2020 in Victoria, British Columbia, where she currently lives.

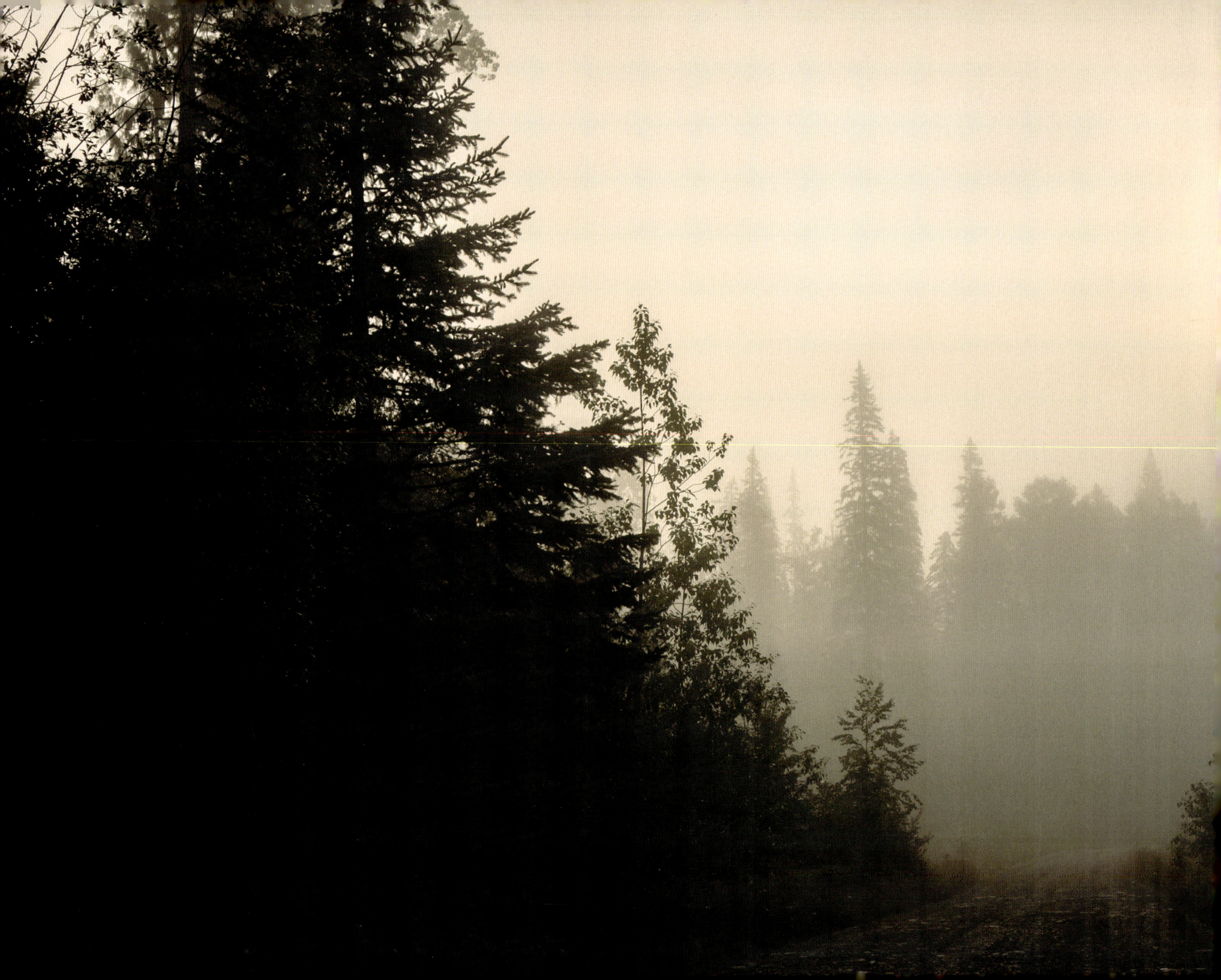

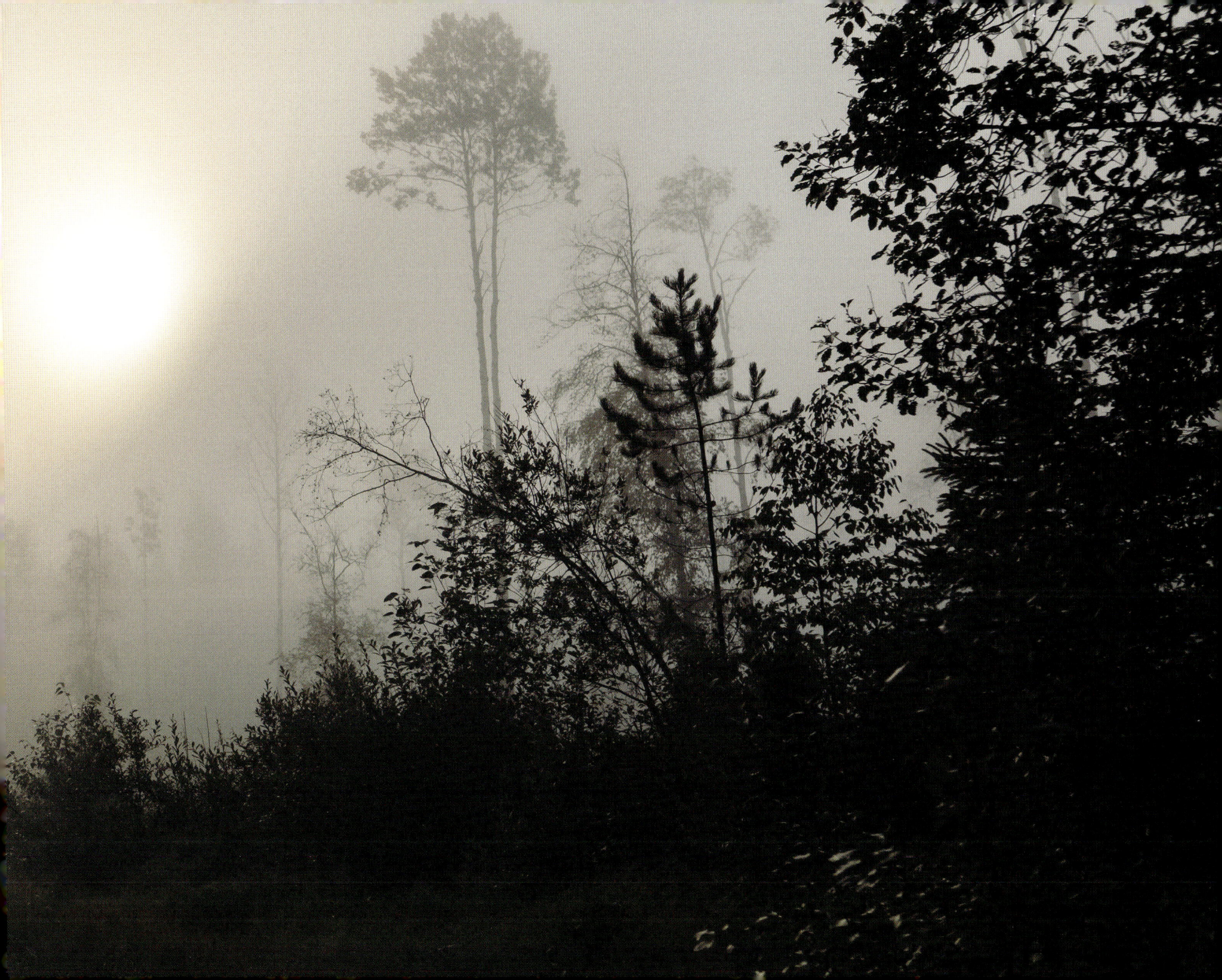

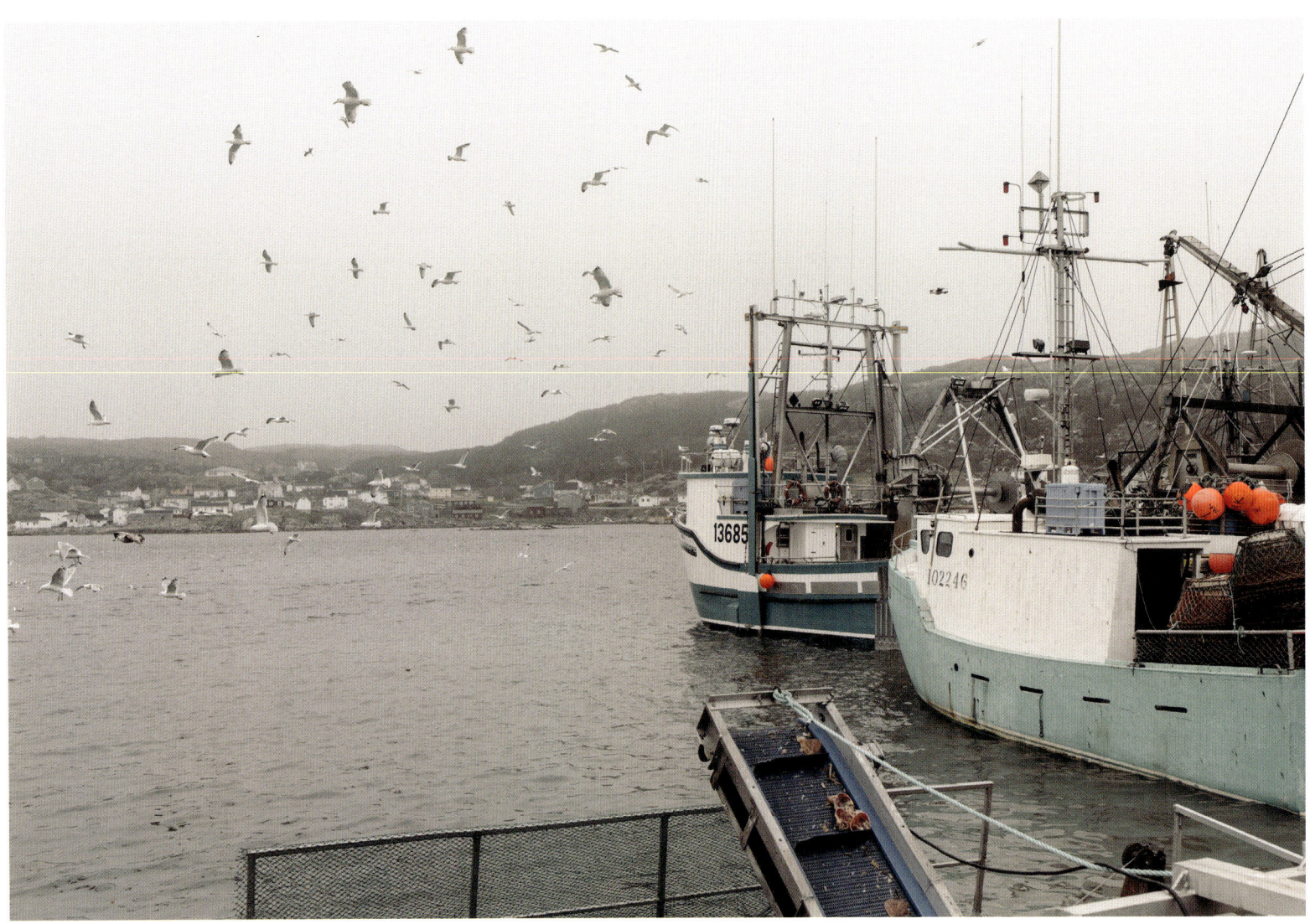